Civil Society Sustainability

This publication focuses on the challenges faced by civil society to remain sustainable in response to major changes in the global political, economic, and social environment. Academics and practitioners from all over the world have contributed original articles, practical notes, and viewpoints which critically examine the ways in which civil society organisations are affected by and are responding to political and financial dynamics. These include reductions in traditional external aid for civil society activities, but also the growth of new forms of funding through social enterprise, philanthropy, fundraising, and contractual relationships with national government. The operating environment for civil society is a central theme, with authors exploring the legitimacy and credibility of different types of civil society organisation, as well as the effects of legislative and regulatory restrictions on their sustainability. The contributions finally examine new opportunities for civil society and the prospects for organisations to emerge that are less dependent on foreign aid funding, that are more embedded in local communities, and that can bring about lasting and sustained social and economic change.

This book was originally published as a special issue of *Development in Practice*.

Brian Pratt is currently the Editor-in-Chief of *Development in Practice*, and previously founding Director of INTRAC. He has worked for OXFAM both in the UK and Andean countries. His research interests include sustainability and other aspects of the development of civil society, and he has written and published widely on these topics.

Rachel Hayman is Director of Research, Learning and Communications at INTRAC, where she is currently leading INTRAC's work on the impacts of the changing global political economy on the sustainability of civil society organisations. Rachel's role at INTRAC focuses on bridging academic research, policy-making and practice.

Civil Society Sustainability

New Challenges in Organisational Legitimacy, Credibility, and Viability

Edited by
Brian Pratt and Rachel Hayman

LONDON AND NEW YORK

First published 2018 by Routledge

2 Park Square, Milton Park, Abingdon, Oxfordshire OX14 4RN

52 Vanderbilt Avenue, New York, NY 10017

Routledge is an imprint of the Taylor & Francis Group, an informa business

First issued in paperback 2019

British Library Cataloguing in Publication Data
A catalogue record for this book is available from the British Library

ISBN 13: 978-1-138-06357-0 (hbk)
ISBN 13: 978-0-367-32190-1 (pbk)

Typeset in Myriad Pro
by RefineCatch Limited, Bungay, Suffolk

Publisher's Note
The publisher accepts responsibility for any inconsistencies that may have arisen during the conversion of this book from journal articles to book chapters, namely the possible inclusion of journal terminology.

Disclaimer
Every effort has been made to contact copyright holders for their permission to reprint material in this book. The publishers would be grateful to hear from any copyright holder who is not here acknowledged and will undertake to rectify any errors or omissions in future editions of this book.

Contents

CONTENTS

Citation Information

The chapters in this book were originally published in *Development in Practice*, volume 26, issue 5 (August 2016). When citing this material, please use the original page numbering for each article, as follows:

Editorial
Special issue overview: civil society sustainability
Brian Pratt
Development in Practice, volume 26, issue 5 (August 2016), pp. 527–531

Chapter 1
Unintended consequences: DAC governments and shrinking civil society space in Kenya
Jacqueline Wood
Development in Practice, volume 26, issue 5 (August 2016), pp. 532–543

Chapter 2
Lessons for supporting policy influencing in restrictive environments
Anique Claessen and Piet de Lange
Development in Practice, volume 26, issue 5 (August 2016), pp. 544–554

Chapter 3
Advancing post-2015 Sustainable Development Goals in a changing development landscape: Challenges of NGOs in Ghana
Albert Arhin
Development in Practice, volume 26, issue 5 (August 2016), pp. 555–568

Chapter 4
Non-governmental development organisations' sustainability, partnership, and resourcing: futuristic reflections on a problematic trialogue
Alan Fowler
Development in Practice, volume 26, issue 5 (August 2016), pp. 569–579

Chapter 5
New routes to CSO sustainability: the strategic shift to social enterprise and social investment
John Hailey and Mark Salway
Development in Practice, volume 26, issue 5 (August 2016), pp. 580–591

For any permission-related enquiries please visit:
http://www.tandfonline.com/page/help/permissions

Notes on Contributors

Mário Aquino Alves is currently Associate Dean for the Graduate Program on Public Administration at Fundação Getulio Vargas, São Paulo, Brazil.

Albert Arhin is currently completing his PhD studies at the Department of Geography, University of Cambridge, Cambridge, UK.

Charles Buxton is a Senior Capacity Building Specialist for INTRAC (International NGO Training and Research Centre), and is based in Bishkek, Kyrgyzstan.

Anique Claessen was a Researcher at the Policy and Operations Evaluation Department (IOB), The Hague, the Netherlands.

Anabel Cruz is the Founder Director of the Instituto de Comunicación y Desarrollo (ICD) in Montevideo, Uruguay.

Elsa L. Dawson is a Gender and Development Consultant and Trainer based in Oxford, UK.

Piet de Lange is an Evaluator at the Policy and Operations Evaluation Department (IOB), The Hague, the Netherlands.

Naila Farouky is CEO of the Arab Foundations Forum (AFF). She is currently based in Cairo, Egypt.

Alan Fowler is Emeritus Professor at the International Institute of Social Studies, The Hague, the Netherlands.

John Hailey is a Professor at the Cass Business School, City University, London, UK.

Rachel Hayman is Head of Research at INTRAC, a role that bridges practical and academic contributions in support of civil society. She is based in Oxford, UK.

Orysia Lutsevych is Manager of the Ukraine Forum in the Russia and Eurasia Programme at Chatham House, London, UK.

Patricia Mendonça is Professor of Public Policy and Management at the School of Arts, Sciences and Humanities, University of São Paulo, Brazil.

Fernando Nogueira is a Lecturer at FGV-EAESP, São Paulo, Brazil.

Inés M. Pousadela is a Policy and Research Officer at CIVICUS and an Associate Researcher at the Instituto de Comunicación y Desarrollo (ICD), Montevideo, Uruguay.

Brian Pratt is currently the Editor-in-Chief of *Development in Practice*, and previously founding Director of INTRAC. He has worked for OXFAM both in the UK and Andean countries.

Mark Salway is Director of Social Finance at Cass Business School's Centre of Charity Effectiveness, City University, London, UK.

James Taylor is an Associate Practitioner at CDRA, Cape Town, South Africa.

Robert Wiggers is Deputy Director of Wilde Ganzen and owns the consultancy firm Wiggers Funding Advice, Hilversum, the Netherlands.

Jacqueline Wood is a PhD candidate at Carleton University, Ottawa, Canada.

Special issue overview: civil society sustainability

This special issue of *Development in Practice* focuses on the challenges faced by civil society to remain sustainable. The dominant model for many developing country NGOs and other civil society groups is one of depending on grants from international donors. However, this option is changing, often dramatically. In our 2013 special issue on civil society at a crossroads, the challenges faced by the part of civil society dependent on external funding were already being raised.[1] That issue noted that in some parts of the world new civil society groups were emerging which had their roots in citizen activism rather than the well-established agencies. In many countries the successful graduation to middle-income status results in donors curtailing previous aid programmes. Indeed, some donors have a legal obligation not to provide funds in middle-income countries.

This special issue will, through a range of contributions, review the more obvious challenges to civil society sustainability, including those posed by the reduction and often removal of external funding. The articles will also highlight many other aspects to sustainability, which are perhaps prompted by financial challenges but which are not necessarily just about the flows of funds. There are underlying questions about the nature of civil society, perhaps sometimes masked by the dominance of funded, professionally staffed NGOs. Questions are being raised about what civil society is, whether is it at heart about local participation through voluntary action, or about not-for-profit service delivery, or indeed both and possibly yet more. Thus when we ask about the nature of civil society sustainability, we also need to ask whether we are really clear about what we mean by civil society and which types of organisation we are referring to. This is not the place to define or redefine civil society, but we should always bear in mind the great variety of forms and functions of civil society organisations; from large service delivery groups, professional associations, chambers of commerce, trade and peasant unions, membership and non-membership groups, the list sometimes seems endless. In considering our major question around sustainability we should also take into account the debates about specific types of organisation, especially the decline in funding for developmental NGOs, but also keep in focus what this and other changes entail for local civil society overall. The political and social implications of changes in funding may not be the most important challenges to a given civil society sector: there are other pressures, including state intervention to control and constrain civil society in general, political populism, nationalism, religious fundamentalism, and state corruption, all of which provide new challenges to a diverse and democratically based civil society sector.

The problem of some alternatives

A few years ago a number of large NGOs in Bangladesh were already claiming that they had found the answer to long-term sustainability. This was to create their own incomes from microcredit and savings programmes, the model being that through providing the poor with microcredit they could charge interest which included within it a contribution to administrative and other costs. As early as the 1990s, they were advertising their success in reducing the proportion of their income derived from international donors in favour of their own generated income. I am aware of many criticisms of microcredit and of many who argue its strengths, and *Development in Practice* has carried a number of articles on the subject in the past. There is, however, an argument that charging relatively high interest rates in order to provide an income for an NGO is tantamount to making the poor pay for their own development. Others would go further and claim it to be immoral to exploit the poor in order to maintain the staff salaries and infrastructures of NGOs. We contacted several Bangladeshi academics to see if we could get a contribution for this special issue in favour or against this practice, but were unable to find an author willing to write about this model of sustainability. Given the dependence of the largest NGOs in Bangladesh on their incomes from microcredit (a practice now increasing in India as well), it would be a brave person who would talk about it. For even if it is argued that such a model does protect certain services to the poor, it is still a controversial model which has slipped into being almost without comment. The idea of microcredit was initially proposed as a mechanism to supply capital, and sometimes funds for emergency consumption, for the poorest. It was not designed as a mechanism to provide incomes for NGOs, which it now seems to have become in many organisations. Even the concept of Bangladesh NGOs being self-funded is probably misleading, given their receipt of a considerable flow of funds from international donors including subsidised credit, the latter of which is in turn converted into profit-making microloans for the poor.

Do donors have a strategic view of local civil society as opposed to a functional delivery perspective?

From the recent experiences of those of us working with official donors, we seem to be witnessing a move by official agencies away from the socio-political value of a strong civil society in favour of the view that regards civil society as being primarily a not-for-profit service delivery mechanism. Many NGOs and others provide laudable services and are willing to accept a role either filling gaps or acting as privatised services on behalf of the state. Such a model, it can be argued, ties neatly to one form of longer-term sustainability through local government funding. However, in focusing on the immediate results of services, many donors seem to have lost the ability and commitment to funding essential programmes covering human rights, independent research, or interest-based coalitions and networks. Given that some governments are consciously constraining the use of foreign funds for such activities (for example, Ethiopia, Russia, and possibly Israel) this challenges local middle classes and businesses, who could be important donors and supporters of local human rights groups, if human rights are to be protected in the absence of foreign funds. It can be argued that it is precisely the issue-based civil society organisations which must find a sustainable alternative to external funding or to local government contracts. A key challenge for many previously dependent civil society groups is how to gain local support for controversial programmes, campaigns, and services.

Failures by donors and recipients to plan for change

What is surprising is the failure of both donors and recipients to plan for the changes in funding that are now being experienced in an increasing number of countries. It should not be a surprise to such groups that once middle-income status is achieved, donors will be obliged to run down their programmes. There are examples where donors tried to give fair warning of such changes, sometimes with a number of years notice (for example, Scandinavian government donors gave more than two years' warning of the closure of their programmes in South Africa, yet local NGOs and even sometimes INGOs failed to act on this information). Is this an issue of poor communication, an unwillingness to face up to the inevitable, or just another sign of how poor many agencies are at planning for the future?

One of our contributors, Alan Fowler, concludes that non-governmental development organisations need to be agile rather than seeking security, and as the world changes it does seem that too much debate is around just maintaining formally structured organisations and their professionally paid staff, rather than thinking of the best ways to meet the emerging and continuing challenges in different contexts.

Overview of contributions

Anique Claessen and Piet de Lange note the decreasing space generally for civil society due to local government constraints, in particular on local human rights groups, and difficulties for them to obtain support for policy influencing in light of these constraints. Their findings and lessons learnt are based on a detailed evaluation of Dutch support for policy influencing.

Jacqueline Wood also looks at the shrinking space for civil society, in this case in Kenya. She reviews the challenges in terms of ensuring the sustainability of past gains in human rights, and out-lines how foreign official donors have previously supported human rights and democratisation work through Kenyan CSOs. Such support has led to the government of Kenya trying to reduce the space open for civil society. This "push back" is due to several reasons, including the more autocratic nature of the government, and anti-terrorism concerns.

Inés M. Pousadela and Anabel Cruz provide an overview of civil society in Latin America, noting the historical dependence of CSOs on foreign funding and the impact of the significant reduction in such funds. This reduction has been the result of the majority of countries in the region obtaining middle-income status, as well as economic recession in certain key donors, especially Spain. Further-more, what funds do exist now tend to be used directly by international NGOs rather than being passed onto local groups. There are some funds available from local government, especially in countries where social services are contracted out to CSOs. Private sector funding is growing slowly but, with a few exceptions such as Colombia, it is still not a major aspect.

Patricia Mendonça, Mário Aquino Alves, and Fernando Nogueira provide a fascinating overview of advocacy and human rights civil society groups in Brazil, using a historical analysis to explain how they developed after the return to democracy supported by international funding, especially during the post-military period through to the end of the 1980s. When certain funding began to change, although many groups failed to adapt to these changes and hence many organisations have closed, others have been obliged to change their approach to a more contractual service delivery model.

It would be interesting to take these studies from Latin America further, given that civil society groups have moved from foreign dependency to coping with the advantages and disadvantages of new-found affluence and middle-income status, and their journey may well have more lessons for CSOs in other parts of the world. We are aware of major changes in civil society in some Latin American countries, with reductions in the size and incomes of agencies which were once well funded. In Peru, many NGOs have closed down while others survive as a shadow of their former selves through, for example, renting out their premises. What is also clear is that many membership groups in particular seemed to have survived despite these changes, while others have not coped with the political and financial pressures on them. Exceptions in Peru are those organisations working with indigenous Amazonian groups and on related environmental issues which gain from contemporary concerns about climate change. Further research could explore what it took for civil society groups to survive when the funding, and in some cases the need, for NGOs seemed to have shrunk.

Our contribution by *Albert Arhin* on Ghana notes that the identity of civil society is changing, not just because of funding and capacity challenges, but because the whole nature of civil society is being realigned from NGO delivery to a civil society engaged in local contexts and issues, putting a greater emphasis on local political, economic, and social problems. This study notes the massive jump from being a very aid dependent country (10% of GDP) to being a middle-income country. Existing funding now seems to be more likely to be tightly projectised, which has weakened the overall capacity of civil society. Many groups have converted into "social enterprises" working on con-tracts to maintain an income stream, while doubts remain as to the future of independent advocacy from civil society groups in the country.

John Hailey and Mark Salway argue that, before looking at the purely financial nature of sustain-ability, it is important to analyse other organisational and contextual indicators relevant to CSO sustainability: everything from organisational objectives, to relationships and the strength of a CSOs' internal organisation. They then move to discuss the global financial challenges to civil society, and describe some of the emerging options, including social enterprises, social investing, and for-profit subsidiaries of NGOs.

Alan Fowler provides a thought-provoking contribution by outlining research which shows the disassociation between many non-governmental development organisations (NGDOs) and citizens, and their own civil society organisations. He suggests that his model of a trialogue between official donors, INGOs, and local NGOs has broken down and failed to prepare civil society for the future. He continues to then look at longer-term changes which have affected development and the role of NGDOs, whilst pointing out the health of non-funded "under the radar" civil society groups. This point was made in the 2013 *Development in Practice* special issue on civil society at a crossroads. Finally, he argues that organisational sustainability is more likely in organisations which remain agile and flexible, rather than those which seek security while they ignore the changes around them.

Elsa L. Dawson's practical note argues the importance of ensuring a strong gender and diversity analysis as a component of any sustainable development activity and in ensuring sustainable and inclusive organisations. She uses the example of the work of the Civil Society Support Programme in Ethiopia, providing six guidelines to help ensure equitable development. The case examples highlight some of the small but emblematic successes resulting from the improved gender analysis within the Ethiopian programme.

In his practical note, *Robert Wiggers* shares the experience of the Wilde Ganzen foundation, which sought to encourage local resource mobilisation in four lower and higher middle-income countries. The fundraising was set at national level and local community levels. Wilde Ganzen provided incentives in terms of co-funding against progress by partners and communities in raising their own funds locally. The author both explains the model as well as the results up to the end of 2015, noting some of the challenges as well as ultimate successes.

Charles Buxton provides an update on the contentious development of civil society in the former Soviet Union, especially Russia.[2] The attempts to curtail foreign funding by the Russian government, and conflict in Ukraine have brought many challenges to local civil society groups. Meanwhile, new initiatives are being offered by the Russian government, which presents a dilemma for local NGOs: whether to accept government funding and collaboration or to continue to protest and lobby against the abuses of human rights and state-sponsored corruption. He concludes that the future will continue to be difficult, and that civil society will have to rely on its own modest resources.

The viewpoint by *Orysia Lutsevych* notes how the process of reforms in Ukraine has been stymied by both the recent conflict, as well as the failure to resolve serious corruption in the government and state. The lack of citizen engagement is, to outsiders, surprising given the huge wave of protest which brought down the previous government. There are, however, considerable local level, volunteering, and other individual activities in the absence of a coherent movement to resolve the country's issues, which possibly points to people waiting for the conflict to subside before confronting other issues around corruption and poor governance.

Naila Farouky's viewpoint discusses Arab philanthropy and the challenges confronting it in a post-Arab Spring world. These challenges include the continuing political landscape, but also problems in the voluntary sector itself with its lack of transparency and accountability, or even the expectation of these. There is also a lack of information about needs in the region and how philanthropy is or could respond to needs that exist. The article presents a realistic assessment of the challenges ahead.

James Taylor discusses the tensions and challenges to organisations in South Africa adjusting to a post-apartheid reality as well as a reduction in external funding. New issues bring new challenges, while old forms of working and organising require new solutions which are aimed at achieving social and political transformation that build on the successes of earlier struggles.

The issue is completed by a concluding chapter from my co-guest editor **Rachel Hayman**, who brings together the key themes running through our different contributions, reviewing what has changed from previous analyses, and proposing ideas for what needs to change as we move forward.

Notes

1. See "Special Issue: Civil societies at crossroads: eruptions, initiatives, and evolution in citizen activism." *Development in Practice* 23 (5&6).
2. See also Buxton, C. 2013. "Russian civil society – background, current, and future prospects." *Development in Practice* 23 (5&6): 771–783.

Brian Pratt

Unintended consequences: DAC governments and shrinking civil society space in Kenya

Jacqueline Wood

ABSTRACT

In the post-Cold War era, rights and democracy promotion became a significant component of Western governments' developing country engagement, including through CSOs. Today, a backlash against CSOs is evident in many developing countries. Drawing from interviews in Kenya, this article reflects on the potential unintended consequences of Western government actions that may be contributing to the backlash, undermining the sustainability of rights and democracy gains, and of CSOs. Autocratic leaders' hostility toward reformist voices; counter-terrorism and security; emphasis on the private sector and trade; and modalities of CSO support, all suggest the need for careful consideration of Western governments' actions.

Durant la période de l'après-Guerre froide, la promotion des droits et de la démocratie sont devenus un élément considérable du dialogue entre les gouvernements occidentaux et les pays en développement, y compris à travers les organisations de la société civile (OSC). Aujourd'hui, on observe une réaction violente à l'encontre des OSC dans de nombreux pays en développement. Cet article se base sur des entretiens menés au Kenya pour réfléchir aux conséquences potentielles imprévues des actions entreprises par des gouvernements occidentaux qui contribuent peut-être à cette réaction violente, ce qui nuit à la durabilité des droits et des progrès effectués sur le plan de la démocratie, et à celle des OSC. L'hostilité des dirigeants autocratiques à l'égard des voix réformistes ; le contre-terrorisme et la sécurité ; l'accent mis sur le secteur privé et le commerce ; et les modalités du soutien apporté aux OSC — autant de facteurs qui suggèrent la nécessité de bien réfléchir aux actions des gouvernements occidentaux.

En la era posterior a la Guerra Fría, los gobiernos occidentales hicieron de la promoción de los derechos y la democracia un aspecto significativo de su relación con los países en desarrollo, impulsando esta agenda incluso a través de las organizaciones de la sociedad civil (OSC). Hoy, en muchos países en desarrollo resulta evidente la existencia de un ambiente hostil contra las OSC. A partir de entrevistas realizadas en Kenia, el presente artículo analiza las posibles consecuencias surgidas de las acciones promovidas por los gobiernos occidentales. De manera involuntaria, éstas podrían haber provocado tal hostilidad, socavando al mismo tiempo la sostenibilidad de los avances logrados en términos de derechos y de democracia, y debilitando a las OSC. Un conjunto de factores —la hostilidad expresada por líderes autocráticos contra las opiniones reformistas; el antiterrorismo y la seguridad; la importancia otorgada al sector privado y al comercio; y las modalidades del apoyo brindado por las OSC— obliga a seguir con atención las acciones emprendidas por los gobiernos occidentales.

Introduction

Since independence, Kenya has experienced high levels of diplomatic and development engagement with Organisation for Economic Cooperation and Development (OECD) countries. The post-Cold War era saw the growth of rights and democracy promotion as a significant component of OECD countries' engagement. This has included financial support and policy dialogue with relevant Government of Kenya (GoK) institutions, along with support to civil society organisations (CSOs) operating in Kenya for a range of activities from service provision to advocacy.

Today in Kenya, as in other developing countries around the world, we are witnessing a rights and democracy pushback. CSOs are finding themselves on the frontlines of the pushback as the ways in which they are regulated and treated shrink the political, operating, and legislative space available to them (hereinafter referred to as "space" or "environment").

While the phenomenon is not limited to Kenya, the Kenya case allows an exploration of the place that OECD-Development Assistance Committee (DAC) governments (hereinafter "DAC/Gs") may have in it. Four factors present in Kenya and in other developing countries need consideration to understand the unintended mitigating influence DAC/Gs may have on CSO space.

First, real or perceived, historical and current DAC/G–CSO alliances and successes in rights and democracy promotion contribute to an autocratic GoK's hostility toward CSOs that motivates GoK efforts to shrink CSO space. Second, new dynamics emerging from DAC/G–GoK counter-terror alliances suggest that DAC/Gs may be less inclined to defend CSO space from encroaching GoK restrictions. Third, the tipping of DAC/G priorities towards the private sector and wider trade and investment interests, particularly in the face of competition from new players such as China, suggests a further challenge to DAC/Gs' post-Cold War rights and democracy efforts, inclusive of defending CSO space. Fourth, modes of DAC/Gs' financial support for CSOs and associated accountability requirements have been long understood to have a direct influence on CSOs' ability to function. The impact is also an indirect one when DAC/Gs' support fuels the type of concerns about CSOs' local legitimacy used by the GoK to justify closing CSO space.

In keeping with the subject matter of this special issue, the underlying challenge is the sustainability of long-fought for advances in rights and democracy, of CSO space, and of CSOs themselves, all of which are under strain. The availability of CSO space depends on the state of rights and democracy, while such space also enables CSOs to advance and sustain rights and democracy gains. It is also integral to the sustainability of individual CSOs and the CSO sector.

This research draws on 49 interviews conducted in 2015, 45 of which were undertaken in Kenya primarily with representatives from DAC/Gs, CSOs, and local and national GoK officials, to assess DAC/G–CSO–GoK relationships and developments over recent years.

The CSOs interviewed and addressed here cover the range of not-for individual-profit organisations, including but not limited to local and international NGOs. This article's focus is on formal CSOs, that is, those with some form of legal status. While CSOs working in rights and democracy are given particular attention, the phenomenon of shrinking space affects all CSOs.

Features of shrinking CSO space in Kenya

The CSO–GoK relationship has, over the years, been characterised by mutual suspicion. Still, the 1990 NGOs Coordination Act (RoK 1990), while far from perfect, had allowed for a relatively independent functioning of the CSO sector, with registration and annual reporting requirements to the NGOs Coordination Board largely unproblematic. Inspired by their own self-regulation efforts and by opportunities provided by Kenya's new 2010 Constitution, in 2011 CSOs spearheaded the development of a new legislative framework for CSOs in Kenya. This CSO-led initiative went through a meaningful negotiation process with GoK representatives and in Parliament and led to a broadly supported Public Benefit Organisations (PBO) Act.

In January 2013 the PBO Act was assented into Kenyan law (RoK 2013a). Touted as a progressive and comprehensive improvement on the NGOs Coordination Act it would replace, the PBO Act was in part designed as a means to strengthen accountability and build trust between the GoK and CSOs. According to one Kenyan CSO representative, *"the natural progression in the [CSO–GoK] relationship would have been ongoing and increased collaboration between CSOs and government"* (I5).[1]

Yet at the time of writing, almost three years after presidential assent, the PBO Act has yet to be implemented. Myriad obstacles thrown in its path attest to a deep challenge for the PBO Act and for the wider environment for CSOs in Kenya. Over less than three years the GoK has made five attempts to amend the Act. Observers, including those from CSOs, DAC/Gs, and within the GoK, see the thrust of the amendment efforts as undermining the Act's intent to enable an independent and accountable CSO sector in Kenya. CSOs claim they are subject to a *"legislative and smear campaign to reduce space for PBOs to operate"* (Ondieki 2015, par. 9). Throughout this period there has been a growing sense that collectively the backlash against CSOs is designed to instil fear in CSOs and their supporters (I4, I7, I15).

The PBO Act was subject to three amendment attempts in 2013/14 (RoK 2013b, 2014a; CSORG 2014), many of which CSOs considered as *"substantive, harmful and chang[ing] the letter and spirit of the PBO Act"* (CSORG 2014, par. 2). While the most controversial amendment proposal was for a 15% foreign funding cap on CSOs' revenues, other provisions at issue relate to: discretionary powers and independence of the PBO Regulatory Authority; voluntary or compulsory PBO migration to the Act; incentive-based CSO self-regulation or self-regulation under a quasi-independent, legislated CSO umbrella; channelling CSO funding through this umbrella; space for CSO participation in policy dialogue; tax exemptions and tax incentives for private donations; and access to GoK funding (CSORG 2014; ICNL 2014). Late in 2014 the PBO Act was amended via the Securities Law (Amendment) Act introducing an unspecified "classification" of CSOs (RoK 2014b, par. 96). In 2015 the GoK launched a PBO Task Force that, following cross-country consultations, delivered its report to the GoK (The PBO Taskforce 2015). The report largely fails to declare clearly on key controversial amendment proposals and has yet to be acted on.

Meanwhile, on two occasions during 2014/15, the NGOs Coordination Board undertook a sweep of its registry, first declaring the pending deregistration of over 500 CSOs, then an additional almost 1,000. While it is the regulator's role to monitor its registrants, the manner of its execution of this role raised questions regarding its intent. Affected CSOs sometimes learnt of their pending deregistration via the media, while official statements made reference to the closing of CSOs' bank accounts and repossession of assets, and associated CSOs with money laundering and terrorism (CIVICUS 2015a). Though the second deregistration announcement was retracted, damage had been done to the reputations of affected CSOs, while fuel was poured onto the fire of fear.

Accompanying these regulatory developments has been an anti-CSO public relations narrative, often intertwined with an anti-West-DAC/G narrative. The language of the 2014 sweep of the NGO registry *"put on notice donors who do not demand accountability from the NGOs they fund"* (Jamah 2014, par. 27). In a 2014 Heroes' Day speech, Kenya's President spoke of *"those abroad"* that *"fund and nurture various outfits"*, putting Kenya's destiny *"in the hands of unelected, unaccountable institutions that answer to elsewhere"* (PoK 2014, par. 25). This type of position is echoed in references to CSOs speaking the voice of their *"foreign masters"* (CIVICUS 2015b), while the term *"evil"* versus *"civil"* society is at times used by GoK officials (HRW 2013, par. 8).

The narrative also seeks to equate CSOs with terrorism in Kenya. Kenyatta's above-mentioned Heroes' Day speech reference was immediately followed by a commitment to seek transparency, *"especially important in enabling us to successfully combat the Al-Shabaab terrorists"* (PoK 2014, par. 27). In April 2015, three CSOs were placed on a GoK "List of Entities Suspected to be Associated with Al-Shabaab" (RoK 2015). Two of these CSOs won a court challenge when evidence linking them to terrorism was not forthcoming (Kenya Court Rules HakiAfrica and MHR Not Terrorist 2015).

CSOs have, at each stage of the amendment efforts, expressed their concerns; proposed alternative amendments; presented data on the social, economic, and democratic contribution of CSOs in Kenya; and participated in the PBO Task Force. DAC/Gs have also not remained silent on the issue. They have similarly articulated concerns through bilateral and joint diplomacy efforts. While reassuring the GoK that they are equally concerned with, and demand, accountability from the their CSO partners, they have also quietly communicated that reductions in their CSO funding due to a foreign funding cap would not result in these funds being redirected to government.

Influencing factors? Locating DAC governments in the landscape

Four dynamics in the DAC/G–CSO–GoK relationship may have unintended consequences on CSO space. First, real or perceived, historical and current DAC/G–CSO alliances and successes in rights and democracy reform seeking contribute to an autocratic GoK's hostility towards CSOs. Second, a preoccupation with counter-terror and security alliances may be reducing DAC/Gs' willingness to defend CSO space from restrictive GoK actions. Third, DAC/Gs' shifting priorities toward the private sector, trade, and investment interests suggest DAC/Gs have less room to manoeuvre in their traditional rights and democracy work, including in relation to CSO space. Fourth, DAC/Gs' CSO support and accountability mechanisms directly impact CSOs' operating space and sustainability, while also indirectly providing fodder for the GoK's rationale to restrict CSO space in the name of addressing gaps in CSOs' local accountability and legitimacy.

DAC/Gs have a significant place in these dynamics – and are the focus of this article – although they are not the primary driver in the regulation and treatment of CSOs in Kenya. While other factors that come into play, such as institutional capacities in the GoK, or CSOs' self-regulation efforts, are important, they are not examined here. The purpose in examining the above four factors is not to point fingers at DAC/Gs for what they are or are not doing in relation to CSO space. Rather, it is to highlight increasingly acute inconsistencies in DAC/G approaches and interests vis-à-vis their relationships with development country governments and CSOs, and the potential unintended consequences for CSO space.

DAC/Gs' influence on developing country governments is exercised through the carrot and stick approach. The former comes in the form of "positive" conditionalities, whereby DAC/Gs invest in certain actors and programming areas in developing countries to entice particular outcomes. The latter comes in the form of "negative" conditionalities, whereby the threat of withholding or suspending aid, diplomatic, or trade relations is extended, again to entice particular outcomes. While there is considerable literature on the legitimacy of conditionalities in the aid system, the assumption here is that conditionalities will remain a feature of DAC/Gs' development cooperation for the foreseeable future (Molenaers, Dellepiane, and Faust 2015, 2).

DAC/Gs are far from uniform in whether and when they apply such conditionalities in Kenya and elsewhere. Further, the degree of coordination across aid, trade, and diplomacy functions within a DAC/G's host country operations varies. Although DAC/Gs are not a monolith, space does not allow for accounting for the many differences across or within DAC/G behaviours.

It also needs to be recognised that perceptions of, and relationships with, CSOs vary between levels of the GoK and its ministries. References to the GoK here are to its main power holders and decision-makers.

Opposition in an autocratic environment: the crux of the matter?

When it comes to rights and democracy promotion, DAC/Gs and CSOs have often found themselves on the same side of reforms in Kenya, which has at times posed a threat to GoK power holders. Such threats have not sat well with the autocratic leadership that has largely dominated Kenya's political landscape.

In the post-Cold War era of the early 1990s, DAC/Gs increased funds for CSOs working on rights and democracy reform in Kenya as elsewhere in the developing world. In Kenya, this occurred alongside DAC/Gs' reduction or suspension of aid to the GoK when both macro-economic and political reforms could not be agreed on (I14; Maina 1998, 154). CSOs came to be increasingly seen by GoK leaders as *"fronts for their political opponents"* (Hornsby 2012, 587). CSOs' and DAC/Gs' struggle for a multi-party system was ultimately successful in 1992 (Maina 1998, 162), beginning a slow process toward Kenya's "second liberation" with the 2003 election of President Kibaki. Yet, DAC/Gs' (temporary) enthusiasm for the new GoK left CSOs out in the cold as much of the former's financing was, for a while, diverted from CSOs to the GoK (I8).

More recently, an informal DAC/G–CSO alliance has been evident in relation to Kenya's 2013 elections. At issue has been the participation and ultimate success of President Kenyatta and Deputy President Ruto in the race, despite their indictment to the International Criminal Court (ICC) for alleged crimes in relation to incitement of the post-election violence of 2007/08. In the view of these leaders, CSOs and their DAC/G funders are responsible for their indictments, having *"coached"* witnesses in the independent investigations producing the ICC cases' evidence (Menya 2014, par. 8).

While Kenyatta and Ruto have not been without CSO supporters, other CSOs, alongside DAC/Gs, have defended the ICC trials while opposing the participation of two indictees in the 2013 elections. CSOs' opposition to Kenyatta and Ruto's candidature included an unsuccessful appeal to Kenya's High Court to block the ICC indictees from running (Jacinto 2013, par. 27). Responding to Kenyatta and Ruto's lobbying for deferral or suspension of their ICC cases, a group of CSOs appealed to the ICC to encourage their pursuit (I12). Kenyatta and Ruto have chastised CSOs and DAC/Gs, with Ruto stating: *"NGOs should stop interfering with government matters, writing letters to their donors abroad to support the ICC intervention and compiling reports about post-election violence. It is none of their business"* (HRW 2013, par. 12). Throughout their election campaign and today, the leaders *"effectively cast international responses to the ICC case as a sign of Western interference in Kenya's domestic affairs"* (Jacinto 2013, par. 5).

Many CSOs also ended up on the opposing side of the current GoK when their petition to the Supreme Court regarding the outcome of the extremely close and contested 2013 election results was merged with the official opposition's petition (I3; Long et al. 2013, 142). Major DAC/Gs also took a stance in 2013, with a number of key EU countries stating they would limit contact with a leadership facing ICC charges, and a senior US official cautioning Kenyan voters that *"choices have consequences"* (Jacinto 2013, paras. 32–33). CSOs' reform interventions have been especially unwelcome given the GoK's legitimacy crisis (I22; I7), and reinforce the perception *"that CSOs are opposed to the government"* (USAID 2014, 6). Today there is a GoK contingent that perceives CSOs as *"advancing the interests of Western countries"* (I8).

The Kenyan leadership's animosity toward the ICC, DAC/Gs, and CSOs are intertwined and run deep. A narrative of the ICC as an anti-African tool of the West is advanced by Kenya's leaders, notwithstanding that the ICC was the option chosen by parliamentarians over a special domestic court initially proposed by post-election violence investigators. Kenya's leaders have been pursuing expansion of the African Union's mandate to take over the ICC's role for cases involving African states, including extending immunity to sitting heads of state or senior officials (Kikechi 2015, paras. 3–4).

The ICC is not the only challenge faced by the GoK today when it comes to CSO and DAC/G rights and advocacy reform seeking. The current GoK is the first to have to deal fully with the requirements of accountability, transparency, citizen participation, and an array of rights enshrined in the 2010 Constitution, as well as considerable resource and power sharing under a constitutionally mandated devolution programme. Major DAC/G and multilateral donors are supporting initiatives to implement the Constitution, including through CSOs which are taking up the charge to ensure the Constitution and its progressive Bill of Rights are implemented. Many CSOs are thus increasingly vocal in the pursuit of accountability (I47), though as power holders adjust to the new constitutional requirements CSOs face accusations of *"witch hunting"* (I32; I46).

In December 2014, the ICC's Chief Prosecutor withdrew the charges against Kenyatta due to obstruction of justice in the form of non-provision of records, witness bribery, intimidation, and possible killing (Bowcott 2014). As Ruto's case, equally fraught, struggles on, Kenya's leaders seem emboldened and their anti-West, anti-CSO sentiments seem to gain momentum, perhaps fuelled by the perception that DAC/Gs' continued engagement with the GoK increasingly reveals a lack of resolve in the former's rights and democracy efforts, as discussed below.

Complicating matters: terrorism and security

There is no question that the war on terror is a global preoccupation. Terrorism is not a new threat in Kenya, preceding even the 1998 US embassy bombing. Since Kenyan troops entered Somalia in 2011, Al-Shabaab-linked terror cells and "home-grown" allies have escalated their attacks in Kenya, including the devastating Westgate Mall and Garissa University attacks in 2013 and 2015. Kenyans are well aware of the reality of the terrorist threat and want the GoK to step up efforts to address it, though the question of how is a topic of debate. In December 2014 a new Securities Law (Amendment) was passed amid great controversy and a brawl in Kenya's Parliament. The Act, considered "draconian" by opposition MPs and activists, was defended as being necessary "to fight Islamist militants threatening Kenya's security" (Kenya Security Bill: MPs Brawl as Measures Approved 2014, pars.18 and 4). The GoK's approach is perceived as simultaneously inadequate and "heavy-handed" (York 2015, par. 4). Police and security forces are accused of abuse of power in relation to alleged surveillance, intimidation, excessive use of force, extra-judicial killing, and harassment of Muslim human rights CSOs.

The implications of Kenya's terror threat for CSO space are manifold. Some see that the climate of fear associated with Kenya's terror threat is being used to justify the narrowing of democratic rights and freedoms, and more specifically, restrictions on CSO space. Reflecting on changes in the state–CSO relationship over time, a Kenyan academic suggests that terrorism is today's alternative to the accusations of Marxism heard during the Cold War era, meant to "demonise and vilify" the CSO sector (I39) and "stigmatise dissent" (I11). In the words of another observer, "we begin to think that [the GoK] is using [terrorism] as an excuse to bring in certain dictatorial measures to ensure that people don't have a voice" (I7). Indeed, official justification for the PBO Act amendments included non-specified terror-related concerns (Houghton and Muchai 2014, par. 19). And as noted, CSOs are sometimes targeted by the GoK as perpetrators or facilitators of terrorism, despite questionably reliable or a lack of evidence.

While this climate of fear is not itself attributable to DAC/G influence, it may impact their actions in relation to CSO space. Kenya is a key partner for DAC/Gs in the global war on terror (Menya 2014, par. 33; Obala 2014, 8). The country is of strategic importance given its proximity to volatile South Sudan and Somalia; Al-Shabaab's activism and linkages to global terror perpetrators; the largely underground coastal independence movement; and Kenya's increasingly alienated Muslim minority, around which there are fears of radicalisation. Major DAC/Gs have been closely collaborating with the GoK with counter-terror assistance and intelligence sharing. The interest in a strong Kenyan counter-terror ally reaches across DAC/Gs even if it requires "closer links" with the GoK than DAC/Gs "might otherwise … desire" (Hornsby 2012, 630).

This raises the question as to whether the need for a strong counter-terror alliance, however uneasy, may reduce DAC/Gs' willingness to act on concerns of rights, democracy, and shrinking CSO space in Kenya, as some suggest (Menya 2014, par. 32). Acknowledging a level of DAC/G diplomatic engagement on the shrinking CSO space issue in Kenya, one observer noted that nonetheless, "at the large level, [DAC/Gs] want to work with the Kenyan government, to deal with terrorist issues … those issues are the priority" (I18). The terror climate seems to be making it increasingly delicate for DAC/Gs, familiar with the growing issue of balancing rights and security at home, to step into the fray in defence of CSO space. Following the 2015 and 2016 terror attacks in Paris and Brussels, global security cooperation can only be expected to increase, and so too may DAC/Gs' willingness to see rights compromised over security in Kenya.

Thus, while DAC/G-CSO alliances and actions in rights and democracy reform have raised GoK ire as previously discussed, the growing imperative of government-to-government security alliances may well be giving rise to new parameters around the old rights and democracy endeavours. Questions of whether counter-terror concerns may be undermining DAC/Gs' intent and efforts in the rights and democracy realm, inclusive of protecting CSO space, are worthy of deeper exploration.

Trade, investment, and rights: competing priorities?

A further complicating factor when it comes to DAC/Gs' rights and democracy efforts relates to developments in the economic and aid landscape in Kenya. Kenya's dependence on foreign aid has been decreasing, down to 6% of Gross National Income in 2012 from 14% in 1992, and from 52% of central government expenditures in 1992 to 27% in 2012. This latter ratio is considerably less than neighbouring countries, including Tanzania at 41% of central government expenditures, or Uganda at 52%. Still, aid to Kenya has remained noteworthy and shown incremental increases in absolute terms over the past decade, with some surges and dips, reaching US$3.2 billion in 2013 (All figures W B 2015). A characteristic of aid flows to Kenya is that they have for the most part not included the substantial government-to-government flows popular since the early 2000s. Largely due to corruption concerns, DAC/Gs have shied away from general budget support (Fengler 2011), especially so under the current GoK (I3).

Concomitantly, DAC countries' trade and foreign direct investment in Kenya have been on the rise. EU members remain Kenya's largest trading partners, with trade between the EU and Kenya increasing almost steadily since 2004 (EC 2015). Foreign direct investment doubled between 2013 and 2014 (ADB, OECD, and UNDP 2015a, 49) and is expected to grow further in 2015 (Masinde 2015). Increasingly Kenya is *"becoming a favoured business hub, not only for oil and gas exploration, but also for manufacturing, transport and information communication technology"* (ADB, OECD, and UNDP 2015a, 49). Since 2014 Kenya has been one of a handful of countries newly minted with lower middle-income status and is Africa's fifth largest economy (WB 2014).

Amidst this trend lies the new private sector thrust that has emerged in DAC/G development cooperation policies. Across many DAC/Gs, and reflected in global agreements such as the 2011 Busan Partnership Agreement and the new Sustainable Development Goals 2030, *"the private sector has become the new donor darling"* (Kindornay and Reilly-King 2013, 31). The private sector is seen as the cornerstone to achieving decades long sought-after development progress, almost the "magic bullet" that CSOs were seen to be two decades ago, and a way to leverage dwindling aid budgets. While private sector development is not a new theme in development cooperation, what is new is its prevalence across DAC/Gs' policies, and the emphasis on private sector partnerships, including as a means to foster the private sector at home, with *"developing countries … as key markets or investment sites for donor countries' firms and investors"* (36, 31). DAC/Gs for which this policy angle holds true to greater or lesser degrees of explicitness are all present in Kenya.

The result of this new private sector thrust so far does not seem to be a reduction in flows to CSOs. In absolute terms, on average, DAC/Gs' CSO flows globally have increased, from US$18.2 billion in 2009 to US$19.6 billion in 2013 (OECD 2015, 5), and have also been increasing in Kenya, though also with surges and dips (I3; I43).

However, observers suggest a risk that DAC/Gs' private sector priority may be muddying the waters of their rights and democracy interests. In the words of one multilateral agency interviewee:

"We're shying away and cowering to what governments are trying to do … It's very subtle … There is just a tepid approach to this issue that says, 'You know what? In the broader scheme of what I'm dealing with here on loan X and loan Y for the hydroelectricity dam, and for the road, and for that, and the wide range of the things that I'm doing here, I do not want to commit to rattling the Kenyan government on the issue of foreign funding for NGOs.'" (I19)

In this vein, a *"deference afforded by States to economic considerations over other interests"* may be taking hold in DAC/Gs' engagement in Kenya and elsewhere (UNSR 2015, par. 99). The reality of this risk is reflected in a recent DAC peer review cautioning one DAC/G to *"remain vigilant to avoid commercial interests over-riding development priorities"* (OECD 2014, 30).

The growing presence of China in Kenya may also render DAC/Gs more sensitive to the need to protect their commercial relationship with the GoK. Reflecting on DAC/Gs' engagement on the shrinking CSO space issue, a CSO interviewee shared:

> "I feel right now, donors are a let-down. Because since [Kenya] was upgraded to middle income, there have been more business opportunities … So everybody's starting to see how much money they can get out of business, since [China] is taking off. So [DAC/Gs] are really not very keen … to antagonise [the GoK] … Because most of the tenders, they're coming from the government anyway. And they want to use public–private partnership … And the government is going to provide the guarantee of cheaper land and whatever." (I6)

China's investment in Kenya is high, if rife with *"procurement questions"*, and less welcomed by Kenya's private sector and citizens than by decision-making politicians and officials (Obala 2014, 3). Despite positive trade and investment figures for DAC countries, there is a sense that in Kenya, China is winning *"the battle for business as their 'ask-no-questions' and 'bribe-all-who-matter' model has stumped their Western competitors"* (Menya 2014, par. 33).

The GoK understands well the country's attractiveness for DAC/Gs in relation to trade and foreign direct investment, and seems to be using this not only to its economic but political advantage. An official narrative of turning east to China among other BRIC-type countries has been in place, with a slightly veiled threat to DAC/Gs (Obala 2014). While some Kenyan and DAC/G observers see the turning east narrative as *"rhetoric"* (I3) meant to *"hoodwink and cajole"* (I39), it seems nonetheless to provide the GoK with *"leeway"* (I3). As DAC/Gs remain concerned with *"retaining [their] wider relationship with Government"* (I24), their position in relation to rights and democracy is weakened with a GoK message that they are being held over a barrel. According to one DAC/G representative, DAC/Gs *"have been intimidated by Government … they are on the defensive and ceding ground"* (I16). Meanwhile, DAC/Gs' tendency to avoid government-to-government aid flows creates *"discomfort"*, if not outright perturbs the GoK (I7), not least of which is due to missed opportunities for state patronage. When political tensions around the ICC and terror-related nervousness are thrown into this mix, DAC/Gs are on tenterhooks, and are seen to be *"shying away"* from speaking out when it comes to issues of rights and democracy (Menya 2014, par. 32).

As with DAC/Gs' counter-terror priority, questions arise as to whether DAC/Gs' shifting priorities toward the private sector, trade, and investment interests and the associated imperative of maintaining trade and investment doors wide open may be at the expense of their rights and democracy interests, inclusive of the defence of CSO space, and counter to DAC/Gs' purported intent.

DAC/G modalities of CSO support and perceptions of CSO legitimacy

There is no shortage of literature on the ways in which the support DAC/Gs provide to CSOs facilitates or hampers CSOs' ability to operate effectively and accountably (e.g. INTRAC 2013). A mitigating factor in Kenya, as in other developing countries, is CSOs' dependence on foreign funding, which though it can hardly be blamed on DAC/Gs, nonetheless fuels concerns over CSOs' sustainability and legitimacy (PEN 2007). Taking this dependence as a given even in the medium term, there are ways in which DAC/Gs extend their financial support to CSOs in Kenya that leave room for improvement.

In Kenya as elsewhere, CSO funding is often short-term and project-based, while also largely directed to donor-defined thematic and geographic areas of priority (I2; I13; I15; I36). CSOs reflect that DAC/Gs' funding priorities affect the programming that they are able to do (USAID 2014, xv). DAC/Gs' increasing emphasis on accountability through rigid results reporting has also been a source of unease, especially when it comes to the long-term, process-oriented, and qualitative changes sought through rights and democracy work (I11). These factors combined mean that CSOs find themselves placing greater emphasis on "upward" accountability to donors, rather than on the "downward" or "horizontal" accountability necessary to the local constituents they seek to serve or represent (I5; I10).

DAC/G support that is less directed toward DAC/G priorities and leaves room for CSOs to be responsive to and invest in *"building a local constituency that would then give the local impression that* [CSOs] *have the interest of the citizens at heart and not someone else's agenda"* (I10) is insufficiently available in Kenya. This type of support, generally understood in its "best" form as core or institutional support, can enhance local ownership of CSO initiatives, while reducing the results monitoring and reporting requirements to DAC/Gs that can distort domestic accountability relationships. It also allows CSOs to invest in organisational strengthening to meet their self-assessed governance and accountability gaps. These could include, for example, investments in the communications and public relations that CSOs need to raise awareness, with the GoK and the public, of their quieter con-tributions to Kenya's development so that they are not just seen as *"making noise in Nairobi"* (I5).

A further challenge relates to the availability of information on DAC/Gs' CSO support. Making DAC/Gs' support objectives and criteria fully transparent can help avoid accusations of *"political meddling"* (Youngs 2015, 46). An oft-heard justification from the GoK for stricter CSO regulation is that, *"we don't know what* [CSOs] *are doing"*, which poses not only coordination and duplication challenges, but con-tributes to mistrust [I14]. That the regulations under the NGOs Coordination Act and PBO Act necessi-tate annual activity and financial reporting from CSOs to the GoK means that information sharing and data compilation are in a sense a shared CSO–GoK responsibility. Arguably DAC/Gs also have a responsibility for full and coordinated transparency here, even simply as a means of providing assur-ances that their CSO support is fully accounted for.

Overall, CSOs' financial dependence, combined with DAC/Gs' financing modalities and account-ability requirements that underemphasise responsiveness and accountability to in-country constitu-ents, not only has a direct impact on CSO sustainability. It also leaves CSOs vulnerable to accusations that they lack accountability and legitimacy locally, while they speak for "foreign masters". Combined with insufficiently available information on DAC/Gs' CSO funding, these provide additional rationale for any GoK intent to shrink CSO space.

Conclusion

The unintended consequences of DAC/Gs' CSO support and policy dialogue efforts, or lack thereof, to influence developing countries' rights and democracy landscape are evident in Kenya. The sustain-ability of rights and democracy gains of the past 25 years, of the CSO space that is part and parcel of these gains, and ultimately of CSOs and the CSO sector, are at risk.

DAC/Gs could do more to avoid some of the pitfalls posed by their CSO support modalities. Greater sensitivity is needed to the fact that DAC/G funders often have more leverage with CSOs than do CSOs' constituents or beneficiaries, and that there are implications for CSOs' relationships of local accountability and, by extension, their legitimacy. The challenge of CSOs' financial depen-dence is not one easily addressed. No amount of DAC/G-supported CSO capacity development in fun-draising will address the absence of alternative GoK, private, or income-generation sources. Such sources are not expected to fill financial sustainability gaps for Kenya's CSOs any time soon, and cer-tainly won't have a chance if resource diversification provisions such as in Kenya's PBO Act are amended as proposed by the GoK.

DAC/Gs can also steer a course of "sectoral equity" in which the CSO and private sectors are each treated with fairness and impartiality, including with regulation grounded in law, standards, and norms, rather than a course that privileges the private sector as is the noted tendency (UNSR 2015, pars. 16–17). There is no reason not to see protection of CSO space as part and parcel of any DAC/Gs' holistic, coherent, long-term strategy in a country like Kenya. Rights and democracy pro-motion and the protection of CSO space that goes with it are easily reconcilable with that of private sector promotion. After all, *"the presence of a critical civil society can be viewed as a barometer of a State's confidence and stability – important factors for businesses looking to invest their money"* (par. 18). Equally when it comes to counter-terrorism, a narrative in which Kenya's CSOs are touted as the peace and security-building allies they can be, for example, in discouraging violence before and after the 2013 elections (Long et al. 2013, 149), rather than as subjects of blanket condemnation, could help turn the current narrative on its head.

DAC/Gs can help resist the challenges to CSO space by bearing in mind that the categorisation of their own and CSOs' rights and democracy pursuits as representing *"foreign values"* is *"insulting to every Kenyan citizen"* (Kiai 2013, par. 23). Where the regulation and treatment of CSOs flies in the face of international human rights commitments and Kenya's Constitution, defending CSO space is hardly "imperialist", nor unpatriotic. Undoubtedly DAC/Gs' financial support has allowed for greater CSO rights and democracy activism than would be the case in its absence. Nevertheless, such activism is not a foreign concept. Kenyans have organised themselves into CSOs for many years as a means to channel their *"political energies"* in the pursuit of reform and in the face of limited opportunities to do so otherwise (Hornsby 2012, 449).

Certainly Kenya's political leaders have seen that DAC/Gs and CSO rights and democracy efforts can alter Kenya's political and governance landscape, sometimes to the leadership's detriment. DAC/Gs need to tread carefully but decisively regarding their approach to political conditionalities related to rights and democracy, as CSO space is the easy target for GoK retaliation. DAC/Gs' historical *"stop-and-go' behaviour"* (Fengler 2011, par. 4) as they divert funding flows between CSOs and the GoK depending on satisfaction or not with GoK behaviour contributes a volatility to both the GoK and CSOs. It leaves the latter on financial and political shaky ground as it may reinforce GoK perception that CSOs are an opposing force to be reckoned with. Moreover, in countries like Kenya – with growing economies, decreasing aid dependency, the Chinese non-interference option, and the terrorist threat – the state's ample *"room to manoeuvre in their responses to Western powers"* (Obala 2014, 6) calls for delicate consideration by DAC/Gs of their actions and how they are framed. DAC/Gs' rights and democracy efforts *"need to be refashioned as a more subtle and sensitive endeavour, but must also not become overly defensive"* (Youngs 2015, 46).

In commenting on DAC/G actions it must be acknowledged that an outside observer cannot readily understand the nuances in any DAC/G's approach to the gamut of its development, democracy, trade, investment, and security objectives. Yet in an era where DAC/Gs seem to be finding themselves increasingly challenged to operate coherently, there is room for policy learning toward a twenty-first century approach to CSO support, financial and otherwise; to rights and democracy promotion; and to political conditionalities. Such learning is imperative to avoid collateral damage to the sustainability of the rights and democracy gains of the past 25 years, of CSO space, and of the CSO sector itself. A greater awareness of the potential unintended consequences of DAC/G actions is one step toward that learning.

Note

1. Bracketed numbers preceded by "I" denote interviewee sources.

Acknowledgements

The perspectives contained in this article are the author's own and reflect findings from her PhD research.

Disclosure statement

No potential conflict of interest was reported by the author.

References

ADB (African Development Bank), OECD (Organisation for Economic Cooperation), and UNDP (Development, and United Nations Development Programme). 2015. "External Financial Flows and Tax Revenues for Africa." *African Economic Outlook.* doi:10.1787/aeo-2014-en.

Bowcott, O. 2014. "ICC Drops Murder and Rape Charges against Kenyan President." *The Guardian*, December 5. www.theguardian.com/world/2014/dec/05/crimes-humanity-charges-kenya-president-dropped-uhuru-kenyatta.

CIVICUS. 2015a. "Intimidation of Kenyan NGOs Unwarranted." *News*, November 3. www.civicus.org/index.php/en/media-centre-129/news-and-resources-127/2325-intimidation-of-kenyan-ngos-unwarranted.

CIVICUS. 2015b. "Attacks on Civil Society Undermining Democracy and Development in Kenya." Johannesburg, SA. Accessed March 5, 2016. http://civicus.org/images/Kenya Policy Action Brief.pdf.

CSORG (CSO Reference Group). 2014. "Briefing Note on the Memorandum to the Public Benefits Act 2013." Naibori: CSORG.

EC (European Commission). 2015. "European Union, Trade in Goods with Kenya." Accessed March 5, 2016. http://trade.ec.europa.eu/doclib/docs/2006/september/tradoc_113407.pdf.

Fengler, W. 2011. "Three Myths about Aid to Kenya." *The World Bank - AfricaCan End Poverty Blog*, November 14. Accessed March 5, 2016. http://blogs.worldbank.org/africacan/three-myths-about-aid-to-kenya.

Hornsby, C. 2012. *Kenya: A History since Independence.* London: I.B. Tauris.

Houghton, I., and S. Muchai. 2014. "Protecting Civic Space against #NGOMuzzle Laws in Kenya." Accessed March 5, 2016. https://irunguh.wordpress.com/2014/03/31/protecting-civic-space-against-ngomuzzle-laws-in-kenya/.

HRW (Human Rights Watch). 2013. "Kenya: Rights Defenders under Attack." *News*, October 4. https://www.hrw.org/news/2013/10/04/kenya-rights-defenders-under-attack.

ICNL. 2014. "NGO Law Monitor: Kenya, July 29." Accessed March 5, 2016. www.icnl.org/research/monitor/kenya.html.

INTRAC (International NGO Training and Research Centre). 2013. "Support to Civil Society: Emerging Evaluation Lessons." *Evaluation Insights* (8). Accessed March 5, 2016. www.oecd.org/dac/evaluation/Evaluation Insight Civil Society FINAL for print and WEB 20131004.pdf.

Jacinto, L. 2013. "Kenyatta Blasts UK – With a Little Help from British PR." *France 24*, March 7. www.france24.com/en/20130307-kenyatta-blasts-uk-with-little-help-british-pr-firm.

Jamah, A. 2014. "Kenya Jobs to Go as Uhuru Adminstration Revokes Registrations of 525 NGOs in Kenya, Freezes Their Accounts." *Standard Digital News*, December 17. http://standardmedia.co.ke/article/2000144966/govt-revokes-registrations-of-510-ngos-freezes-their-accounts?

"Kenya Security Bill: MPs Brawl as Measures Approved". 2014. *BBC News*, December 18. www.bbc.com/news/world-africa-30530423.

"Kenya Court Rules HakiAfrica and MHR Not Terrorist". 2015. *BBC News*, June 11. www.bbc.com/news/world-africa-33092786.

Kiai, M. 2013. "In Kenya, Averting a Move to Strangle Civil Society with the Financial Noose." *Open Democracy*, December 18. www.opendemocracy.net/openglobalrights/maina-kiai/in-kenya-averting-move-to-strangle-civil-society-with-financial-noose.

Kikechi, B. 2015. "Kenyan Team in Addis Leads Push for African Alternative to ICC." *Standard Digital News*, February 1. www.standardmedia.co.ke/?articleID = 2000150054&story_title = Kenya-kenyan-team-in-addis-leads-push-for-african-alternative-to-icc.

Kindornay, S., and F. Reilly-King. 2013. "Promotion and Partnership: Bilateral Donor Approaches to the Private Sector." In *Private Sector Development - Business Plan or Development Strategy?*, 31–38. Vienna: Österreichische Forschungsstiftung für Internationale Entwicklung. http://www.oefse.at/Downloads/publikationen/oeepol/Artikel 2013/3_Kindornay_Reilly.pdf.

Long, J. D., K. Kanyinga, K. E. Ferree, and C. Gibson. 2013. "Choosing Peace over Democracy." *Journal of Democracy* 24 (3): 140–155. doi:10.1353/jod.2013.0048.

Maina, W. 1998. "Kenya: The State, Donors and the Politics of Democratization." In *Civil Society and the Aid Industry*, edited by A. Van Rooy, 134–167. London: Earthscan.

Masinde, J. 2015. "Kenya Eyes Sh200bn in Foreign Investment." *Daily Nation*, August 23. www.nation.co.ke/business/Kenya-eyes-Sh200bn-in-foreign-investment/-/996/2843746/-/68b6f0z/-/index.html.

Menya, W. 2014. "State Targeting Us over Support for Hague Cases, Civil Society Protests." *Daily Nation*, October 25. http://mobile.nation.co.ke/news/Civil-Society-ICC-Hague-Cases-Jubilee-Government/-/1950946/2499628/-/format/xhtml/-/15mi3qz/-/index.html.

Molenaers, N., S. Dellepiane, and J. Faust. 2015. "Political Conditionality and Foreign Aid." *World Development* 75: 2–12. doi:10.1016/j.worlddev.2015.04.001.

Obala, L. 2014. "The Myths and Realities of Kenya's Turning to the East." Accessed March 5, 2016. http://studies.aljazeera.net/ResourceGallery/media/Documents/2014/5/22/201452212924830734Kenya and China.pdf.

OECD (Organisation for Economic Co-operation and Development). 2014. "OECD Development Co-Operation Peer Reviews: United Kingdom, 2014." Paris: OECD. doi:10.1787/9789264226579-en.

OECD. 2015. "Aid for CSOs." Paris: OECD. Accessed March 5, 2016. www.oecd.org/dac/peer-reviews/Aid%20for%20CSOs%20in%202013%20_%20Dec%202015.pdf.

Ondieki, E. 2015. "Civil Societies Call for NGOs Board Overhaul." *Daily Nation*, October 31. www.nation.co.ke/news/Civil-societies-call-for-NGOs-board-overhaul/-/1056/2937096/-/wafslq/-/index.html.

PEN (Poverty Eradication Network). 2007. "Enhancing the Competence and Sustainability of High Quality CSOs in Kenya." Nairobi: PEN. Accessed March 5, 2016. www.akdn.org/publications/civil_society_kenya_competence.pdf.

PoK (President of Kenya). 2014. "Speech by His Excellency Hon. Uhuru Kenyatta, C.G.H., President and Commander-in-Chief of the Defense Forces of the Republic of Kenya during the Fifth Mashujaa Day, 20th October 2014." http://allafrica.com/stories/201410202625.html.

RoK (Republic of Kenya). 1990. The Non-Governmental Organizations Co-Ordination Act, 1990. Kenya. Accessed March 5, 2016. http://andalucia.isf.es/guia_kenia/anexos/3/3_2.pdf.

RoK. 2013a. "Public Benefit Organizations Act, 2013 No. 18." www.khrc.or.ke/component/search/?searchword=public+benefits&ordering=&searchphrase=all.

RoK. 2013b. The Statute Law (Miscellaneous Amendments) (No. 2) Bill, 2013 - Kenya Gazette Supplement No. 146 (Bills No. *32)*. Vol. 147. Kenya. http://kenyalaw.org/kl/fileadmin/pdfdownloads/bills/2013/TheStatuteLaw(Miscellaneous Amendments)Bill2013.pdf.

RoK. 2014a. The Statute Law (Miscellaneous Amendments) (No. *2) Bill, 2014 - Kenya Gazette Supplement No. 75 (National Assembly Bills No. 24)*. Vol. 19. Kenya. http://kenyalaw.org/kl/fileadmin/pdfdownloads/bills/StatutesLawMiscellaneous(Amendments)Bill2014.pdf.

RoK. 2014b. The Security Laws (Amendment) Act, 2014. Kenya. www.cickenya.org/index.php/legislation/acts/item/447-the-securtty-laws-amendment-act-2014.

RoK. 2015. "Gazette Notice No. 2326." *The Kenya Gazette*, April 7. http://puntlandi.com/wp-content/uploads/2015/04/TERROR-LIST.pdf.

The PBO Taskforce. 2015. "Taskforce Report on the Public Benefit Organizations Act, 2013 (PBOs Act, 2013)." Accessed March 5, 2016. http://www.ngobureau.or.ke/?wpdmpro = final-task-force-2014-15-report-on-the-pbos-act-2013.

UNSR (United Nations Special Rapporteur on the rights to freedom of peaceful association and assembly). 2015. "Report of the Special Rapporteur on the Rights to Freedom of Peaceful Assembly and of Association (A/70/266)." http://freeassembly.net/rapporteurreports/sectoral-equity/.

USAID (United States Agency for International Development). 2014. "The 2013 CSO Sustainability Index for Sub-Saharan Africa." Washington, DC: USAID. Accessed March 5, 2016. www.usaid.gov/sites/default/files/documents/1866/2013_Africa_CSOSI.pdf.

World Bank. 2014. "Kenya: A Bigger, Better Economy." *News*, September 30. www.worldbank.org/en/news/feature/2014/09/30/kenya-a-bigger-better-economy.

World Bank. 2015. "World Development Indicators." Accessed March 5, 2016. http://databank.worldbank.org/data/reports.aspx?source=2&series

York, G. 2015. "Anti-Terror Tactics Targeting Muslim Leaders Provoking Tensions in Kenya." *The Globe and Mail*, July 2. www.theglobeandmail.com/news/world/anti-terror-tactics-targeting-muslim-leaders-provoking-tensions-in-kenya/article25236344/.

Youngs, D. 2015. "Rethinking Civil Society and Support for Democracy." Accessed March 5, 2016. http://eba.se/wp-content/uploads/2015/04/Rapport-2015-01-med-framsida_för_web.pdf.

Lessons for supporting policy influencing in restrictive environments

Anique Claessen and Piet de Lange

ABSTRACT

Donors have rediscovered the importance of civil society in creating the political conditions for sustainable development. This article describes trends in diminishing space for civil society organisations (CSOs) and presents findings and lessons based on an evaluation of Dutch support for policy influencing. Restrictive environments for policy influencing engagement affect levels of effectiveness and threaten the sustainability of civil society. Aspects that are particularly important are civic engagement and cooperation between civil society actors. Building a strong support base is key, and local networks and international contacts are crucial. Furthermore, donors can help defend CSOs' operating space.

Les bailleurs de fonds ont redécouvert l'importance de la société civile au moment de créer les conditions politiques requises pour le développement durable. Cet article décrit les tendances de l'espace de plus en plus étroit réservé aux organisations de la société civile (OSC) et présente les conclusions et les enseignements basés sur une évaluation du soutien apporté par les Pays-Bas aux activités d'influence des politiques générales (IP). Des environnements restrictifs pour l'action d'IP ont une incidence sur le niveau d'efficacité et menacent la durabilité de la société civile. Les aspects qui sont tout particulièrement importants sont le dialogue civique et la coopération entre les acteurs de la société civile. Il est essentiel de bâtir une base de soutien solide, et les réseaux locaux et les contacts internationaux sont cruciaux. Qui plus est, les bailleurs de fonds peuvent contribuer à défendre l'espace d'opération des OSC.

Los donantes han redescubierto el importante papel desempeñado por la sociedad civil en la creación de condiciones políticas propicias para el desarrollo. El presente artículo describe la tendencia a disminuir el espacio de participación de las organizaciones de la sociedad civil (OSC), presentando los hallazgos y los aprendizajes surgidos de una evaluación encaminada a valorar el apoyo otorgado desde Holanda para hacer incidencia en políticas (IP). Aquellos ambientes que restringen la IP afectan los niveles de eficacia, amenazando la sostenibilidad de la sociedad civil. Los aspectos que revisten particular importancia tienen que ver con la participación civil y la cooperación entre actores de la sociedad civil. En este sentido, adquiere relevancia la construcción de una fuerte base de apoyo y el enlace con las redes locales y los contactos internacionales. Asimismo, los donantes pueden contribuir a defender el espacio en que se desenvuelven las OSC.

Introduction

Civil society agency is not uncontested and is continually under threat. The enabling environment for civil society, which depends on freedom of expression, assembly, and association, is under pressure in many countries. This jeopardises the sustainability of civil society. In some countries, the environment is so restrictive that civil society organisations (CSOs) fear for their survival and their staff for their lives. These restrictions seriously limit CSOs' campaigns and the extent to which they are able to achieve their goals.

The main purpose of the "Evaluation of Policy Influencing, Lobbying and Advocacy" by the Policy and Operations Evaluation Department (IOB) of the Netherlands Ministry of Foreign Affairs was to contribute to insights and lessons that support the development of lobbying and advocacy policies and, in particular, to gain a better understanding of how the ministry may best support CSOs working on influencing policy in developing countries.[1] Many policy choices by donors are mainly politically motivated and are hardly substantiated by evidence on the effectiveness of donor assistance. This is particularly the case when it comes to policy influencing. There is little systematic knowledge and information available about the effectiveness of support provided for lobbying and advocacy, nor about the factors leading to or impeding success. The evaluation focused on understanding and iden-tifying the factors explaining the results of external support. The main evaluation question was: !What are the lessons for donors and Northern non-governmental development organisations (NGDOs) for improving the effectiveness of their support for Southern CSOs' capacity to influence policy?!

This article presents the findings and lessons on the effectiveness of support for PI in restrictive environ-ments, and links these findings to the opportunities for, and challenges to, the sustainability of civil society.

Evaluation findings

This section describes trends in diminishing space for civil society activities and organisations and discusses some key findings of the evaluation of the effectiveness of policy influencing (PI) in restric-tive environments.

Environments for civil society engagement are becoming more restrictive

Establishing an enabling environment for civil society engagement entails guaranteeing freedom of expression, association, and assembly, as enshrined in international human rights standards. These freedoms are under pressure in many countries (Shrinking Political Space of Civil Society Action 2011; Poskitt 2011; Trócaire 2012; CIVICUS 2013). Shrinking or restrictive space for civil society is often associated with authoritarian governments (Calingaert 2013). However, although room for manoeuvre is influenced by state capacity and the type of regime, CSOs increasingly face difficulties in fulfilling their mandates even in democratic countries like India or Brazil (Shrinking Political Space of Civil Society Action 2011).

These restrictions threaten the sustainability of civil society, as it cannot function optimally and fulfil the roles that are so important to achieving inclusive development. Especially for policy influen-cing, the enabling environment defines the scope for engagement and the success of interventions. Policy influencing aims to create conditions for social justice and political and civil liberties, and its reach and success are determined by levels of political freedom and respect for fundamental rights.

Restrictions on the space for civil society – a disabling environment

The extent to which the environment in which CSOs operate is enabling or constraining is first and foremost determined by the presence or absence of formal provisions safeguarding this space. However, "informal conditions that facilitate or hinder CSO engagement", such as political, socio-econ-omic, and cultural attitudes and practices, also need to be taken in to account (ITAD and COWI 2012,

51). Common restrictions on civil society and CSOs include barriers to entry, interference with activities, and limitations or restrictions on foreign funding (Bruch et al. 2013).

The CIVICUS State of Civil Society Report 2013 convincingly illustrates how space for civil society is curbed by governments and elites and faces threats from big business. According to the report, *"Russia was perhaps the most prominent example* [of countries that restricted funding for CSOs in 2012], *but Bangladesh, Kazakhstan, Malaysia, Nicaragua and Pakistan were also considering or have already adopted foreign funding restrictions"* (CIVICUS 2013, 74). When we look at this trend, Egypt, Ethiopia, and Russia appear to have spurred a "contagion effect", with their laws and behaviour setting an example for other countries (CIVICUS 2013, 74; see also Bruch et al. 2013).

Some types of CSOs, especially those focusing on policy or advocacy, struggle to raise domestic resources and rely heavily on foreign funding. Attempts to limit the supply of foreign funding to such CSOs have therefore become a tactic for governments seeking to silence critics in civil society. In addition to funding constraints, a wide range of governments have continued to impose measures restricting individuals' ability to dissent, demonstrate, and exercise their freedoms of assembly and expression. According to CIVICUS (2013, 75):

> "A number of countries also introduced laws that prohibit certain types of online content or seek to impede bloggers and other internet users. Such measures stifle the right of individuals and CSOs to receive and provide information and to exchange ideas with civil society counterparts inside and outside their home countries."

Governments have used a variety of arguments to rationalise restrictions on the operating space for civil society organisations (Poskitt 2011; Trócaire 2012; WMD 2012). Anti-terrorism laws, for example, are used to limit international support for CSOs. Furthermore, CSOs are perceived (or framed) as being part of the opposition or rebel movements, and their operations are restricted in the name of stability. Other arguments for regulation include the need to enhance the accountability and transparency of CSOs, counter corruption, and ensure results. Furthermore, harmonising CSO activities with government plans and coordinating development activities are frequently used as reasons for influencing what activities CSOs can engage in. Perhaps the most common argument for restricting foreign funding is that it interferes in domestic affairs and therefore constitutes a breach of sovereignty. This is related to the argument of a *"perceived lack of legitimacy with the local population"* (Trócaire 2012, 16).

These arguments do have some legitimate grounds, but they are generally put forward by governments wishing to restrict critical voices. Furthermore, they are based on a state-centric perspective and are not necessarily valid from a human rights-based perspective.

Cases illustrating trends of diminishing space

The literature review and case studies underlying the evaluation delivered interesting findings on the importance of an enabling environment for CSOs to conduct PI activities and the prospects for PI in restrictive environments.[2]

A significant finding from the ACT Alliance and CIDSE report, "Space for Civil Society" (2014), is that many civil society actors feel unsafe on account of the work that they do. CSOs may work amid threats to organisational or even personal security. The report describes how the large majority of CSO leaders in Colombia and Zimbabwe work in conditions in which they sometimes or frequently feel unsafe. Threats may come from the state or from other actors, such as opposition or paramilitary groups (ACT Alliance and CIDSE 2014).

It is often the *perception* of a security threat that can determine the boundaries within which CSOs feel comfortable to operate. These perceptions do not necessarily reflect the prevailing legal framework; CSOs may engage in a degree of "self-censorship". The 2014 ACT Alliance and CIDSE report describes this phenomenon for Malawi, where the lingering legacy of past events determines many CSOs' perceptions of their current operating space. From 2009 to 2011, *"CSO offices in Malawi were raided and CSO leaders were arrested or attacked"* and some *"CSO leaders still do not feel safe carrying out their activities"* (ACT Alliance and CIDSE 2014, 22). According to the report, past trauma is an important factor, but there is also a lack of confidence about real changes within the political culture in government (ACT Alliance and CIDSE 2014, 22–23). This finding is similar for Mozambique, where the historical background has a restricting effect on CSOs' perceptions of what is possible with regards to PI, especially when it comes to more sensitive issues and more confrontational strategies.[3]

Ethiopia is an example of a country with an environment for civil society that is generally classified as very restrictive.[4] Freedom of expression, association, and assembly, a strong opposition and an independent judiciary are imperative for meaningful PI activities, but are currently severely restricted in the country. Engaging in PI openly and freely in an institutional setting is very difficult, especially for CSOs classified as Ethiopian resident charities and societies by the Charities and Societies Proclamation (CSP). The restriction on CSOs that receive more than 10% of funding from foreign sources from participating in any human rights and advocacy activities *"may effectively silence civil society in Ethiopia by starving NGOs of resources, and thus essentially extinguishing their right to expression"* (ICNL 2015a). Consequently, the government has become the sole agent in control of policy development and the only practitioner in the public and private sector (Article 19, 2003). These restrictions in general, and prohibitions on external resources in particular, have forced many CSOs to close down or abandon activities since they were unable to raise sufficient funds locally (ICNL 2015a). Many CSOs that have been involved in advocacy activities have had to change their approach to encompass other types of development activities in order to keep generating financial resources from donors outside the country (Denu and Zewdie 2013).

However, even in countries that are generally perceived as having a more open environment for civil society, CSOs may feel that their operating space is confined. In Mozambique, there is a widening gap between a relatively progressive legal and policy framework, the practice of public institutions, which is characterised by a lack of implementation, and people's living conditions. Socio-cultural arguments are often deployed to legitimise the infringement of civil liberties and rights of association, whilst political rhetoric is used to intimidate increasingly assertive and vocal civil society actors. In addition, legal instruments addressing the freedom of assembly and demonstration allow excessively restrictive interpretations and have often been used to justify repressive action by the police. Access to information about approved legislation and rights for citizens and institutions (including public institutions) is still limited.

In Kenya, although there are officially no legal barriers to CSOs speaking out or engaging in advocacy on any issues of public importance, CSOs feel that the political environment is increasingly restrictive. According to the ICNL Kenya NGO Law Monitor (2015b), *"the Kenyan Public Benefits Organization (PBO) Act provides that PBOs may engage freely in research, education, publication, public policy and advocacy"*. Moreover, *"in general, Kenyan law provides a conducive framework for CSOs to seek and secure funding"* (ICNL 2015b). There are no special rules relating to the receipt of foreign funds by CSOs. However, the PBO Act, which was passed in 2013, is still not in operation and the government has proposed several amendments. ICNL (2015b) finds that CSOs have worked continuously to push the government to commence the PBO Act, saying *"they have written a number of letters to the Cabinet Secretary of Devolution and Planning and presented a public petition to Parliament that was supported by Kenyans from across the country"*. These campaigns were successful: the proposed amendments to the PBO Act, which would have imposed restrictions comparable to the Ethiopian proclamation, were abandoned by the Kenyan Government after extensive protest in Kenya and international criticism (ACT Alliance and CIDSE, 2014). However, CSOs continue to face challenges, as the government has still not implemented the PBO Act and is finding opportunities to stall (for example, through a task force set up in 2015 to consult with stakeholders on proposed amendments) (ICNL 2015b).

In addition, a report by CIVICUS and the Kenya Human Rights Commission (KHRC) on attacks on civil society in Kenya highlights that government officials accuse CSOs working on politically sensitive issues of acting for foreign parties.[5] The report reveals acts of self-censorship by CSOs for fear of bureaucratic reprisals, including arbitrary cancellation of their registration and/or freezing of their bank accounts.

Policy influencing activities and issues are more risky than others

Certain situations, activities, and organisations face higher risks. According to Van der Borg and Terwindt (2012, 1072), *"an important distinction is whether organisations are 'primarily service-oriented or claim-making and policy-oriented"*. In general, CSOs that advocate and make claims are more vulnerable to restrictions, since these activities lead to tensions (Van der Borg and Terwindt 2012; Trócaire 2012). According to CIVICUS (2014, 26):

> *"Charitable organizations and CSOs that deliver vital services, which governments are unable to provide, are rarely challenged. However, when CSOs question policy implications or undertake advocacy to influence government actions, they tend to face challenges to their legitimacy. When CSOs are vocal in opposing government policies, accusations of being partisan or being tools of vested interests and foreign governments tend to fly thick and fast."*

The ACT Alliance and CIDSE report (2014, 44) notes how in Malawi, *"CSOs working on human rights and democracy issues perceive government-CSO relations as confrontational"*, while CSOs providing emergency relief and delivering other services *"view relations in a more positive light"*. The report mentions Rwanda as another example where service delivery is welcomed, while policy influencing is not. The government is willing to engage and there is space for informed dialogue, but CSOs still do not feel comfortable addressing sensitive issues with the government or criticising government policy or practice (ACT Alliance and CIDSE 2014).

Another aspect that may determine the extent to which PI is possible in restrictive environments is the issue being addressed. Sensitive issues like minority rights and sexual and reproductive rights are more likely to elicit resistance from PI targets. However, the most important factor is whether they challenge the status quo in terms of political power, economic relations, or social norms. Therefore, what exactly is perceived as sensitive depends on the political and social context.

Furthermore, the idea that there is one enabling (or disabling) environment for a whole country is flawed. Often, whether civil society space is open or restrictive varies considerably within a country. According to the ACT Alliance and CIDSE report (2014, 90) for example, CSOs in urban areas in Colombia experience *"a general improvement in atmosphere and working environment, whereas those in rural areas reported a restricted operating space for CSOs working on extractives, land restitution and victims' rights"*.

Conducting policy influencing in restrictive environments is possible, but means taking precautions

Although there is growing concern about the deteriorating environment for CSOs in many countries, it is often still possible for them to effectively influence agendas and policies. INTRAC (2013, 6) finds that *"even in restrictive contexts, CSOs have sometimes been able to build constructive relationships with and influence the government on social issues, particularly at a sub-national level"*. It can be effective to shift the focus from the national government to local authorities, which may offer closer and more direct links and open relations. According to ITAD and COWI (2012), engagement with local authorities often offers an avenue for constructive and productive dialogue, even though this takes place within controlled space.

Strategic and careful approach – cooperative strategies

If their operating space is restricted, CSOs have to engage in PI strategically and carefully; cooperative strategies generally work better and confrontational approaches are risky (or are perceived as such). Working closely with authorities and focusing on inside-track strategies (advising and lobbying) is less threatening and therefore more effective in a restrictive context. Cooperative strategies may not make authorities or decision-makers feel challenged by CSOs' approaches and the issues they try to promote through PI. Findings from the ACT Alliance and CIDSE report (2014, 73) for Zimbabwe show that *"an individual CSO's relations with the authorities, and the government's treatment of that CSO, depends to a large extent on whether it adopts a confrontational strategy"*. Even in less restrictive environments like Mozambique and Kenya, confrontation is not generally considered desirable. There is a shared perception among CSOs that collaboration is the best approach to influence policies, given the political context.

The fact that the distinction between service delivery work and PI is not always clear cut can work to the advantage of CSOs wishing to engage in PI in restrictive environments. Van der Borg and Terwindt (2012, 1072) note for instance that *"an organisation delivering health services to women can become engaged in claim-making about the provision of contraception"*. This means that there may be room for PI "behind the scenes" of service delivery. Moreover, a strong reputation based on a long track record of providing services can strengthen the legitimacy of a claim-making organisation in the eyes of both the government and the public. CSOs in Ethiopia, for example, may look for opportunities for silent and low profile PI, for example behind a mandate of service delivery or capacity development. This allows them to work closely and in a cooperative manner with government officials and policymakers, giving them room to influence attitudes, policies, and perhaps even practices. Even in countries like Ethiopia, if CSOs are not critical in the public sphere and try to engage government behind closed doors, they may be able to contribute to improvements. Another tactic can be to incorporate human rights issues in sectoral work, for example on education, health, and access of marginalised groups, and work directly with sectoral government offices and representatives.

Civic engagement and the need for national CSO coalitions

Extra precautions are needed in restrictive circumstances to influence policies effectively and ensure the sustainability of civil society. The evaluation found that three aspects are of critical importance: (1) a strong support base that is sympathetic to the cause; (2) strong national coalitions of CSOs; and (3) the support of international networks, including donors.

Civic engagement is important, regardless of the context, when it comes to civil society work, especially if civil society is to be a sustainable force to be reckoned with. In restrictive environments, it is even more important, though in such environments it is likely to be even more difficult to achieve. If civil society is weak and governments are not receptive to CSO influence, donors may find it easier to support service delivery CSOs. However, policy influencing work may pay off, as it can help to raise awareness, build public confidence, and encourage citizen participation (Devlin-Foltz 2012).

For CSOs in restricted environments, it is especially important to be connected to their support base, stay in tune with local sentiments, and connect to citizens. The ability of CSOs to rally support, mobilise their constituencies, and ensure civic engagement to back their campaigns is crucial, as they need the weight of citizen participation to substantiate and legitimise their claims and to gain leverage in their dealings with state authorities. Civic engagement is therefore an important ingredient for the sustainability of civil society.

What are also needed for effective influence in restrictive environments are local/national networks to share and mitigate risks and combine their strengths. According to ACT Alliance and CIDSE (2014, 83), in some restrictive environments *"CSOs have developed strong co-ordination networks to spread the risk of insecurity and deal with threats to their liberty and physical integrity."* For example, in Colombia (ACT Alliance and CIDSE 2014, 100):

> "CSOs have often adopted highly collaborative approaches to their work, presenting issues with one voice and ensuring that the issues presented are well-evidenced and well-documented, in an effort to overcome the difficulties faced by human rights defenders and community leaders. They have worked collaboratively on their own protection and engaged effectively with INGOs."

However, even though the benefits of cooperation and coordination among CSOs are clear, especially in restrictive environments, in practice this seems to be quite difficult to achieve. Building trust is hard. In Ethiopia, there are regulatory restrictions on contact between CSOs. Alliance formation or networking is allowed only among organisations classified under the same category by the CSP.[6] Besides the regulatory challenge, CSOs do not appear to engage in dialogue on consensus building or mutual support. This can be caused by a fear or uncertainty of being associated with organisations that are seen in a negative light by the authorities. The other reason for weak dialogue is that CSOs may opt to focus on issues of individual interest rather than joint engagements. Some studies also indicate that CSOs in Ethiopia tend to compete for resources rather than work on collective agendas (Horn Consult 2003). Similar rationales are at work in Kenya and Mozambique; the need for closer collaboration is voiced frequently, but putting this into practice seems to be hard, for various reasons. In Kenya, CSOs compete with each other for donor funding and attention, attempting to put their own organisations in the spotlight. In Mozambique, there is a lack of trust and feeling of insecurity stemming from the civil war.

The ACT Alliance and CIDSE report (2014, 73) found that *"co-ordination and sharing of information and strategies between different groups of CSOs … has been minimal and marked by tension"*. Additionally, political, geographical, or ethnic differences have sometimes undermined effective collaboration between CSOs. The report mentions an example in Zimbabwe, where CSOs leaders in rural areas *"are concerned that national civil society groups based in Harare neglect issues specific to their geographical regions. They believe that this geographical disconnect has contributed to tension and suspicion among CSOs"* (ACT Alliance and CIDSE 2014, 74).

Similar regional differences are also experienced in Mozambique and Kenya. Despite efforts to increase civil society support in Mozambique, there are marked geographical inequalities, with a sharp urban–rural discrepancy in civil society's access to resources and capacity. In Kenya, local CSOs have stronger links with grassroots actors than with national CSOs. Interestingly, this weak link is often experienced by local CSOs, while national CSOs claim their relations are strong.

Donor support and international networks

Donors and international partners can play an important role in restrictive environments. They can be witness to and assist in monitoring human rights violations and obtain international attention and publicity for them. They can also support and protect local CSOs against government repression and provide assistance in emergency situations. Furthermore, international connections can be helpful in lobbying for donor support for specific issues, themes, or programmes and can help local CSOs to continue to work in difficult rural areas. The ACT Alliance and CIDSE report (2014, 23) notes, for example, that *"Zimbabwean CSOs credit international solidarity as having contributed significantly to the release of* [a human rights activist] *in late 2008 after abduction and torture by state actors"*. The report also notes that, in Malawi, CSOs believe that Amnesty International and Human Rights Watch protected CSO leaders by speaking out publicly, and members of international church-based networks provided financial assistance to CSO leaders (ACT Alliance and CIDSE 2014, 23).

In Mozambique, international pressure has contributed to the emergence of formal spaces for policy dialogue, which have been created to comply with the conditions defined by international financing institutions and multilateral/bilateral donor agencies and funds. For instance, the Development Observatories took account of criticism from these institutions about the lack of consultation and civil society participation when drawing up the first Poverty Reduction Strategy Paper. In addition, creating space for civil society participation in the National AIDS Response was one of the conditions of multilateral/bilateral agencies and funds for supporting the National AIDS Council. Unfortunately, these formal spaces have not necessarily translated into increased openness to civil society voices and alternative ideas (ITAD and COWI 2012).

According to ITAD and COWI (2012, 105), besides supporting specific CSOs working on issues that are considered controversial, donors can play *"a key role in the promotion of the role of CSOs in host countries"* – towards both government authorities and the broader public. They have political and financial leverage to push governments to respect and promote the role of civil society in the public sphere. In Ethiopia, for example, international donors have tried to engage the government in regular dialogue to consider possibilities for relaxing the restrictions on CSOs to create an enabling environment for free and independent engagement. This external pressure has somewhat opened the door for CSOs (Hyden and Hailemariam 2003).

However, ITAD and COWI (2012, 15) note that, because of the politically sensitive nature of supporting an enabling environment for civil society, donors are often *"too cautious in challenging diminishing freedoms and the lack of political space to support CS engagement"*. This goes for Ethiopia, for example, where donors are still cautious when it comes to supporting advocacy CSOs and tread carefully. They do not want to be in confrontation with the government since Ethiopia is considered an important ally in the fight against terrorism in the region. Donors often face a dilemma as they may not want to risk bilateral relations in other fields of national or international interest, such as security or trade. Moreover, there is a fine line between defending space for civil society and keeping a foot in the door or a seat at the table to avoid deteriorating relations.

Lessons for more effective policy influencing in restrictive environments

The evaluation found that the operating space for CSOs is perceived as restricted and, more than other activities or issues like service delivery or capacity development, policy influencing entails risks. However, even in restrictive environments, PI is possible and CSOs continue their work despite facing opposition. They do, however, have to go about it carefully and strategically – cooperative strategies generally work better than more confrontational approaches. One aspect that is particularly important for effective PI in restrictive environments and civil society sustainability in general, is civic engagement; building a strong support base is key. Furthermore, local networks and international contacts are crucial, but it is difficult to build trust among CSOs (and other organisations).

Donors can play an important role in creating space for CSOs in restrictive environments, for example by providing political backing or intervening in individual cases. However, they are often too cautious in challenging diminishing freedoms and the lack of political space for civil society engagement, for example because of economic and security interests.

When it comes to effective strategies for supporting policy influencing efforts in restrictive environments, there is no blueprint for success. The lessons from the evaluation offer directions for improving support, but it is up to the stakeholders involved to translate them into concrete measures tailored to their own situation. There is room for improvement in practice; support for PI in restrictive environments could be provided more effectively if the insights generated by the evaluation were to be addressed systematically by all development actors. Moreover, these lessons address some critical issues that may stand in the way of a forceful and sustainable civil society.

Donors can help defend the operating space for conducting policy influencing

Freedom of expression, assembly and association – required for an active civil society – are often under threat. This happens even in countries where the constitution and regulations formally provide for freedom to engage in PI. Donors can play a role in defending the space for civil society to conduct PI in countries where the environment becomes seriously restricted, but they may need to rethink how best to support CSOs in these situations. Authorities are probably not very cooperative, it might mean putting other interests at risk, and the results are unlikely to be on a large scale or clearly visible. This makes support politically sensitive, at home and abroad. Since the influence of individual donors is increasingly limited, donors may need to mobilise broader coalitions to build up sufficient leverage. The EU and the UN could be logical entry points.

In working to expand the space for CSOs' engagement in PI, it is important to realise that legal provisions for participation do not necessarily work unless people feel able to claim that space. Therefore, it is important to empower those directly affected by policy to assume their own agency. By endeavouring to contribute to the conditions needed for civil society to flourish and claim a role in society, donors can help civil society secure a more independent and sustainable role. It is then up to civil society organisations themselves to take advantage of this opportunity.

A Theory of Change based on political economy analysis is indispensable

The trend of diminishing space means that it is very important for CSOs to gain a thorough understanding of the environment in which they operate. They urgently need to keep track of political and socio-economic changes and should monitor the narrow margins that remain for them to conduct their PI work. It is therefore indispensable that they continually conduct political economy analyses (PEAs). The evaluation found that a strong and well-thought-out Theory of Change (ToC) is important for the effectiveness of PI. A ToC entails thinking strategically about the demands CSOs make and how they are rooted, on what demands the targets of PI can be expected to give in, whose support is needed to back these demands, what strategies are most suitable for reaching out to this support base, and which partners are needed to convene enough power to challenge the status quo. It also implies that CSOs and their donors should think beyond traditional developmental interventions and might need to work in unconventional ways with unconventional partners. CSOs need to be able and willing to continuously reflect on their goals and strategies and the context in which they are to be applied if they are to be reliable, sustainable partners and an enduring force to be reckoned with.

Customised approaches are required and donors need to allow room for failure

The evaluation found that it can take many years, even decades, for PI to achieve changes in policy, or even to get issues on the agenda. It may be uncertain whether envisaged changes will be achieved at all. The long term and unpredictable nature of PI processes and results have implications for all the development actors involved.

For donors this implies that support should be long term, or should at least be seen as contributing to processes that may take much longer than their own financial budgeting cycles. It is therefore important that donors ensure the solidity and continuity of their policies. Furthermore, they should be realistic about the results that can be achieved and indicators should reflect intermediate results. It is advisable to accommodate a certain degree of flexibility in the programme design and implementation, in order to respond to changes in local realities.

For CSOs, this implies that, when designing their campaigns, they should be realistic about their sphere of influence and base them on a deep understanding of the incentives of specific lobby targets to change (or not). They therefore have to think about changes that can realistically be achieved and should not fall into the trap of inflating projected results to satisfy unrealistic donor expectations.

Coalitions pursuing a common goal are paramount

The evaluation found that it is becoming increasingly difficult for individual CSOs to be effective in their PI campaigns. Their legitimacy is often at risk and the harsher environment in which Southern CSOs have to operate requires a heavier countervailing power. CSOs that receive donor support face two constraints: (1) their claim to represent the interests of the population is seriously questioned; and (2) the coalitions in which they work are weak or tend to fall apart. Unless they are able to overcome these constraints, CSOs run the risk of being portrayed as foreign agents and of becoming further marginalised.

Donors could encourage CSOs to enhance their legitimacy by reflecting on the issue of linkages to their constituencies and building a firm support base. They can also encourage CSOs to work in strong and lasting coalitions that pursue a common goal. This means supporting cooperation and coordination – perhaps even facilitating networking and coalition-building – without intruding on and steering cooperative processes. The nature of the relationship between donors, Northern NGDOs, and Southern CSOs is of the utmost importance and work is needed to ensure that it is based on symmetry and equality.

Conclusions and implications for the sustainability of civil society

A sustainable civil society is difficult to attain in general, but even more so in restrictive environments. These restrictions threaten the sustainability of civil society, as they prevent it from functioning optimally and fulfilling the roles that are so important in achieving inclusive development. Furthermore, limitations on the operating space for CSOs restrict their organisational sustainability and decrease the possibilities for engagement and the success of interventions, especially in the long term.

Besides furthering a specific theme, which can also be related to political and civil liberties, policy influencing work often aims to create or maintain democratic conditions. Therefore, the sustainability of the outcomes has a positive effect on the sustainability of civil society itself.

Two aspects are of vital importance in ensuring a sustainable civil society: civic engagement and more cooperation between civil society actors. It is crucial for CSOs to build their legitimacy and a support base in order to have long-term influencing power. Southern CSOs have a number of options to strengthen their position and ensure sustainability, including revising their strategies, systematically involving and mobilising their constituencies, linking up with other CSOs with more legitimacy in representing citizens' interests, supporting their work with more evidence-based research, and operating in local, national, and international networks and coalitions that add value to their work. Furthermore, it is possible to derive legitimacy from other sources than a strong support base, for example from universal values, new ideas, knowledge and expertise or experience, for instance in service delivery. Working on human rights can be difficult when it comes to LGBT (lesbian, gay, bisexual, and transgender) issues, for example, but the lack of a broad support base does not make it less important.

Lastly, it is important to note that "sustainable" does not necessarily mean "without donor funding". Donor funding entails dilemmas. For donors, it is difficult to reach out to organisations beyond their established network of NGDOs, which are often based in the North or in capital cities in the South. This means that grassroots actors, which make up an important part of a sustainable civil society, may not be heard or included. Furthermore, donor policies, financial support, and the related administrative demands encourage upward accountability at the expense of downward accountability from the CSOs to their constituencies. This may cause problems, in terms of a perceived lack of legitimacy in the eyes of both local communities and the state.

Even though these are valid points, they do not mean that donors should stop financing NGDOs and CSOs altogether. After all, given the increasingly restrictive environments facing civil society in more and more parts of the world, it is unrealistic to expect local organisations to spring up and evolve independently. Sustainable civil society thus implies a strong, popular force bringing together the state, the market and the family that can claim its space and influence policies and practices for those parts of the population that might otherwise not be heard.

Notes

1. The full evaluation report on "Policy Influencing, Lobbying and Advocacy" is available on the IOB website: (www.iob-evaluatie.nl/PILA). Responsibility for any errors and omissions in the article lies with the authors. The findings from Mozambique, Kenya, and Ethiopia are based on studies commissioned by IOB as part of the evaluation. The study on Mozambique is available on the IOB website.
2. IOB commissioned two country studies as part of the evaluation, focusing on the practice of policy influencing, lobbying, and advocacy (PILA) by CSOs in Mozambique and Kenya. The Mozambique report is available on the IOB website. Findings from the country studies draw on literature and interviews with several local CSOs and other stakeholders.
3. Views expressed during CSO workshops in Maputo, Mozambique, in February 2015.
4. Ethiopia scores 0.36 on the CIVICUS Enabling Environment Index (EEI), putting the country in the bottom ten, just above countries like Zimbabwe, Burundi, and Iran. Mozambique and Kenya both score 0.43.
5. Preliminary report shared with the IOB research team, but not yet publicly available.
6. For example, CSOs which are presumed to generate 90% of their budget domestically cannot form networks with Ethiopian resident charities or Ethiopian resident societies that generate 90% of their budget externally and which are prohibited from engaging in advocacy and human rights issues.

Disclosure statement

No potential conflict of interest was reported by the authors.

References

ACT Alliance. 2011. Shrinking political space of civil society action. Accessed March 16, 2016. http://www.kpsrl.org/browse/download/t/shrinking-political-space-of-civil-society-action.

ACT Alliance, and CIDSE. 2014. "Space for Civil Society: How to Protect and Expand an Enabling Environment." Accessed February 14, 2016. www.cordaid.org/media/publications/SpaceForCivilSociety.pdf.

Article 19. 2003. "The Legal Framework for Freedom of Expression in Ethiopia." Accessed February 14, 2016. www.article19.org/data/files/pdfs/publications/ethiopia-legal-framework-for-foe.pdf.

Bruch, A., et al. 2013. "NGO Legal Enabling Environment Program (LEEP): Performance Evaluation." Unpublished paper. Washington, DC: USAID and ICNL.

Calingaert, D. 2013. "Resisting the Global Crackdown on Civil Society." Freedom House, Policy Brief. Accessed July 1, 2016. https://freedomhouse.org/article/resisting-global-crackdown-civil-society.

CIVICUS. 2013. "State of Civil Society 2013: Creating an Enabling Environment." Accessed February 14, 2016. www.3sektorius.lt/docs/2013StateofCivilSocietyReport_full_2013-05-02_10:53:58.pdf0i.pdf.

CIVICUS. 2014. "State of Civil Society Report 2014: Reimagining Global Governance." Accessed February 14, 2016. www.civicus.org/images/SOCS%20SEPT_2014.pdf.

Denu, B., and A. Zewdie. 2013. "Tracking Trends in Ethiopia´s Civil Society Sector (TECS) Project: Impact of the Guideline to Determine Charities' and Societies' Operational and Administrative Costs (70/30 Guideline) – Phase III." Accessed February 14, 2016. http://esap2.org.et/wp-content/uploads/2014/11/Report-10_7030-Phase-III_Sep2013.pdf.

Devlin-Foltz, D. 2012. "Civil Society Advocacy in Uganda: Lessons Learned." The Aspen Institute Advocacy Planning and Evaluation Program. Accessed February 14, 2016. www.aspeninstitute.org/publications/civil-society-advocacy-uganda-lessons-learned.

Horn Consult. 2003. "Constituency Building: Diagnostic Survey on Ethiopian NGOs." Unpublished paper. Addis Ababa: CRDA and Oxfam.

Hyden, G., and M. Hailemariam. 2003. "Voluntarism and Civil Society: Ethiopia in Comparative Perspective." *Afrika Spectrum* 38 (2): 215–234.

ICNL (The International Center for Not-for-Profit Law). 2015a. "NGO Law Monitor: Ethiopia." Accessed February 5, 2016. www.icnl.org/research/monitor/ethiopia.html.

ICNL (The International Center for Not-for-Profit Law). 2015b. "NGO Law Monitor: Kenya." Accessed February 5, 2016. www.icnl.org/research/monitor/kenya.html.

INTRAC. 2012. "Enabling Space for Civil Society Action." Accessed February 14, 2016. www.intrac.org/data/files/resources/751/ONTRAC-52-Enabling-space-for-civil-society-action.pdf.

INTRAC. 2013. "Support to Civil Society: Emerging Evaluation Lessons." Accessed February 14, 2016. www.oecd.org/dac/evaluation/Evaluation%20Insight%20Civil%20Society%20FINAL%20for%20print%20and%20WEB%2020131004.pdf.

ITAD, and COWI. 2012. "Joint Evaluation of Support to Civil Society Engagement in Policy Dialogue: Synthesis Report." Ministry of Foreign Affairs of Denmark. Accessed February 14, 2016. www.oecd.org/derec/denmark/cso_indhold_web.pdf.

Poskitt, A. 2011. "Accountability in a Restricted Civil Society Environment: International Initiatives for common frameworks." CIVICUS. Accessed February 14, 2016. http://lta.civicus.org/download/Accountability_in_a_Restricted_Civil_Society_Environment%20_ INTRAC_June_011.pdf.

Trócaire. 2012. "Democracy in Action: Protecting Civil Society Space." Accessed February 14, 2016. www.trocaire.org/sites/trocaire/files/resources/policy/democracy-in-action.pdf.

Van der Borgh, C., and C. Terwindt. 2012. "Shrinking Operational Space of NGOs – A Framework of Analysis." *Development in Practice* 22 (8): 1065–1081.

WMD (World Movement for Democracy). 2012. "Defending Civil Society Report." Accessed February 14, 2016. www.defendingcivilsociety.org/dl/reports/DCS_Report_Second_Edition_English.pdf.

Advancing post-2015 Sustainable Development Goals in a changing development landscape: Challenges of NGOs in Ghana

Albert Arhin

ABSTRACT

In September 2015, the UN General Assembly formally adopted 17 Sustainable Development Goals (SDGs) that aim among other things, to end poverty and hunger, protect the planet, and promote prosperity by 2030. The SDGs were, however, adopted at a time when an increasing body of research is drawing attention to a series of game-changing trends in international development and funding landscapes. This article considers the ways in which the changing development landscape is affecting the ability of NGOs to perform their expected roles towards the attainment of the SDGs. Drawing on in-depth qualitative interviews with NGOs in Ghana, the article contends that expectations of the roles of NGOs in advancing the cause of SDGs in Ghana are being affected by three main factors: (i) uncertainty of income generation and funding sources; (ii) changing operational capacity; and (iii) changing NGO identity.

En septembre 2015, l'Assemblée générale des Nations Unies a formellement adopté 17 Objectifs de développement durable (ODD) visant, entre autres, à mettre fin à la pauvreté et à la faim, à protéger la planète et à promouvoir la prospérité d'ici à 2030. Les ODD ont, cependant, été adoptés alors même que des recherches de plus en plus nombreuses attirent l'attention sur une série de tendances qui changent la donne dans le développement international et les paysages du financement. Cet article considère l'incidence qu'a un paysage du développement en évolution sur l'aptitude des ONG à assumer leurs rôles prévus vers la réalisation des ODD. Cet article se base sur des entretiens qualitatifs approfondis avec des ONG au Ghana pour soutenir que les attentes relatives aux rôles des ONG au moment de promouvoir la cause des ODD au Ghana sont influencées par trois facteurs principaux : (i) l'incertitude relative à la génération de revenus et aux sources de financement ; (ii) les capacités opérationnelles en évolution ; et (iii) l'identité en mutation des ONG.

En septiembre de 2015, la Asamblea General de la ONU adoptó formalmente los 17 Objetivos de Desarrollo Sostenible (ODS), entre cuyos fines para 2030 se encuentran la eliminación de la pobreza y el hambre, la protección del planeta y la promoción de la prosperidad. Sin embargo, dichos objetivos fueron adoptados en un momento en que las cada vez más numerosas investigaciones registran la presencia de varias tendencias que están modificando el panorama en los ámbitos de desarrollo internacional y de financiación. El presente artículo examina cómo este cambiante ambiente de desarrollo afecta la capacidad de las ONG para desempeñar sus funciones habituales, orientadas a lograr los ODS. Basándose en entrevistas cualitativas a profundidad realizadas en varias ONG de Ghana, el artículo sostiene que las expectativas en torno a las funciones cumplidas por las ONG en aras de impulsar los ODS en este país se han visto afectadas por tres factores torales: (i) la incertidumbre respecto a las fuentes de financiamiento y a la generación de ingresos; (ii) su variable capacidad operativa; y (iii) su identidad inestable.

Introduction

In September 2015, the UN General Assembly formally adopted 17 Sustainable Development Goals (SDGs) that would, among other things, end poverty and hunger, protect the planet, and promote prosperity by 2030 (see Figure 1). The SDGs are the successors to the Millennium Development Goals (MDGs) launched in 2000 to mobilise resources and political support towards meeting some of the world's pressing challenges such as poverty, hunger, gender inequality, unmet schooling, diseases, and environmental degradation (Sachs 2012; Karver, Kenny, and Sumner 2013). Accompanying the 17 universal goals are 169 targets and about 330 indicators that are expected to frame development policies across all countries over the next 15 years. By packaging these global priorities into a set of goals, targets, and indicators, the SDGs are expected to not only become a global report card for the fight against poverty, but also to help promote global awareness, political accountability, social feedback, and public pressures (Sachs 2012).

As the SDGs are about to be translated into specific policies and practices, there have been increasing calls and interest in NGOs as stakeholders to play major roles towards attaining the

Figure 1. Overview of the Sustainable Development Goals.

SDGs at both global and national levels (Salamon and Haddock 2015). However, the SDGs have been adopted at a time when an increasing body of research is drawing attention to a series of game-changing trends in international development and funding landscapes. These shifting trends include, but are not limited to, indications of considerable aid withdrawal and policy shifts by donors and international NGOs in developing countries, increasing restrictions on foreign funding, and restrictions on political and operating space in various countries (Dubochet 2012; Mawdsley 2012; Hayman 2015). Other trends include the increasing voice of the global South as both recipients and providers of development assistance, and the increasingly complex geographies of poverty and wealth, where a growing proportion of the world's poor are living in what are being (re)classified as middle-income countries (Kanbur and Sumner 2012; Sidaway 2012).

The past few years have seen discussions about the challenges and opportunities of shifting development trends on the sustainability of the roles of civil society organisations (CSOs) across different countries, although there is still very limited empirical research on this (Bandyopadhyay 2013; Goswami and Tandon 2013). Within this context, this article asks in what ways the changing development landscape is affecting the ability of NGOs to perform their expected roles towards the attainment of the SDGs. It addresses this by drawing on an exploratory study examining the challenges and opportunities of the changing landscape for NGOs in Ghana. The article contends that expectations of the roles of NGOs in advancing the SDGs in Ghana are affected by three main factors: (i) uncertainty of income generation and funding sources; (ii) changing operational capacity and competences; and (iii) changing NGO identity. This paper, therefore, adds to the empirical evidence of the challenges of the changing development landscape on the sustainability of civil society organisations (see Bandyopadhyay 2013; Goswami and Tandon 2013). While the issues discussed focus largely on NGOs, other works (e.g. Arhin, Adam, and Akanbasiam 2015) corroborate how it is a reflection of the broader civil society in Ghana and elsewhere.

The article is structured as follows. The analytical framework for examining the roles of NGO is introduced, followed by the explanation of the study methodology. The roles of NGOs and the changing development landscape in Ghana are then presented, along with a discussion of the challenges they face.

Figure 2. Analytical framework for understanding the triple roles of NGOs.

Understanding the expected roles of NGOs in a post-2015 world

Lewis and Kanji (2009) have argued that NGOs are high-profile actors in the field of international development. Despite the recognition of their centrality in international development, the definition of an NGO is contested. The frequent references to interchangeable terms such as "non-profit", "third sector", "charity", "voluntary", and "civil society" organisations, further compound a clear definition. Najam (1996) recorded at least 47 different labels given to NGOs. While recognising the challenge of explicitly defining NGOs, this study follows the World Bank (1999) in defining NGOs as organisations that are largely independent of government and characterised principally by humanitarian or cooperative, rather than commercial, objectives. In particular, this study identified NGOs as organisations that exhibit the five key characteristics proposed by Salamon and Anheier (1992), namely that NGOs should be *formal* (institutionalised to regular meetings, having office bearers, and some form of organisational permanence); *private* (institutionally separate from government, even if it receives some support from government); and *non-profit distributing* (where financial surplus is not distributed among the owners or directors). NGOs should also be *self-governing* (having the ability to control and manage its own affairs) and *voluntary* (at least some degree of voluntary participation in the conduct or management of the organisation).

The analytical framework for examining the expected roles of NGOs in the context of the SDGs builds on the work of Lewis and Kanji (2009) and Banks and Hulme (2012). According to these works, the roles of NGOs in advancing development can broadly be categorised into three main functions: service delivery (or implementers), advocacy (or catalysts), and facilitation and brokering (or partners) (Figure 2).

As service providers, NGOs mobilise resources to provide goods and services to specific groups of people or communities who need them (Lewis and Kanji 2009). It involves the big "D" development activities linked to the provision of tangible outputs (Bebbington et al. 2008; Hulme 2008). Examples of these services include education and health services to marginalised areas, livelihood interventions, human rights, democracy building, finance, policy analysis, and environmental management (Banks and Hulme 2014; Lewis and Kanji 2009). Such services also include provision of water supply systems, public health facilities, and microcredit facilities. These services place greater emphasis on material poverty and tangible project outputs, with little attention to structural changes that challenge society's institutional arrangements. While NGOs have been able to make critical social services accessible to so-called hard-to-reach areas and people through their service provision function (Clayton, Oakley, and Taylor 2000), one of the weaknesses of the service provision role is that it fails to acknowledge the foundational causes of poverty (Banks and Hulme, 2012). It is in this context that the emphasis of NGOs' roles had predominantly shifted towards advocacy by the turn of the millennium – and in the context of the expired MDGs. This shift changed the emphasis and orientation of NGOs in their operations, rather than completely supplanting the service provision role.

In their roles as advocates, NGOs place greater emphasis on radical and systemic alternatives which advance different ways of organising the economy, social relationships, and politics – the little "d" development (Bebbington et al. 2008; Lewis and Kanji 2009; Banks and Hulme 2012). The turn to advocacy focuses on the underlying causes of development issues, with NGOs playing the role of catalysts to *"to inspire, facilitate or contribute to improved thinking and action"* that promote change (Lewis and Kanji 2009, 13). Such advocacy may include gender and empowerment work, policy-oriented research, lobbying, and attempts to influence wider policy processes (Lewis and Kanji 2009). Advocacy may be directed towards individuals or groups in local communities to change or promote attitude and particular practices, or among other actors such as government, businesses, or donors for wider improvement in policies and practices that facilitate poverty reduction efforts.

The role of NGOs as facilitators or brokers is concerned with connecting, integrating, and *"bringing together diverse social economic and political actors so as to achieve goals that neither would be able to achieve individually"* (Lewis 2014, 293). Lewis and Kanji (2009) highlight capacity building work to develop and strengthen capabilities, and partnerships of NGOs with government, donors, and the private sector on joint activities, as some of the activities undertaken by NGOs in these roles. Here, NGOs act as intermediaries or partners and play a bridging role that contributes to improved policy and practice for particular groups of people or communities. It is important to stress that particular NGOs are rarely confined to a single role. It is common practice for NGOs to engage in all three types of activities at once, although as contexts and opportunities change, there could be a shift in emphasis from one to the other over time (Lewis and Kanji 2009).

Research methodology

The study relied predominantly on qualitative research design. In collecting data for this research, semi-structured interviews were conducted with the leaders of 22 NGOs (20 local and two international) in Accra, Ghana from August to September 2013. The NGOs varied in terms of their size and thematic areas of operation. Interviews were conducted largely with chief executive officers and/or nominated senior programme officers. Organisational leaders were interviewed because they are the custodians of organisational information due to shaping decision-making processes. Qualitative research methods were the most appropriate method to capture the views and experiences of NGOs (Creswell 2012). All the interviews were conducted in English. Findings reported here also draw partially on insights from a research commissioned by the West Africa Civil Society Institute (WACSI), in which the author was involved (see Arhin, Adam, and Akanbasiam 2015). This latter research examined perceptions of the state of sustainability of about 100 civil society organisations across all Ghana between November 2014 and March 2015.

Some caveats are in order. First, the study was designed to be exploratory and illustrative rather than comprehensive and exhaustive of all the challenges and opportunities related to the changing development landscape in Ghana, hence the findings must be interpreted with caution. Second, since the research was largely exploratory, the scope was limited to a smaller number of NGOs operating in one region of Ghana (Accra), hence the findings may not be generalisable across the wider NGO sector. Nonetheless, the issues discussed here are very important, as the research findings are reflective of the findings from the WACSI research which covered a broader section of CSOs in all ten regions of Ghana.

The MDGs, NGOs, and the changing development landscape in Ghana

The Millennium Development Goals have been acclaimed as *"having produced the most successful anti-poverty movement in history"* (UN 2015), even though their achievements were generally uneven. Between 2000 and 2015, the MDGs served as an important political and policy reference point for the assessment of progress of efforts geared towards meeting some of the pressing development challenges confronting Ghana. According to the Government of Ghana (2015), targets such as halving extreme poverty (MDG 1A), achieving universal primary education (MDG 2A), achieving gender parity in primary schools (MDG 3), and halving the proportion of people without access to safe drinking water (MDG 7B), were attained. Substantial progress was also made in reducing HIV prevalence (MDG 6C) and increasing access to ICT (MDG 8F). However, slow progress was made towards reducing under-five and child mortality (MDG 4), reducing maternal mortality (MDG 5), achieving equal share of women in wage employment in non-agriculture sectors and women's involvement in governance (MDG 3), and reversal of the loss of environmental resources (MDG 7).

Civil society organisations in Ghana, including NGOs, played significant roles in complementing the efforts of government in the progress made under the MDGs (Ghana Integrity Initiative et al. 2013; Government of Ghana 2015). NGOs in Ghana played diverse roles spanning across service provision, advocacy, and facilitation. Generally, some NGOs played facilitation roles by being represented on various state committees charged with achieving the MDG targets of specific thematic areas such as health and education. Respondents interviewed highlighted some of the specific roles played by

NGOs as mobilising financial, human, and material resources to pursue specific programmes on both advocacy and service provision across the focus sectors of the MDGs; advocacy and policy influencing in democratic governance and accountability at various levels of government; creation of awareness of government policies among rural populations; capacity building initiatives to enable communities to participate in public policy; and facilitation of self-help groups and community development. These roles expressed by respondents are consistent with the observations of the Ghana Integrity Initiative et al. (2013). A significant part of the response to the MDGs by NGOs also involved the formation of coalitions and networks. Coalitions included the Ghana Civil Society Coalition on the MDGs, which focused on building the capacity of citizens to hold government accountable on the progress of the MDGs; the Ghana Coalition of NGOs in Water and Sanitation (CONIWAS), which focused on promoting and influencing policies to remove barriers to access to potable water, sanitation, and improved hygiene; the Ghana National Education Campaign Coalition, which focused on influencing policies on education; and the Essential Services Platform (ESP) whose advocacy effort was directed towards the government to commit adequate resources that would ensure the attainment of the MDG targets in education, health, and agriculture.

Following the expiration of the MDGs, many NGOs expect to continue working on the broad roles of service provision, advocacy, and facilitation to ensure that the goals set out in the newly launched SDGs are achieved. For instance, Ghana Action 2015, a coalition of NGOs, has been formed to mobilise resources and raise public awareness about the SDGs. Also, within two months of the adoption of the SDGs, CONIWAS began advocacy efforts to input into the development of national indicators, national baseline report, and nationwide dissemination of the SDGs (CONIWAS 2015). Yet, the translation of the SDGs into policy and practice is occurring at a time when NGOs in Ghana are increasingly confronted with a new development landscape. This changing development landscape, it is argued, could have implications on the roles that NGOs can play in the context of the SDGs. While one must be careful in establishing a date signifying this important turning point, most of the changes occurring are gradual and even those that are not, are products of both global processes described above and also other national events that are redefining the landscape for NGOs in Ghana. These trends are setting a new scene for NGOs and civil society in general, albeit one that is in dynamic interplay with past trends and patterns. Three particular trends were identified by the respondents as increasingly redefining the development and funding landscape for the NGOs in Ghana.

The first notable shift is the changing political and socio-economic position of Ghana in the international aid architecture. In 2010, Ghana's recalculation of its gross domestic product (GDP) led to an overnight graduation from being a poor country to a lower middle-income country (LMIC) with a per capita income of about US$1300 (Moss and Majerowicz 2012). This LMIC tag is shifting Ghana's position in the international aid system and increasingly changing her relationship with her bilateral and multilateral (traditional) donors/development partners in notable ways – which further leads to a new landscape for CSOs (Zeitz 2015). Closely linked to the country's shifting position is a historic Compact (Government of Ghana 2012) signed in 2010 by development partners on one hand and the Government of Ghana and CSOs on the other. This Compact expects Ghana to be an aid-free country by 2020. It therefore provides a reference point for development partners to channel their development assistance to specific critical sectors until 2020 (Embassy of the Kingdom of the Netherlands 2011; 2014; SECO 2012). The Compact places full financial responsibility on the Ghanaian government to invest in accelerated development to reduce poverty and inequality. This compact has also paved way for many development partners to put exit strategies in place (DFID Ghana 2012). The shifting position of Ghana and the changing donor relationship have ushered in a period of reprioritisation, reductions, and withdrawal of budgets from several of Ghana's traditional donors. For example, traditional donors such as DFID and CORDAID, which have been instrumental in supporting NGOs in the performance of their roles, have cut their funding for their operations in Ghana. DFID indicated that it would reduce the level of general support for the country from UK£36 million in 2010/11 to around UK£10 million in 2014/15 (DFID Ghana 2012). Many respondents interviewed therefore expected external funding to be more competitive and lesser in volume than it had been under the MDGs. Third, while the traditional donors are revising and preparing their exit strategies, there are also new actors emerging in the development landscape in Ghana, both as development partners and as trade partners. These include Korea, China, Brazil, and India. However, unlike the traditional donors, the new actors have so far paid very little attention towards strengthening or supporting the civil society sector. While recognition is being given to the changing landscape among leaders of NGOs (Arhin, Adam, and Akanbasiam 2015), an increasingly concern emerging but that has not been systematically explored relates to the various ways through which the roles of NGOs may be affected in advancing the SDGs.

Advancing SDGs: to what extent is the changing development landscape affecting the roles of NGOs?

As the previous section showed, Ghana made mixed progress towards the MDGs. For instance, Ghana reduced the proportion of the poor living in extreme poverty from 51.7% to 28.5% between 2000 to 2005, and further down to 24.2% in 2012/13 (Government of Ghana 2015). The under-five mortality rate reduced from 122 per 1,000 live births in 1990 to 82 per 1000 live births in 2012, although it fell short of the MDG target of 40 per 1,000 live births. Similarly, institutional maternal mortality ratio reduced from 216 per 100,000 live births in 1990 to 144 per 100,000 live births in 2014 (Government of Ghana 2015). In spite of these national averages, there are significant disparities among the three regions in northern Ghana and those in the south. There is also heightened inequality between the rural and urban poor (Abdulai and Hulme 2015; Government of Ghana 2015). The advent of SDGs enjoins governments across the world to, among other things, eradicate extreme poverty, end hunger, achieve food security, improve nutrition and agriculture, and ensure healthy lives. For the government and civil societies alike, the SDGs provide avenues for *"tackling some of the unfinished business of MDGs"* (Government of Ghana 2015, vii).

Findings from the research suggested that many NGOs expect to play significant roles in promoting and protecting the interests of poor and disadvantaged people through advocacy (such as pressure on government to distribute local and national services in favour of the poor), service delivery (such as provision of schools, water facilities, health centres), and capacity building and facilitation (such as empowering local people to demand accountability and rights from duty-bearers) in the context of the SDGs. In particular, NGOs expressed the need to complement the state's effort in various sectors such as health, education, gender, and the environment to accomplish the SDGs. Some respondents made reference to the fact that, in light of Ghana's transition as a LMIC, the government had announced the removal or reduction of subsidies on critical social services such as electricity, petroleum, and water which would significantly affect poor people. For these respondents, NGOs would be critical to promote social protection policies for the poor. Others highlighted how advocacy from NGOs would be vital in pressuring government to be transparent in distributing national resources beneficially, especially as Ghana begins to produce oil in commercial quantities. The research findings show that in view of the changing landscape, the roles of NGOs in advancing SDGs would be affected by at least three main ways: uncertainty in mobilising financial resources; changing competencies, skills and capacities; and a changing identity for NGOs.

Uncertainty of income generation and funding sources

As several researchers (e.g. Golub 2000; Banks and Hulme 2012) have emphasised, the 1990s and 2000s saw significant amounts of financial resources from donors in support of the various roles of played by CSOs in the global South. Ghana enjoyed its share of this boom, which contributed to significant rise in the number of NGOs. USAID's 2014 CSO sustainability index for Ghana reported an increase in the number CSOs from 5,714 in 2012 to 6,019 in 2013, and 6,258 as at 2014. As has been widely documented elsewhere (e.g. Edwards and Hulme 1996; Banks, Hulme, and Edwards 2015), NGOs in Ghana rely heavily on bilateral and multilateral donors – especially the traditional ones – for their operations.

Yet, the current aid withdrawal, reprioritisation, and dwindling donor resources characterising the shifting development context in Ghana are seriously affecting NGOs' revenue mobilisation. This should not be interpreted entirely negatively. Indeed, respondents highlighted how the changing landscape has been embraced as an opportunity for reflection and action that would reduce dependence on traditional sources. Several respondents also mentioned how the changing landscape is forcing their organisations to explore different sources of funding, including social enterprise, private sector funding, social media marketing, and many others. Others showed how they were *"becoming more innovative and adaptive"* to the changing environment – which is expected to lead to increased volume of funding even if the number of available sources reduces. This finding is in tandem with those reported elsewhere (Arhin, Adam, and Akanbasiam 2015).

In spite of the opportunities that the changing landscape presents, respondents consistently articulated how uncertainty of revenue mobilisation was significantly affecting their expected roles of advocacy, service provision, and facilitation in the context of the SDGs. In Ghana, official public aid inflows have fallen from 6.09% of GDP in 2009 to 2.8% of GDP in 2014 (Government of Ghana 2015). While official figures on donor commitments to NGOs were not readily available, there was a general perception among respondents that funding to support NGOs' work was generally dwindling. As an example, several respondents referred to limited calls for proposals/expressions of interest for projects. Others also mentioned that unsolicited funding approaches of many CSOs to donors are increasingly being rejected. Even more profound are the statements from many traditional donors such as DFID and CORDAID that they were cutting funding for their operations in Ghana. The perception of dwindling external sources of funding is creating anxiety and uncertainty among NGOs. As one respondent summed it up: *"we have so much to do; but we do not know whether we will do it all because funding sources are now very competitive and to be frank dry"*. Respondents increasingly narrated stories of how it was becoming more difficult for NGOs to find sufficient, appropriate, and continuous funding for their work. Many described the situation as very challenging and competitive. For instance, one respondent explained that:

> "last year by this time we were having over eight big time active projects going on. We made a huge contribution in our operational areas. But this year, we have had less than three projects that are running. What has actually kept us busy has been the mopping up the programmes we did last year."

Another respondent gave the example that: *"since the year began, we have been submitting at least two proposals to different organisations. It was only one that we were successful."* Several respondents highlighted that although some local fundraising efforts have been attempted, the overall contribution to revenue streams has been minimal. This could be attributed to low philanthropic culture and the general higher levels of poverty in developing countries (Kakava, Mbizi, and Manyeruke 2013).

What is even more challenging for the NGOs is that while traditional donors are often frustrated with state inefficiency in programme management and increasingly supporting and strengthening civil society groups to perform their roles, emerging donors such as China and India have largely bypassed non-governmental entities in many of their operations. As one respondent recounts: *"we are very much side lined! They deal largely with the government."* This was corroborated by another respondent who mentioned that: *"the new actors have less focus on how to build a strong civil society. Nearly all their grants and assistance go to government functionaries."* However, funding is not the only channel that appears to be significantly affecting NGOs and their sustainability to advance the SDG agenda.

Changing operational capacities of organisations

NGOs in Ghana expect to play the diverse roles of delivering specific services for marginalised population, advocacy for improved policy and practices that favour poor and marginalised people, and facilitation and brokering functions. Through their work with communities and other stakeholders, NGOs expect to work to complement and challenge the efforts of government in pursuing the post-2015 development agenda. As the development context is gradually changing, some NGOs have taken the opportunity to improve the efficiency and impact of their operations through measures such as cost-cutting, increasing visibility through media reportage, and also enhancing their legitimacy, developing credibility building and policy influencing skills.

Yet, concerns about the insidious effect of the changing landscape on the operations and the difficulty of meeting the changing capacity and competence needs of staff, especially in the area of technology, could affect the role of NGOs in advancing the SDGs. Respondents narrated how the changing development landscape is increasing the difficulty of investing in new skills and maintaining competent staff, as well as the high cost of training and investment into organisational systems and structures. In many ways, the research findings suggested a possible weakening of the very institutional capacity (human capacity such as staff and partner skills, experiences, and competencies, as well as organisational capital such as structures, financial resources, and organisational culture and learning) that NGOs need to advance the SDGs. In one interview, a respondent stated that:

> "Unlike when we started [operations], office spaces are now in hot demand here in Accra because of the proliferation of banks, telecoms and some of these rich businesses. Look at our office. We pay $6000 every month as rent and utilities alone. You dare not pay and you will be thrown out. Left to me alone, we would have left this place but you know this kind of work requires physical address and a well maintained office for you to be credible. It is not easy."

Other respondents also highlighted how the changing funding landscape is contributing to increased staff turnover and the general challenge to maintain competent and well-trained staff. As one respondent mentioned:

> "unlike previously the government policy … has brought strong competition and we quickly lose our staff. In fact, we find ourselves in a perpetual cycle of having had to build capacity almost every time. But this is costly at a time our volume of funding and projects is going down."

These statements draw attention to some of the challenging environment through which the capacity of NGOs to execute programmes might be affected. The implications of this changing institutional capacity were summed up by one respondent as:

> "NGOs are basically in existence to serve as the voice for the voiceless … but if you as the organisation is not able to see how you are going to be in existence, then this obviously has several implications for the poor. Very soon, the poor will be on their own because there will be no NGOs to fight their cause."

Other respondents also mentioned that the challenge for many NGOs is how to continue to make post-2015 investments into capacity building and empowerment processes for groups such as small-scale farmers, girls, adolescents, disabled people, and local communities in mining areas that are likely to be stalled – or abandoned – as the changing development landscape raises the possibility that they will have to close aspects of their programmes.

Changing identity and legitimacy of NGOs

In Ghana, NGOs distinguish themselves as development actors largely by highlighting their differences and distance from the state, political parties, and private sectors. This was very prevalent in the course of our interviews. For instance, when asked to describe who they are and what they do, several respondents emphasised that they are non-profit-driven, non-government, and non-partisan entities whose primary aim is meeting the interests of the poor and disadvantaged groups. This observation has also been made by White (1999) in other contexts. The research findings show that NGOs expect to play critical roles of the implementation processes of the SDGs because of their distinctive character as non-profit, non-partisan, and close to (grassroots) communities which permits flexibility to provide innovative and people-centred approaches to service delivery, advocacy, and empowerment initiatives. As Bebbington (2004, 2005) observed, the grassroots linkages which NGOs offer have been one of their major strengths which enables them to design tailored services and programmes that empower disadvantaged groups and consequently help them gain voice in the governance spaces from which they have so often been excluded.

While the identity of NGOs in Ghana has long been known as not-for-profit organisations with clear legitimacy driving altruistic interventions, respondents particularly emphasised two nascent developments which have been occasioned by the changing development landscape. The first issue relates to what we would call the "social enterprise craze", which refers to the speed at which several organisations are rebranding themselves as social enterprises. The concept of social enterprise is increasingly gaining popularity among donors and CSOs as an important model for building and advancing the sustainability of NGOs (Alter 2006; Griffin and Darko 2014). Social enterprises allow NGOs to provide social services while also generating significant income from their activities (Khieng and Dahles 2015; Maier, Meyer, and Steinbereithner 2016). The research suggested that NGOs are developing "business minds" and consequently establishing income-generating wings to support their revenue generation efforts as a result of the uncertainty and dwindling volume of funding sources. While the attention to social enterprise could be considered an innovative strategy and an important part of the sustainability of NGOs, many feared that it would gradually change the identity of NGOs which could affect the different roles that NGOs play in the SDGs agenda. The concern expressed during the research was summarised by one respondent as:

> "Many organisations are now rebranding themselves as social enterprises. This way, they will be able to generate income and promote social good. But if all of us become social enterprises, what do you think will happen to advocacy programmes which ensure that duty-bearers perform their duties responsibly for poor people? You know that you cannot charge fees for advocacy functions."

What this quote demonstrates is that the speed and potential superficiality by which NGOs are redefining as social enterprises could lead to neglect of advocacy roles played by civil societies in the context of the SDGs. This is because while it is possible to charge user fees from service delivery functions and also facilitation roles to generate income, the same cannot be said of advocacy functions. Our respondents worried that advocacy roles of *"pressuring government and other duty-bearers to do the right thing"* should play significant roles in shaping the outcomes of the SDGs in Ghana by 2030, but the prominence given to activities where fees can be charged would divert attention largely towards service delivery and facilitation roles at the neglect of advocacy programmes in a post-2015 world. This might lead to NGOs being perceived largely as profit-making entities whose activities can run counter to the traditional spirit of voluntarism characterising the third sector.

A second concern about how the changing development landscape is affecting the identity of NGOs relates to the increased alienation of organisations from the grassroots due to the professionalisation of the sector and alignment of interests to donors rather than communities. This finding is a much older trend, but one that is arguably accelerating and finding new forms in Ghana (for example, the pressure to act more like and with the private sector). As highlighted above, one of the distinctive values and features of NGOs has been their linkage with grassroots. However, as Edwards and Hulme (1996) have argued, the strong dependence of NGOs on donors can affect their relationship with the grassroots. Indeed, Banks and Hulme (2012) have argued that donor priorities and funding can cause a shift to a poverty-focused agenda and in the process move away from objectives of empowerment which recognise that while poverty reduction is an important goal in itself, it is also a condition within the broader goal of empowerment. Our research reflected these concerns and particularly how they are endangering the identity of NGOs. We gathered narratives about how the changing landscape and the drive for NGOs to be visible to gain donors' attention is seriously compromising their grassroots orientation, autonomy, and even legitimacy. This was expressed by one respondent as:

> "We are supposed to be operating in a bottom up era but this hardly happens. The usual practice nowadays is for NGOs to align their interests to donors, particularly on advocacy issues. This keeps such organisations going but then questions about legitimacy and independence naturally arise."

Another respondent noted that:

> "survival remains a topmost priority for several NGOs. In view of this, they follow the things donors are interested in rather than what communities are interested in. So, you only see them working with the grassroots once they get some donor money."

Respondents also highlighted how some NGOs were *"twisting their missions and goals"* to suit funding requirements, forming or becoming part of networks and coalitions they share little values with, and occasionally revising strategic plans to suit areas where there seem to be an increase in funding. Such mission-twisting exercises, it is argued, can affect the legitimacy, credibility, and ultimately the identity of these NGOs, which can further affect their functions and how they are perceived by those they engage and the poor that they purport to represent. Indeed, research suggests that attention towards donors rather than the grassroots could further compromise some of the values and expected roles that underpin NGOs as not profit-driven and non-partisan entities in the context of the SDGs.

Discussion and conclusion

An increasing body of research is currently drawing attention to a series of global trends that are changing the socio-economic and political tableau in several countries in the global South (Dubochet 2012; Hayman 2015). In particular, the challenges and opportunities being offered by these game-changing trends for civil society organisations have become topical issues for academics, activists, and development practitioners at large (Bandyopadhyay 2013; Goswami and Tandon 2013). However, with the adoption of the SDGs as the overarching framework for solving pressing global development challenges, there has been limited research into how the changing development landscape can or is affecting the roles that NGOs can play in the post-MDG development agenda.

In answering the question as to what extent the changing development landscape will affect the roles of NGOs in advancing SDGs in Ghana, this article has argued that NGOs will play critical roles spanning service provision, advocacy, and facilitation to advance the 17 broad goals enshrined in the SDGs. Yet, this exploratory study suggests that the changing development landscape can affect the expected roles of NGOs in at least three ways. First, although the changing development landscape in Ghana presents opportunities, it is also generally causing uncertainty in the mobilisation of financial resources that NGOs need to perform their diverse roles. In Ghana, NGOs rely significantly on external donor support rather than internally generated funds or the government (Arhin, Adam, and Akanbasiam 2015). Thus, unlike India (Goswami and Tandon 2013) and Latin America (Pousadela and Cruz, this issue) where the state provides significant funding to support the activities of CSOs, the reprioritisation and withdrawal of general funding support by the traditional donors has been noted by NGO leaders as one significant way through which their roles in advancing the SDGs would be affected.

Second, the study findings have also shown that the changing development landscape may affect the institutional capacity of several NGOs to deliver programmes that would advance the SDGs. Respondents highlighted the difficulty in maintaining office and operational costs, the high turnover of competent staff, closure of programmes, and difficulty in investing in the capacity of staff to meet changing technological development as some of the specific reasons that could lead to a weakening of the institutional capacity for NGOs. This does not mean the changing development landscape is producing only negative impacts, as some research has shown other opportunities such as the implementation of cost-cutting measures (Arhin, Adam, and Akanbasiam 2015).

The third way through which the roles of the NGOs may be affected by the changing landscape concerns the identity of NGOs. Following Bebbington (2004; 2005), this study has reported that many NGOs draw their strength and legitimacy from their closeness to grassroots populations and the fact that they are non-profit and non-partisan. But the study also gathered concerns about how the impact of the changing development landscape is likely to affect the image and identity of NGOs in the context of the SDGs. The study identified how the effect of the changing landscape and the need to generate resources to survive can place commercial interests above the voluntarism and altruistic motivations that have driven NGOs. In particular, the study showed how the necessity to charge user fees for services provided by NGOs can potentially shift attention away from advocacy functions to predominantly service provision and facilitation. Because the implementation of the SDGs is in its early stages the concerns reported in this article may largely be speculative. Nevertheless, they provide important windows for understanding areas of capacity building and support that should be directed towards NGOs to enable them play significant roles to advance the SDGs.

This article contributes to the literature on sustainability of the third sector by outlining three challenges facing NGOs in Ghana and how these are affecting their roles of service delivery, advocacy, and facilitation in the operationalisation of the SDGs. Elsewhere, we have highlighted some of the strategies being devised by the NGOs to overcome the challenges (Arhin, Adam, and Akanbasiam 2015). Future research could examine the dynamics of the effects of the changing development landscape with a focus on geography (for example, urban-based versus rural based organisations), type (local, national, and international), as well as by specific sectors (for example, health, education, environment, etc.). Further work could also focus on coping strategies for NGOs and alternatives sources of their funding mobilisation efforts such as engagement with the private sector and government.

Acknowledgements

The author wishes to thank Dr Emma Mawdsley for leading and providing advice on the research design for the article, and two anonymous reviewers for their constructive comments on earlier drafts of the paper.

Disclosure statement

No potential conflict of interest was reported by the author.

Funding

This paper is based primarily on research on a "changing development and civil society: implications, strategies, impacts", funded by the Cambridge Humanities Research Grant. The Cambridge Humanities Research Grant is an internal funding scheme at the University of Cambridge. More information is here: http://www.csah.cam.ac.uk/Research/CHRGS.

References

Abdulai, A. G., and D. Hulme. 2015. "The Politics of Regional Inequality in Ghana: State Elites, Donors and PRSPs." *Development Policy Review* 33 (5): 529–553.

Alter, S.K. 2006. "Social Enterprise Models and Their Mission and Money Relationships." In *Social Entrepreneurship: New Models of Sustainable Social Change*, edited by A Nicholls, 205–231. Oxford: Oxford University Press.

Arhin, A.A., M. S. Adam, and A. C. Akanbasiam. 2015. "The State of Civil Society Sustainability in Ghana: Striving, Surviving or Thriving?" West Africa Civil Society Institute Research Report.

Bandyopadhyay, K. 2013. "Civil Society at Multiple Crossroads in Asia." *Development in Practice* 23 (5-6): 644–652.

Banks, N., and D. Hulme. 2012. "The Role of NGOs and Civil Society in Development and Poverty Reduction." *Brooks World Poverty Institute Working Paper* 171.

Banks, N., Hulme, D., and Edwards, M. 2015. NGOs, States, and Donors Revisited: Still too close for comfort?. *World Development* 66, 707–718.

Bebbington, A. 2004. "NGOs and Uneven Development: Geographies of Development Intervention." *Progress in Human Geography* 28 (6): 725–745.

Bebbington, A. 2005. "Donor–NGO Relations and Representations of Livelihood in Nongovernmental Aid Ahains." *World Development* 33 (6): 937–950.

Bebbington, A. J., S. Hickey and D. Mitlin. 2008. "Introduction: can NGOs make a difference? The challenge of development alternatives." In: A. J. Bebbington, S. Hickey, and D. C. Mitlin (eds.), Can NGOs Make a Difference? The Challenge of Development Alternatives, London: Zed Books, 3–37.

Clayton, A., P. Oakley, and J. Taylor. 2000. "Civil Society Organizations and Service Provision." Washington, DC: United Nations Research Institute for Social Development.

CONIWAS. 2015. "CONIWAS Mole conference Communique." Accessed April 14, 2016. www.washghana.net/content/download/ … /Draft%20Communique.pdf.

Creswell, J. W. 2012. *Qualitative Inquiry and Research Design: Choosing among Five Approaches.* London: Sage.

DFID Ghana. 2012. "Operational Plan 2011-2015." Accessed January 8, 2016. www.gov.uk/government/uploads/system/uploads/attachment_data/file/67396/ghana-2011.pdf.

Dubochet, L. 2012. "Civil Society in a Middle-income Country: Evolutions and Challenges in INDIA." *Journal of International Development* 24 (6): 714–727.

Edwards, M., and D. Hulme. 1996. "Too Close for Comfort? The Impact of Official Aid on Nongovernmental Organizations." *World Development* 24 (6): 961–973.

Embassy of the Kingdom of the Netherlands. 2014. "Multi-Annual Strategic Plan Ghana, 2014–2017." Accessed January 8, 2016. www.rijksoverheid.nl/binaries/rijksoverheid/documenten/rapporten/2014/02/05/meerjarige-strategische-plannen-mjsp-2014-2017/ghana-multi-annual-strategic-plan-2014-2017.pdf.

Mawdsley, E. 2012. *From Recipients to Donors: The Emerging Powers and the Changing Development Landscape.* London: Zed Books.

Ghana Integrity Initiative. 2013. "A Civil Society Review of Progress Towards the Millennium Development Goals in Commonwealth countries: Ghana Report." London: The Commonwealth Foundation.

Golub, S. J. 2000. "Democracy as Development: A Case for Civil Society Assistance in Asia." In *Funding Virtue: Civil Society Aid and Democracy Promotion*, edited by M Ottaway, & T. Carothers, 135–158. Washington, DC: Carnegie Endowment for International Peace.

Goswami, D., and R. Tandon. 2013. "Civil Society in Changing India: Emerging Roles, Relationships, and Strategies." *Development in Practice* 23 (5–6): 653–664.

Government of Ghana. 2012. "Leveraging Partnership for Shared Growth and Development: Government of Ghana-Development Partners Compact." Accessed January 8, 2016. www.epd.eu/wp-content/uploads/2014/10/Leveraging-Partnership-for-Shared-Growth-and-Development-2012-2014.pdf.

Government of Ghana. 2015. "Ghana Millennium Development Goals-2015 Report." Accessed January 8, 2016. www.undp.org/content/dam/ghana/docs/Doc/Inclgro/UNDP_GH_2015%20Ghana%20MDGs%20Report.pdf.

Griffin-EL, E., and E. Darko. 2014. "A case study of health and agriculture social enterprises in Kenya." Accessed January 8, 2016. www.odi.org/sites/odi.org.uk/files/odi-assets/publications-opinion-files/8876.pdf.

Hayman, R. 2015. "NGOs, Aid Withdrawal and Exit Strategies." *Austrian Journal of Development Studies* 31 (1).

Kanbur, R., and A. Sumner. 2012. "Poor Countries or Poor People? Development Assistance and the New Geography of Global Poverty." *Journal of International Development* 24 (6): 686–695.

Karver, J., C. Kenny, and A. Sumner. 2012. "MDGs 2.0: What Goals, Targets, and Timeframe?" *IDS Working Papers* 2012 (398): 1–57.

Kakava, N. Z., Mbizi, R. and Manyeruke, J. 2013. Beyond philanthropy to sustainable community development – evaluation of corporate social responsibilities activities in Zimbabwe Interdisciplinary journal of contemporary research in business.

Khieng, S., and H. Dahles. 2015. "Commercialization in the Non-Profit Sector: The Emergence of Social Enterprise in Cambodia." *Journal of Social Entrepreneurship* 6 (2): 218–243.

Lewis, D. 2014. "Understanding the Role of Non-government Organizations (NGOs) as cultural brokers: a review of approaches." Osterreichische Zeitschrift fur Volkskunde.

Lewis, D., and N. Kanji. 2009. *Non-governmental Organizations and Development.* London: Routledge.

Maier, F., M. Meyer, and M. Steinbereithner. 2016. "Nonprofit Organizations Becoming Business-Like: A Systematic Review." *Nonprofit and Voluntary Sector Quarterly* 45 (1): 64–86.

Moss, T. J., and S. Majerowicz. 2012. "No Longer Poor: Ghana's New Income Status and Implications of Graduation from IDA." *Center for Global Development Working Paper* 300.

Najam, A. 1996. "NGO Accountability: A Conceptual Framework." *Development Policy Review* 14 (4): 339–354.

Netherlands Embassy. 2011. "Multi Annual Strategic Plan 2012-2015." Accessed January 8, 2016. www.rijksoverheid.nl/binaries/rijksoverheid/documenten/jaarplannen/2012/02/15/meerjarige-strategische-plannen-ghana/meerjarige-strategische-plannen-ghana.pdf.

Sachs, J. D. 2012. "From Millennium Development Goals to Sustainable Development Goals." *The Lancet* 379 (9832): 2206–2211.

Salamon, L. M. and Anheier, H. K. 1992. In search of the non-profit sector. I: The question of definitions. Voluntas: International Journal of Voluntary and Nonprofit Organizations, 3 (2): 125–151.

Salamon, L. M., and M. Haddock. 2015. "SDGs and NPIs: Private Nonprofit Institutions—The Foot Soldiers for the UN Sustainable Development Goals." Baltimore: Johns Hopkins Center for Civil Society Studies.

SECO. 2012. "Swiss Economic Cooperation and Development Ghana Country Strategy 2013-2016." Accessed January 8, 2016. www.eda.admin.ch/content/dam/countries/countries-content/ghana/en/Ghana-Country-Strategy-2013-16_en.pdf.

Sidaway, J. 2012. "Geographies of Development: New Maps, New Visions?" *The Professional Geographer* 64 (2): 1–14.

United Nations. 2015. "The Millennium Development Goals Report 2015." Accessed April 15, 2016. www.un.org/millenniumgoals/2015_MDG_Report/pdf/MDG%202015%20rev%20(July%201).pdf.

White, S. C. 1999. "NGOs, Civil Society, and the State in Bangladesh: The Politics of Representing the Poor." *Development and change* 30 (2): 307–326.

World Bank. 1989. "Involving Nongovernmental Organizations in World Bank-Supported Activities." Operative Directive 14.70. Washington, DC: The World Bank.

Zeitz, A. 2015. "The Changing International Political Economy of Development Assistance: The Ghanaian Case." *GEG Working Paper* 2015/104.

Non-governmental development organisations' sustainability, partnership, and resourcing: futuristic reflections on a problematic trialogue

Alan Fowler

ABSTRACT

The CIVICUS Civil Society Index Report 2011 highlights a disassociation between non-governmental development organisations (NGDOs) and the general population. The vulnerability of aided development CSOs is systemic. This can often be traced to a failed trialogue between NGDOs, their partners, and resource providers. This article argues that NGDOs share co-responsibility for their sustainability predicament. Signs of aid uncertainty in the last decades of the millennium were not heeded, nor strategies developed for life beyond aid. Instead, NGDOs were saved by the advent of, and prescribed roles in reaching, the Millennium Development Goals. A repeat performance with the new Sustainable Development Goals is unlikely.

Le Rapport de l'Indice CIVICUS de la société civile 2011 met en relief une dissociation entre les organisations non gouvernementales de développement (ONGD) et la population dans son ensemble. La vulnérabilité des OSC de développement recevant une aide est systémique. On peut souvent faire remonter ce problème à un trialogue échoué entre les ONGD, leurs partenaires et les fournisseurs de ressources. Cet article soutient que les ONGD sont co-responsables de leur situation difficile en matière de durabilité. On n'a pas tenu compte des signes indiquant une incertitude de l'aide au cours des dernières décennies, et on n'a pas non plus mis au point de stratégies pour la vie après l'aide. Au lieu de cela, les ONGD ont été sauvées par l'arrivée des Objectifs du Millénaire pour le développement et par les rôles prescrits pour les atteindre. Il est peu probable que cela se reproduise avec les nouveaux Objectifs de développement durable.

El Informe "Index", presentado por la Sociedad Civil CIVICUS en 2011, resalta la disociación existente entre las organizaciones no gubernamentales de desarrollo (ONGD) y la población en general. Las OSC de desarrollo que han recibido apoyo adolecen de vulnerabilidad sistémica; a menudo, ésta es atribuida al fallido *triálogo* entre las ONGD, sus contrapartes y los donantes. El presente artículo sostiene que las ONGD comparten la responsabilidad por su dilema de sostenibilidad, argumentando que no prestaron atención a las señales de incertidumbre financiera surgidas durante las últimas décadas del milenio anterior y que tampoco desarrollaron estrategias para sobrevivir sin la ayuda externa. Al respecto, entiende que fueron rescatadas por la aparición de los Objetivos de Desarrollo del Milenio y las funciones que se les asignaron para alcanzarlos. Tomando en cuenta estos antecedentes, no parece factible que las ONGD puedan repetir el esquema, ahora con los nuevos Objetivos de Desarrollo Sustentables.

Introduction

In 1998, I was in conversation with Mariano Valderrama, the leader of a prominent local non-governmental development organisation in Peru, on the withdrawal of funding by and through Northern partners. He described the experience as seeing the sea of external resources ebbing away to find his organisation, with many others like it, stranded on socio-economic and political islands amidst a mass of civil society to which, despite original local roots, it was no longer well connected. Now fast forward almost 20 years to an article in September 2015 on Malawi. It reports that:

> "Malawi has almost 500 NGOs, most of which are funded by international donors. But many NGOs don't work closely with local communities, so when they leave, projects collapse.
> Malawi's dependence on foreign-funded NGOs puts the country in a vulnerable position. The only way to step away from that is community engagement that goes beyond lip service to genuine involvement." (*The Guardian*, September 28, 2015)[1]

These examples are not exceptions. The CIVICUS Civil Society Index Summary Report of 2011 speaks about a disassociation between NGDOs – both local and foreign – and the population at large (CIVICUS 2011). The issue of the vulnerability of aided development CSOs – that is NGDOs – is systemic. One could go on and on about NGDOs being semi-detached from the populace or public policy without cutting through to a long-term problem. This organisational unsustainability outcome can often be traced to a failed trialogue between international NGDOs (INGDOs), their local partners, and their resource providers, often referred to as "back donors". The (historical) argument put forward in the following sections is that INGDOs have a large share of co-responsibility for finding themselves and local partners in a sustainability predicament. Signs of aid uncertainty and the end of their golden age of the last decades of the millennium (Fowler 2011) were not heeded, nor strategies for "life beyond aid" pursued with vigour (Fowler 2000a). While a notable few such as Amnesty International, Greenpeace, and Transparency International chose for autonomy, often with member funding, many others opted to be "saved", so to speak, by the expansion of official grant aid for North and South NGDOs tied to the advent of, and prescribed roles in reaching, the Millennium Development Goals (MDGs).

The concluding section argues that resource pluralisation and straitjackets suggest that a repeat performance with the newly minted Sustainable Development Goals (SDGs) will be wishful thinking. Exploring this line of argument raises issues of aid pathology and perverse incentives. But we begin by dispelling a myth and getting a sense of proportion.

Getting a sense of proportion

Within a wide universe of civil society, NGDOs – both international and local – are one organisational field among very many others (Edwards, 2011). If properly understood as the associational life of some seven billion citizens, civil society across the globe is not in a crisis of sustainability. Self-sustaining, self-governed "under the radar" formations that people create are the dense fabric of civil society that remains unseen by many external (aid) observers (Fowler 2013). More visibly, one just has to look at the mushrooming of churches on the African continent to see that there is more than enough in the way of resources for people to come together in faith and worship. As noticeable is diaspora financing which, at US$600 billion, dwarfs aid flows and which, while often kept within a family, is also used for community betterment which maintains social capital and reputation.

> "Once the money is back in an expatriate's homeland, it is put to good use. Remittances have reduced poverty in Bangladesh, Ghana, and Nepal. Children from recipient households in El Salvador have a lower school-dropout rate; in Sri Lanka, they have more access to private tutors. The money finances health care, housing, and businesses. Micro-finance borrowers can even use remittance receipts as evidence of credit history."[2]

Moreover, the rise of "new (struggling) middle classes" across the world, away from a hand-to-mouth existence, offers a perspective of more citizens with time, money, and interests to invest in and expand associational life. To what purposes remains an open question (Wiemann 2015; Biekart

2015), which calls for dedicated empirical study of living civil society and its class ecology (Knorringa 2015). But the notion that civil society in its full sense is facing a crisis of sustainability must be questioned. Moreover, it is beholden on analysts to avoid using the "inflationary" blanket term of civil society when their terrain is far more limited.

The current sense of anxiety and stress about the sustainability of civil society is tied to a relatively small, vocal, and media-visible set of mostly, but not exclusively, aid-related NGDOs, many without a membership base. But numbers – big or small – are a poor proxy for impact on livelihoods and on social-political processes. For example, relying on international law and financed by members, Amnesty International can exert influence disproportionate to its small size. But these types of NGDOs are not the mainstream of other-serving, aided entities that have achieved a relatively significant (inter)national presence that is now, it is argued, under threat.

Today's INGDOs can employ thousands of staff with US$1 billion plus annual budgets, operating in more than a hundred countries. This community is said to be responsible for intermediating the disbursement and application of annual amounts in the range of US$50.8 to 76 billion which has to be raised from sources that are proving to be less and less reliable but not, if OECD data are to be believed, less generous (Tomlinson 2013). Between 2008 and 2013 official aid to and through NGDOs increased from US$18.5 billion to US$21 billion (Baobab 2015a). In spending these sums, the delivery of humanitarian aid and social services enjoys relatively more support than does advocacy, lobbying, and human rights (Baobab 2015b).

Access to this volume of funding is not evenly or fairly distributed across INGDOs and their national partners. For example, it is estimated that local NGDOs gain direct finance for only 2% of the total allocated to humanitarian relief, yet they are first at the scene, culturally informed, taking risks, and often more effective than their international counterparts who arrive later.[3] Here, and more widely, a reluctance of INGDOs to treat what is local as sufficiently competent reflects a natural self-interest in enduring self-viability, abetted by back donor reluctance to finance Southern NGDOs directly. The Secretary General of CIVICUS puts his finger of this Northern symbiotic pathology in terms of arguments voiced by back donors:

1. Lots of Southern and smaller CSOs do not have the capacity to fill in all our forms, let alone spend our money effectively.
2. We do not have the administrative capacity to give smaller amounts of money.
3. We need to channel money through a few, trusted partners so that we can manage risk and comply with our own rules.
4. We have strict anti-terror and anti-money laundering rules that make giving directly difficult.
5. We are under domestic political pressure to fund through CSOs in our home country. (Sriskandrajah 2015)

The three-fold combination of Northern NGDO survival, back donors' reluctance to fund directly in the South, and semi-detachment of Southern NGDOs from their domestic economic roots connects the sustainability, partnership, and resourcing story.

To avoid misunderstanding, this article does not argue that NGDOs have not been a valuable part of the development landscape. Through their efforts, lives have been saved, people have risen out of poverty, the abuse of rights has been publicised and redressed, attention to women's issues and their oppression have gained prominence, and so on. Rather, what follows looks at the co-responsibility of NGDOs for the seemingly financially vulnerable position in which they now find themselves. The analytic lens applied is one of organisational ecology (Hannan and Freeman 1989).

Why has it come to this?

An approach to an answer of why NGDOs have brought the problem of viability on themselves is to explore the connection between sustainability, partnership, and resourcing, starting with the ambiguities and unrealism of the former. In doing so, a distinction must be made between the sustainability of development outcomes and that of the organisations. Both perspectives gained momentum in the 1980s and early 1990s (e.g. Honadle and van Sant 1985; Brinkerhoff and Goldsmith 1992; Kadekhodi 1992). This article is about the latter in terms of its theory, practice, and futures.

The project continued to outweigh the organisation

A framework for analysis is provided by a theory of resource dependency: a fundamental way in which most organisations interact with their environments (Pfeffer and Salancik 1978). Organisations are shaped by, but in turn try to shape, external operating conditions in their favour. Advertising and political lobbying – singly or collectively – are common ways of doing so. Business associations and NGDO umbrella bodies often play this type of role.

In the 1980s, INGDOs were claiming distinctive ideologies and competencies which made them an effective alternative to official aid orthodoxies and practices (Drabek 1987). One division was between the political "social solidarity" school of INDGOs and those more aligned with market thinking based on complementary comparative advantages (Brown and Korten 1989). Twenty years on, a review by Bebbington, Hickey, and Mitlin (2008) indicated that the latter, "public service contractor" school had prevailed.[4] One reason was the latent effect on INGDOs of *caritas* which approximated financial disbursement with development achievement, leading to a growth-driven stance towards resource mobilisation. Perhaps, with the exception of child sponsorship and humanitarian disasters, this proved to be easier in terms of gaining large aid grants spurred by official pro-NGDO policies than the task of motivating millions of individuals to donate money in a reliable way. The aid strategy simply had and, despite the advent of crowd-sourcing, still has, lower transaction costs.

A further driver towards market-oriented resourcing behaviour was calls for "professionalisation" of North and South NGDOs without any real intrinsic models of what this meant. Despite many differences in organisational logic and tasks, by default if not design, the practices and metrics of the private sector became the point of reference (Edwards and Fowler 2002). To a large extent, this remains the case, and was reinforced as official aid became more privatised by, for example, the introduction of competitive bidding.

One has to look hard and wide for anything similar to the experience of the Bangladesh Rural Advancement Committee (BRAC), whose founder, Fazel Abed, determined from the outset in 1972 to pursue a strategy of self-financing through enterprises that has become a signature characteristic (Fowler 2000c).[5] Citing examples of Amnesty International, Greenpeace, and so on must not overlook the fact that they are lobbyists that do not provide on-the-ground services to the poor. In sum, the landscape of assuredly viable (I)NGDOs is thinly populated, in part due to their intermediary role.

Application of dependency theory to NGDOs in the North and in the South illustrates the vertical chain structure and patron–client asymmetry between them (Hudock 1995). Disbursement proceeds from resource-rich to resource-poor settings usually via a contractually mediated set of relationships embodying power asymmetry in favour of the initial provider and successive intermediaries (Fowler 2000b).

In the 1990s, an increasing dependency of INGOs on official aid (Development Initiatives 2000) meant shaping the environment constructed by their back donors in favour of modalities to achieve the organisational sustainability of partners. In the words of Richard Holloway (1997), the organisation not the project would have to become the unit of analysis. While NGDOs have generally succeeded in changing the language funders relied on – empowerment, participation, partnership, and so on – a shift in financing models to invest in long-term organisational viability did not occur to any substantive degree. Instead attention focused on capacity development that could increase the attractiveness of Southern NGDOs to other resource providers as proven project implementers (Hailey and James 1994). Holloway's insight did not gain hold. Capacity development of Southern NGDOs was mainly a means for developmental outcomes, not a "civil society" end in itself. Unless Northern NGDOs took it upon themselves to ensure their partners' future viability – which hardly occurred – unsustainability was a predictable outcome somewhere in the future; which for some, if not many, is now.

In turn, Southern NGDOs could have moved towards revising their financing set-up to root themselves in their own economies. Many practical guides were available to help them do so (Fox and Schearer 1997; Gibson 1995; Cannon 1999; Fowler 2000c; Malunga and Banda 2004). Though uneven across the world, ten years on, the CIVICUS (2011) study identifying the semi-detachment of local NGDOs from their societies demonstrates that, for many Southern NGDOs, this was a path less travelled. The reasons are many. One is a simple ecological/economic mismatch between what a (poor) country – often itself heavily aid dependent, like Mozambique and Malawi – could support institutionally set against the unwieldy scale of local NGDOs created through external aid. Inability to raise local resources was exacerbated by the salaries and conditions of service that aid-related Southern NGDOs became accustomed to. For example, with its post-colonial latency, an often tense topic in Northern NGDO relations with local partners was about terms of staff remuneration, usually sharpened when expatriates were also involved. What salaries would be "fair", what other benefits would be "reasonable"? The higher the answer, the bigger the problem of economic embedding.

In addition, incentives and effort required for a local NGDO to mobilise domestic resources were often calculated, respectively, to be too few and too heavy. In the case of the former, evidence in the CIVICUS study suggests that local populations either did not know of, understand, or trust NGDOs functioning in their name. In addition, local NGDOs were often wary of engaging with their governments to access tax-based or official aid: demands for corrupt payments being but one concern, the improbability of finance for advocacy another. Consequently, for all their complicated administrative frustrations, writing proposals was easier, as was adjusting organisational strategies towards shifts in aid priorities and fashions. In short, it made more sense to follow the aid money (Albertyn and Tjønneland 2010) than to take a more demanding path of cultivating financial self-reliance. Understandably, the more entrepreneurial NGDOs tended to fare better, shaping the NGDO ecology country by country as donors' geo-political priorities shifted, as did Northern NGDO priorities in their slipstream (Koch 2009).

Overall, unless self-financing was a Southern NGDO agenda from the outset, motivation to do so down the road typically faced obstacles of inhospitable environments, organisational inertia, and inconvenience, fostering enduring dependency (e.g. Gibson 1995).

Partnership for organisational sustainability: a politically correct myth

The pursuit of authentic partnership has been an enduring narrative of NGDO North–South interactions. This "authentic" relational quality was understood in terms of, for example, of: mutuality in commitment, organisational capabilities and power; sharing in terms of goals and purposes, standards of behaviour, language and understanding of key concepts, such as the causes of poverty; balance in terms of risk and vulnerability, costs and benefits, rights and obligations; and trust based on transparent decision-making and fair allocation of responsibilities and accountability (Fowler 1991).

More often than not, good partnership intentions were simply offset by power asymmetries built into the chain that could not be overcome. For example, an attempt by Kamal Malhotra and myself to establish an ombuds function that could even-handedly hear partnership disputes foundered because it would require a Northern NGDO to forego final relational authority (Fowler and Malhotra 1997).

The presence of disincentives, described above, to financially empower partners become clearer as virtually no progress was made in revising funding and resourcing modalities, for example, by providing investment for buildings and income-generating/expenditure-reducing assets that could start to provide local financial stability for Southern NGDOs. Despite many calls to translate the sustainability rhetoric of partnering into a reality, minimal provision for operational overheads remained the practice.

There was always an element of unreality about an expectation that, in partnering, Northern NGDOs would work to ensure the long-term viability of counterparts, potentially at the cost of themselves in the sense that, for many, their own sustainability was not – and is still not – assured. Doing themselves out of a job was always an INGDO myth (van Rooy 2000).

With a few instructive exceptions (e.g. Hailey 2014), Northern NGDOs choose self-sustainability first, with partnership in an authentic vein seldom a close second. For Southern NGDOs, unless, like BRAC, self-financing was a strategy from day one, expecting a Northern partner to do this for them was a misguided hope. This does imply a cynical interpretation of sincere intentions that partnerships should evolve in this way, but the improbability of this occurring was already apparent at the end of the last millennium.

The scenario sketched above does not do justice to attempts by a few of the smaller official aid agencies – the Scandinavians, Dutch, and, at times, the British – to establish multi-year unrestricted funding windows for their domiciled NGDOs (INTRAC 2014). Greater funding certainty increased the potential for Northern NGDOs to take a strategic approach to supporting the longevity of local counterparts. Seldom, however, was this type of agreement with back donors redeployed along the aid chain in favour of the long-term viability of Southern partners.

By the turn of the millennium, lessons from Latin American and Asian NGDO experience invited questioning about a life for NGDOs beyond aid (Browne 1999; Aldaba et al. 2000). Whatever the model, strategy, or tactics authors proposed, an incentive to look at alternative relational, self-financing scenarios was effectively delayed, if not undermined, by the advent of the MDGs. This focusing of official aid effort included prescribed roles for NGDOs: social service delivery, policy influence/ advocacy, and to watchdog aid recipient governments. The advent of goal-specific finance for these functions – increasingly based on competitive bidding – effectively removed partner sustainability from the frames of reference in favour of NGDOs partnering for operational effectiveness. The data on growth of NGDO disbursements cited previously suggest that the issue of organisational sustainability – the being of an NGDO – was systematically separated out from the availability of finance for the doing, which MDGs stimulated.

What next?

Outlining future scenarios and teasing out their implications for NGDOs is always a tricky enterprise. Doing so at the end of the past millennium pointed towards three major options: more of the same and bigger, social enterprise, and civic innovation (Fowler 2000a). Fifteen years on, to greater and lesser degrees, all these options are in play. NGDOs are more plentiful and (much) bigger if annual budgets are the measure. Social enterprise and "hybridisation" of NGDOs as non+for-profits is gathering traction, while civic innovation is increasing associated by engagement with "netted" social movements, networks, and media. At the risk of the charge of hubris, this section speculates forward on the partnership, sustainability, resourcing trialogue. It does so ecologically in terms of connections between pluralisations and straitjackets, or systemic constraints that NGDOs have to navigate to stay viable in pursuit of social justice and transformation.

Six pluralisations

For NGDOs, the world ecology is becoming more plural at different speeds and scales. Beginning with the big picture, the tectonic plates of geo-political relations are shifting from a Western/Euro-American defined, if not imposed, order, to a condition where other powers have leverage and authority in international affairs to back up a stronger voice. While the BRICS spring to mind, other countries – Mexico, Indonesia, Turkey – are lining up as actors to take into account as pluralisation of global power plays out and feeds through, creating straitjackets discussed later. A historical NGDO reliance on the norms and values of the West to be universally applicable and transmitted through aid and other pathways will be increasingly open to uncomfortable "relativating" challenges. More harshly put, Southern NGDOs will be less and less able to rely on a protective umbrella of Western-backed human rights discourse and associated external pressures from other countries.

Another, simultaneous, site of governance pluralisation is within countries, showing two principle directions. One is vertical, as governance and responsibilities for well-being are devolved downwards towards and through tiers of local government to individual citizens and their collective associational forms. At the same time, authority over life and the rules they require is being spread across all sorts of institutions – market, customary, and virtual – whose governance arrangements make impunity towards citizens for decisions taken more rather than less likely (Fowler and Biekart 2015). Here, North and South NGDOs' focus will need to expand towards the multiple sites from which power is exercised.

Pluralisation is also to be seen in the expansion of sources for development financing (Severino and Ray 2010). While the mega-philanthropies of the living super-rich – such as Bill Gates – are contentious game-changers, corporate social responsibility is being complemented by collective social value (Moore 2014). Alongside are more opportunities for personal giving via internet-mediated markets that are "dis-intermediating" the traditional INGDO financing model. The general point is that resourcing needs to appreciate far beyond the aid system's parameters, which is not say that new sources are qualitatively better or worse – here the jury is certainly out – but they are options to explore. For example, high net-worth individuals in Africa are already becoming an indigenous source of finance for local non-profits, a trend which is set to grow (AGN 2014).

Through SDG 17 the United Nations is pushing hard for relational pluralism. It is doing so by promoting the implementation of sustainable development goals by means of multi-stakeholder initiatives (MSIs) (Dodds 2015). Correspondingly, and reminiscent of the end of the past millennium, new guides, handbooks, and practical tools are coming to redefine NGDO competencies (e.g. Huijstee 2012; Brouwer and Woodlhill 2015). The ability to engage in these complex multi-partner relationships – as a host or as a member – is likely to be a common requirement for accessing resources as well as for tricky decision-making about who to associate with or not. Here, the specification of goals invites (I)NGDOs to articulate a compelling value proposition as participants as well as hosts.

There is also pluralisation going on in the development delivery landscape. That the private sector has been increasingly contracted to provide services to aid agencies is far from new. What is new is an expansion of legal types of business organisations with a social agenda; a process of social enterprise hybridisation. In the United States, this organisational category is referred to as L3Cs (low-profit limited liability company). In the United Kingdom they are charitable incorporated organisations (CIOs). The point is that these entities are bringing a form of competition for resources that may – depending on what is to be delivered – squeeze out traditional NGDOs.

With other forces, such as technology, climate, and demographic changes, these pluralisations are interactively altering the operating environments in different ways for different types of organisations, NGDOs included. Their viability requires adaptation to a shifting ecology, but without losing site of mandate and purpose. Doing so also means awareness and navigation of constraints which are likely have differential impacts.

Five (potential) straitjackets

Opportunities that come with socio-ecological change can also bring constraints or straitjackets, limiting choices and the decisions that can be made. Some constraints are more readily connected than others to the types of pluralisations sketched above. We can start with a large-scale potential straitjacket – the quality of development finance.

To the extent that benevolence was ever part of the aid system's reason for being, the Euro-American 2008 financial crisis brought to the fore the fact that economic fundamentals determine how development cooperation views, values, and allocates resources – a question of relative affordability, not an ethical imperative. A nail in the organisational sustainability coffin through authentic NGDO partnerships was probably delivered by a recalibration of aid for what and for whom, with the

EU's refugee predicament being a more recent reason to redefine what aid is about, for whom, and the geography of application. In terms of EU countries' assistance, over here and overseas are becoming synonymous.

A constraint on adequate finance for development – including the SDGs and climate change – has been the subject of much debate at Addis Abba and at Paris. A reading of these events is that: (a) private rather than public finance will need to play a far bigger proportional role in development investment; while (b) allocations are likely to be biased towards the interface between people and biosphere, with eradicating extreme poverty becoming secondary unless these two overlap each other. This analysis invites questioning around issues of corporate influence, accountability, and a system-wide appetite to finance human rights initiatives which interweaves with the next constraint.[6]

The governance pluralism noted above is already having an adverse effect on Western-backed local NGDOs that are dedicated to issues of basic freedoms of information, association, and respect for human rights. Foreign flows to Southern NGDOs operating in these socio-politically sensitive areas are already being curtailed, as are regimes' constraints on critical advocacy more widely. Emboldened by South-South power emergence and the self-implosion of Europe as a sustainable democratic-capitalist model to be emulated, aided-countries' concern about geo-political repercussions from their behaviour which emanate from Western donor countries seems to be ebbing away. The consequences for overtly rights-driven NGDOs seem particularly dire unless the population is driven to tackle and resource protecting this feature of their lives and prospects.

An additional constraint is a further tightening of the straitjacket known as value-for-money, which will place increasing demands on administering and measuring results of development allocations. A probable outcome is a re-projectisation of allocations after a period of more programmatic and complexity based ways of thinking about how change happens (e.g. Burns and Worsley 2015).

Finally, a very uncertain constraint is around the way in which the internet penetrates virtually all facts of life in whose favour – citizens, or states, or commerce. It seems impractical to ignore how contentions around internet governance and its resolution will play out. Will states take over from a proven transparent and accountable non-profit with the prospect of national cyber-sovereignty prescribing the "free" flow of information with an international mandate to do so?[7] This debate takes place alongside those concentrating on the way that governments can observe and manipulate the associational life and activisms of citizens, with NGDO-ism as but one manifestation of collective civic agency (Morozov 2102, 2014). For example, international NGOs are already discussing what the digital age will mean for their accountability (INGO Charter Company 2015).

An emerging trialogue: challenges of strategy, relational competence, and organisational agility

This sustainability issue of *Development in Practice* can be placed in critical analysis feeding wider debates about the future of INGDOs as we currently know them (Gnärig 2015; Green 2015). Despite differences in conclusions about meeting disruptive changes that NGDOs face – disintermediation, political constraints, public mistrust and so on – a common perspective is one of operating conditions that are the products of the pluralisations and straitjackets described above. Their scenario is one where: (1) as further organisational blending and hybridisations occurs the notion of "sectors" will be increasingly misleading as a way of thinking about how society is structured and works; (2) there will be more and more niches to be filled by organisations that make good strategic readings and choices – climate change, pollution, inequality, youth unemployment – and respond accordingly; and (3) relational competencies will become an even more essential organisational attribute. In relation to the latter, Banks, Hulme, and Edwards (2014) argue for an (I)NGDO future which brings value because of a historically evolved ability to connect and mediate diverse actors, multiple scales, and mixed geographies. What they do not elaborate is how this type of bridging role and relational value proposition will be resourced.

Perhaps or greater significance from this analysis is the need for a mindset shift where sustainability becomes equated with agility rather than a secure "partnership". Put another way, sustainability will have to be sought in agility and adaptability. It will require fine-tuned readings of the qualities of the diverse resources and their providers. Maintaining agendas of social justice, transformation, and treating development as political, rather than technical processes, calls for accurate readings and assessment of who to collaborate with or not. How close to the state and private finance? How close to member-based organisations that can help NGDOs to really root in their own economies? Is the critical NGDO task one of localising to globalise – that is, to actively seek sustainability from below and from within, rather than from above?

Perhaps a closure must return to the beginning. What will a future-oriented trialogue look like? One thing is clear, that trialogue must become a multilogue.[8] The resource and actor landscape is diversifying by type and scale in unprecedented ways that open up space for innovation and responsiveness that cannot be let slip: agility and viability will go hand in hand. In addition, as the potential for in-country resourcing in the South becomes an (uneven) reality across the world the direction of multilogues will need to become more horizontal. Finally, partnerships need to be re-calibrated towards greater clarity and honesty about inherent differences in power and interests to be constructively worked with and not masked by false labels of convenience.

Notes

1. Charles Pensulo, "NGOs in Malawi: What happens when donors leave?" *The Guardian*. September 28, 2015.
2. See www.euractiv.com/section/migrations/opinion/remittances-and-savings-of-the-diaspora-can-finance-development/
3. See www.theguardian.com/global-development-professionals-network/2015/oct/16/less-than-2-of-humanitarian-funds-go-directly-to-local-ngos?CMP=ema-1702&CMP=
4. I am grateful to a reviewer for this observation.
5. Personal communication while advising BRAC on sustainability strategy in 2008.
6. See www.socialwatch.org/node/17062
7. See http://blogs.cfr.org/cyber/2015/12/16/chinas-internet-conference-xi-jinpings-message-to-washington/
8. I must thank a reviewer for this terminology.

Disclosure statement

No potential conflict of interest was reported by the author.

References

AGN. 2014. *Africa's Wealthy Give Back: A Perspective on Philanthropic Giving by Wealthy Africans in Sub-Saharan Africa with a Focus on Kenya, Nigeria and South Africa*. Johannesburg: Trust Africa.

Albertyn, C., and E. Tjønneland. 2010. *Follow the Money! Policies and Practices in Donor Support to Civil Society in Southern Africa*. Johannesburg: Southern Africa Trust.

Aldaba, F., P. Antezana, M. Valderrama, and A. Fowler. 2000. "NGO Strategies beyond Aid: Perspectives from Central and South America and the Philippines." *Third World Quarterly Special Issue* 21 (4): 669–683.

Banks, N., D. Hulme, and M. Edwards. 2014. "NGOs, States and Donors Revisited: Still Too Close for Comfort?" *World Development* 66: 707–718.

Baobab. 2015. "Civil Society Aid Trends 2015." Baobab Briefing No. 3. Accessed March 1, 2016. www.baobab.org.uk/wp-content/uploads/2015/01/BBAidTrends2015.pdf.

Bebbington, A., S. Hickey, and D. Mitlin, eds. 2008. *Can NGOs Make a Difference? The Challenge of Development Alternatives*. London: Zed Press.

Brinkerhoff, D., and A. Goldsmith. 1992. "Promoting the Sustainability of Development Institutions: A Framework for Strategy." *World Development* 20 (3): 369–383.

Biekart, K. 2015. "The Choice of the New Latin American Middle Classes; Sharing or Self-Caring." *European Journal of Development Research* 27 (2): 238–245.

Brouwer, H., and J. Woodlhill. 2015. *The MSP Guide: How to Design and Facilitate Multi-Stakeholder Partnerships*. Wageningen: Centre for Development Innovation, University of Wageningen.

Brown, D., and D. Korten. 1989. *Voluntary Organizations: Guidelines for Donors*. Working Paper WPS 258. Washington, DC: The World Bank.

Browne, S. 1999. *Beyond Aid: From Patronage to Partnership*. Aldershot: Ashridge.

Burns, D., and S. Worsley. 2015. *Navigating Complexity in International Development: Facilitating Sustainable Change at Scale*. Rugby: Practical Action.

Cannon, L. 1999. *Life beyond Aid: Twenty Strategies to Help Make NGOs Sustainable*. Johannesburg: Interfund.

CIVICUS. 2011. *Bridging the Gaps: Citizens, Organisations and Disassociation, Civil Society Index Summary Report 2008–2011*. Johannesburg: CIVICUS.

Development Initiatives. 2000. *Global Development Assistance: The Role of Non-Governmental Organisations and other Charity Flows*. White Paper on Globalisation, Background Note on Section 4.1. Evercreech: Development Initiatives.

Dodds, F. 2015. *Multi-stakeholder Partnerships: Making them Work for the Post-2015 Development Agenda, ECOSOC*. New York: United Nations.

Drabek, A. ed. 1987. *Development Alternatives: The Challenge for NGOs, World Development, Vol. 15*. Oxford: Pergamon Press.

Edwards, M., and A. Fowler. 2002. *The Earthscan Reader in NGO Management*. London: Earthscan.

Edwards, M. ed. 2011. *The Oxford Handbook of Civil Society*. Oxford: Oxford University Press.

Fowler, A. 1991. "Building Partnerships between Northern and Southern Developmental NGOs: Issues for the 1990s." *Development in Practice* 1 (1): 5–18.

Fowler, A. 2000a. "NGOs as a Moment in History: Beyond Aid to Social Entrepreneurship or Civic Innovation?" In Fowler, A. (ed.). "NGO Futures: Beyond Aid." *Third World Quarterly* 21 (4): 637–654.

Fowler, A. 2000b. *NGOs, Civil Society and Social Development: Changing the Rules of the Game*. Geneva 2000 Occasional Paper, No. 1. Geneva: United Nations Research Institute for Social Development.

Fowler, A. 2000c. *The Virtuous Spiral: A Guide to Sustainability for NGOs in International Development*. London: Earthscan.

Fowler, A. 2011. "Development NGOs." In *The Oxford Handbook of Civil Society*, edited by M. Edwards, 42–54. Oxford: Oxford University Press.

Fowler, A. 2013. "Civil Society and Aid in Africa: A case of mistaken identity?" In *Handbook of Civil Society in Africa*, edited by E. Obadare, 417–438. New York: Springer.

Fowler, A., and K. Biekart. 2015. "Navigating Polycentric Governance from a Citizen's Perspective: The Rising New Middle Classes Respond." *European Journal of Development Research*, 18 June. doi:10.1057/ejdr.2015.44.

Fowler, A., and K. Malhotra. 1997. *An NGO Ombudsman: A New Way of Enhancing Development Alliances in a Gobalising World*. Bangkok: FOCUS on the Global South.

Fox, L., and B. Schearer, eds. 1997. *Sustaining Civil Society: Strategies for Resource Mobilization*. Washington, DC: CIVICUS.

Gibson, K. 1995. *Becoming Self-Sufficient: The Experience of US NGOs in Achieving Sustainability*. MULBERRY Series No. 5. Durban: Olive Information Services.

Gnärig, B. 2015. *The Hedgehog and the Beetle: Disruption and Innovation in the Civil Society Sector*. Berlin: International Civil Society Centre.

Green, D. 2015. *Fit for the Future? Development Trends and the Role of International NGOs*. Oxfam Discussion Papers. Oxford: Oxfam.

Hailey, J. 2014. *EveryChild's Journey to a New Model - Transistioning from an INGO to a Network: The First Five Years*. London: EveryChild.

Hailey, J., and R. James. 1994. "Developing the Sustainable NGO: Strengthening the Capacity of Southern NGOs." Paper presented at the Development Studies Association Conference, University of Lancaster, September.

Hannan, M., and J. Freeman. 1989. "Organizations and Social Structure." In *Organizational Ecology*, 3–27. Cambridge: Harvard University Press.

Holloway, R. 1997. *The Unit of Development is the Organisation, Not the Project: Strategies and Structures for Sustaining the Work of Southern NGOs*. Washington, DC: Paul H. Nitze School of Advanced International Studies, Johns Hopkins University.

Honadle, G., and J. van Sant. 1985. *Implementation for Sustainability: Lessons from Integrated Rural Development*. West Hartford: Kumarian Press.

Hudock, A. 1995. "Sustaining Southern NGOs in Resource-Dependent Environments." *Journal of International Development* 7 (4): 653–667.

Huijstee, M. 2012. *Multi-stakeholder Initiatives: A Strategic Guide for Civil Society Organizations*. Amsterdam: SOMO.

INGO Charter Company. 2015. *CSO Accountability in the Digital Age: Outcome Summary*. Berlin: INGO Accountability Charter Company.

INTRAC. 2014. *Comparative Review of Donor Approaches to Unrestricted Funding of CSOs: Final Report*. Oxford: INTRAC.

Kadekhodi, G. 1992. "Paradigms of Sustainable Development." *Development Seeds of Change* 3: 72–76.

Knorringa, P. 2015. "Towards a More Empirical Debate on Middle Classes in the Global South." *The European Journal of Development Research* 27 (2): 254–256.

Koch, D-J. 2009. *Aid from International NGOs: Blind Spots on the Allocation Map*. London: Routledge.

Malunga, C., and C. Banda. 2004. *Understanding Organizational Sustainability through African Proverbs*. Washington, DC: Impact Alliance Press.

Moore, C. 2014. *Corporate Social Responsibility and Creating Shared Value: What's the Difference?* Little Rock: Heifer International.

Morozov, E. 2012. *The Net Delusion: The Dark Side of Internet Freedom*. New York: Public Affairs.

Morozov, E. 2014. *To Save Everything, Click Here: The Folly of Technology Solutionism*. New York: Public Affairs.

Pfeffer, J. and G. Salancik. 1978. *The External Control of Organizations: A Resource Dependence Perspective*. New York: Harper and Row.

Robb, D. 2000. "Building Resilient Organizations." *OD Practitioner* 32 (3): 27–32.

van Rooy, A. 2000. "Good News! You May be Out of a Job: Reflections on the Past and Future 50 Years for Northern NGOs." *Development in Practice* 10 (3/4): 300–318.

Severino, J-M., and O. Ray. 2010. *The End of ODA (II): The Birth of Hyper Collective Action*. Working Paper Number 218. Washington, DC: Center for Global Development.

Sriskandrajah, D. 2015. "Five Reasons Donors Give for Not Funding Local NGOs Directly." Guardian Development Professionals Network, 9 November.

Tomlinson, B. 2013. *Working with Civil Society in Foreign Aid: Possibilities for South-South Cooperation?* New York: United Nations Development Programme.

Wiemann, J. 2015. "The New Middle Classes: Advocates for Good Governance, Inclusive Growth and Sustainable Development?" *The European Journal of Development Research* 27 (2): 195–201.

New routes to CSO sustainability: the strategic shift to social enterprise and social investment

John Hailey and Mark Salway

ABSTRACT

The issue of sustainability is becoming more important for civil society, as non-profits, NGOs, and other civil society organisations (CSOs) face a range of political, regulatory, organisational, and financial challenges. This article focuses on the crucial dimension of financial sustainability and the growing awareness of the importance of accessing alternative sources of funds and developing new funding models. These include accessing social investment, using subsidiary businesses to fund programme work, or developing new social enterprises. The article draws on analysis of the funding environment and specific examples to explore the different dimensions of sustainability, and assess why many CSOs are looking to new funding models and alternative routes to sustainability.

La question de la durabilité revêt une importance croissante pour la société civile, alors que les organisations à but non lucratif, les ONG et les autres organisations de la société civile (OSC) sont confrontées à une variété de défis politiques, organisationnels, financiers et en matière de réglementation. Cet article se concentre sur la dimension cruciale de la durabilité financière et sur la prise de conscience croissante de l'importance de l'accès à des sources alternatives de fonds et de l'élaboration de nouveaux modèles de financement. Il s'agit entre autres d'accéder aux investissements sociaux, de l'utilisation de filiales pour financer les activités de programme ou du développement de nouvelles entreprises sociales. Il s'inspire d'une analyse de l'environnement de financement et d'exemples précis afin d'examiner les différentes dimensions de la durabilité et d'évaluer pourquoi de nombreuses OSC se tournent vers de nouveaux modèles de financement et des voies alternatives vers la durabilité.

En la medida en que las organizaciones sin ánimo de lucro, las ONG y otras organizaciones de la sociedad civil (OSC) deben enfrentar diversos retos políticos, reglamentarios, organizacionales y financieros, la cuestión de la sostenibilidad se ha vuelto cada vez más importante para la sociedad civil. El presente artículo se centra en el aspecto crucial que significa la sostenibilidad financiera y la creciente sensibilización [de las OSC] respecto a la importancia de lograr el acceso a fuentes de financiación alternas, así como de crear nuevos modelos para el financiamiento. Estos incluyen el acceso a inversiones sociales, el uso de negocios filiales para financiar el trabajo programático, o la creación de nuevas empresas sociales. El estudio parte del estudio del ambiente financiero y de ejemplos específicos que permiten explorar las distintas dimensiones de sostenibilidad, analizando por qué muchas OSC están buscando nuevos modelos de financiación y caminos alternos para lograr la sostenibilidad.

Alternative perspectives on sustainability

There are different perspectives on sustainability and what it means in practice. Any analysis of sustainability needs to acknowledge the diversity of these different perspectives, but also the way that they complement each other. What is clear is that perspectives on sustainability are context specific and that it is a generic term with no agreed definition (Benton and Monroy 2004). Recent commentaries on civil society sustainability by CIVICUS (2014) and USAID (2015a) reinforce this perspective and conceptualise sustainability as being the product of the environment in which an individual CSO operates and a particular set of conditions.

For the purposes of this article a sustainable CSO is one that can continue to fulfil its mission over time and in so doing meets the needs of its key stakeholders – particularly its beneficiaries and supporters. As such sustainability should be seen as an ongoing process rather than an end in itself. It is a process that involves the interaction between different strategic, organisational, programmatic, social, and financial elements. A recent study on CSO sustainability in Ghana likened this to a plant that may grow well and thrive if watered and nurtured, but which can wither quickly if not well cared for (WACSI 2015). Such analogies are common throughout much of the literature on the sustainability and viability of non-profits and NGOs generally.

Social sustainability

Perspectives on the sustainability of CSOs vary. For many it is about environmental sustainability and addressing issues of population growth, climate change, and resource imbalances. But in the context of civil society the focus has been social sustainability and the role of viable civil society in ensuring equity and access to justice. Efforts to gauge levels of social sustainability are multi-faceted and complex. This is well-reflected in the methodology used in the CSO Sustainability Index (CSOSI), which relies on a range of indicators to assess the strength and viability of civil society in different countries. This index was first developed by USAID in 1997 to assess the sustainability of the civil society sector in 29 countries in Europe and Eurasia (USAID 2015b). Since 2009 the CSOSI has been expanded to include civil society in sub-Saharan Africa, Afghanistan, and Pakistan.

By using standard indicators and collecting data each year, the CSOSI allows users of the tool to track developments and identify trends in the CSO sector over time while allowing for cross-country and cross-region comparison. It is intended to create a time-series of information which provides development practitioners and policymakers with knowledge on the opportunities and challenges for sustainable CSOs, and insights into how to strengthening their activities. The Index is based on seven dimensions: (1) the legal environment; (2) organisational capacity; (3) financial viability; (4) advocacy capacity; (5) service provision; (6) infrastructure; and (7) public image and reputation. The difficulty of trying to collate and measure this mix of criteria well highlights the complexity and methodological challenges of both preparing and applying such all-embracing measures of social sustainability.

An example of a similar multidimensional model of social sustainability is WACSI's framework designed to assess the sustainability of civil society in Ghana. This is referred to as the *"wheel of sustainability"* and draws on fifteen different criteria based on a range of indicators. This framework identifies four key dimensions as crucial to the sustainability of a local CSO: (1) financial (the continuous availability of financial resources); (2) operational (technical, operational, and administrative capacity); (3) identity (the relevance, legitimacy, and accountability of the organisation in the eyes of the community); and (4) interventions (long-term benefits and viability of specific projects or investments). This model attempts to capture the key generic and sector-specific criteria that determine the sustainability of civil society in Ghana. Specifically, it highlights the holistic and multi-dimensional nature of CSO sustainability and the importance of organisational relations in determining the sustainability of a particular CSO (WACSI 2015, 41).

Organisational sustainability

There is growing recognition of the significance for CSOs of organisational sustainability. New methodologies are being developed to identify and assess the organisational characteristics of effective and sustainable NGOs. Commonly these are based on an assessment of core attributes such as leadership capabilities and management competencies, the capacity to deliver specific services (health, education, etc.) or the ability to pay salaries and cover running costs. Another dimension of organisational sustainability relates to the long-term impact of the programmes or added-value of specific development interventions implemented by individual CSOs. "Intervention sustainability" is commonly used in reference to the viability and effectiveness of health service interventions designed to promote sustainable change in local health services.

Assessment of organisational sustainability commonly reflects a CSOs' ability to anticipate and handle change; in particular adapting to changes in the external environment and the consequences of such changes on their income as well as on existing or outdated systems and processes. In this regard sustainable CSOs are those seen able to respond strategically and effectively to changes in the external environment, revise their mission and objectives accordingly, access new resources, and adapt their systems and processes to meet the new challenges (Hailey 2014a). It is useful to reflect on the criteria for organisational sustainability that was initially developed by Ashoka and has been refined over time. This suggests that the ability of CSOs to manage change and remain sustainable depends on, first, having sufficient and positive public profile, network, and reputation to attract resources. Second, having suitable and appropriate organisational systems and processes to be able to attract resources and retain a relationship with the donor or those making the contribution. Third, having the internal capacity and willingness to learn and evolve (Hamschmidt and Pirson 2011).

Financial sustainability

While social and organisational sustainability are issues of significant concern, most researchers and commentators acknowledge that the issue of greatest concern for most CSOs is economic or financial sustainability and what strategies they can develop to access new funds or ensure their financial viability and survival. In Ghana, for example, recent research has demonstrated that many local CSOs are just surviving, or are struggling to survive financially, in an increasingly competitive market. The evidence suggests that there is limited understanding among local CSOs of the implications of changing funding trends and the consequences of the shrinking funding base. Sustainability indicators suggest that they struggle to generate income and mobilise new financial resources, and lack any effective financial planning system (WACSI 2015, 50).

The consequences of this lack of funds are that projects get cancelled, programme work is curtailed, experienced staff are laid off, and there is less investment in staff development or organisational learning. Investment in new management systems or digital and web-based technologies are put on hold. Partnerships and other collaborative ventures are jeopardised. In general, organisations have to go through a process of significant change and downsizing, all of which create tensions and threaten the trust that has been built between management and staff, as well as with the local community. In this regard organisations are more prone to internal conflict, and personal tensions are exacerbated. As a consequence, internal communication is stymied, morale is low, and productivity reduced. Weakened financial viability seems to lead to a vicious circle that jeopardises long-term sustainability.

Practice and experience tells us that CSO financial sustainability is not just about writing funding proposals, but as much about ensuring that there has been sufficient investment in organisational systems and processes. These include building relationships with potential donors, effective risk management, and basic good financial practice – including ensuring sufficient financial reserves and managing organisational costs and overheads (Mango 2015).

What is notable about both the Ashoka and Mango analysis of the characteristics of sustainable CSOs is the emphasis on their ability to develop and maintain strong external relationships. A recent study of an integrated water project in Kenya highlighted the impor-tance of such personal relationships and effective management in ensuring long-term sustain-ability. The evidence suggested that such sustainable personal relationships promoted internal cohesion, enabled effective decision-making, facilitated accountability, and above all, built trust between the key actors and external stakeholders based on personal rapport and open dialogue (Spalling, Brouwer, and Njoka 2014).

This analysis of CSOs and sustainability has highlighted the need to incorporate the differing, but complementary, views of sustainability, as well as the important role of organisational processes and relationships in ensuring long-term survival and sustainability. But such analysis should not detract from the strategic importance of financial management and that financial sustainability is crucial to CSO sustainability.

CSO financial sustainability

There is a growing body of research that suggests that CSOs face a funding crisis. The growth in the number of non-profits, charities, NGOs, CSOs, and social enterprises means there is strong compe-tition for a limited pool of funds. All the projections suggest that the number of non-profits, NGOs, and charities grows year on year – estimates suggest that there are over 10 million registered CSOs worldwide. The number of NGOs accredited to the United Nations nearly quadrupled between 1995 and 2012. In India alone the number of registered CSOs exceeds three million, an increase of over a million in a decade. Even in mature non-profit sectors, such as the UK, the number of development NGOs continues to grow. The data from the UK Charity Commission (the UK's regulator of non-profits) identifies nearly 12,000 registered charities as being involved in "over-seas aid and famine relief work", of which nearly a thousand had been created in the previous two years (Hailey 2014). In other words, nearly 10% of the UK charities involved in overseas aid work were new start-ups. The picture is that of an increasing number of development non-profits and CSOs com-peting for a relatively limited pot of funds.

CSO funding: public giving and philanthropy

Public giving and philanthropy continues to grow, but not at the same pace as the growth in the number of CSOs internationally. Research in the US shows that public giving only grew by 0.8% in the period 2005–15, as compared with a growth of 8.5% in the previous decade (Birin 2015). Evidence from Australia suggests that public giving to development NGOs has "flatlined" since 2007 (Wilson, Pryke, and Howes 2015). While it is projected that private donations will grow worldwide as individual incomes increase and civil society takes advantage of innovative approaches to fundraising and makes greater use of new digital platforms, it is also apparent that it will only be those non-profits with sufficient capacity and access to technology that will benefit from such advances. Smaller CSOs with limited capacity will struggle in this new marketplace and the digital divide will become even more apparent.

Research also suggests that individual "givers" are more discerning. The evidence suggests that they prefer to donate to "trusted" CSOs that are perceived to have sufficient skills and capabilities, and have effective communication strategies to demonstrate impact and enhance their legitimacy (CAF 2014a). Fur-thermore, a new generation of individual givers see their donations not as "philanthropy" but as "invest-ment", with the inherent expectations that goes with such a shift in thinking. There are also concerns about an over-reliance on donations from an increasingly sceptical general public. Opinion polls highlight increasing public cynicism as to the value of funding development projects, and the ageing profile of those donating to international NGOs (CAF 2014b). The evidence suggests that while many CSOs will con-tinue to generate significant funds from individual givers and philanthropy, a high proportion of CSOs will struggle to access this competitive global marketplace.

CSO funding: aid funding

Similarly, while aid funding to civil society continues to grow internationally, access to official aid funds by the majority of CSOs is limited; partly as result of changing donor sectoral and regional priorities, partly the imposition of more onerous conditions, and partly the preference by some donors to fund larger INGOs with their economies of scale and enhanced capacity. While the share of official aid (ODA) channelled through civil society has risen from 13% of ODA in 2008 to 17% in 2012, the majority of these funds go to a small proportion of large, high profile INGOs (Development Initiatives 2014b).

In 2013 ODA channelled via civil society grew by 2% in real terms, reaching a new high of US$21 billion (a growth in real terms by 11% over the previous four years). But this funding growth is only in specific countries and regions. In the four years to 2013, there were significant declines in aid via civil society in specific regions – most notably South and Central America and South and Central Asia. In contrast the number of aid-funded civil society projects in sub-Saharan Africa grew by 14%. These now make up over half of the total funding to CSOs on a regional basis (Baobab 2015). There were also striking shifts in funding to CSOs with particular sectoral focus. There was a notable decrease in aid to CSOs working in such areas as food aid, education, multi-sectoral, and economic development between 2010 and 2013, while funding for health and humanitarian support grew significantly.

Concurrent with these shifts in the focus of aid funds to CSOs there have been significant changes in the overall aid architecture, with donors identifying new priorities, demanding tangible results or identifiable impact. Some countries have reduced their total aid budgets (such as Australia, Ireland, Italy, and the Netherlands). Other official donors, such as DFID, have introduced new conditionalities around "Value for Money" or "Payment by Results" commissioning. There is also a growing trend for official donors to contract a range of development activities and projects to the private sector. DFID's spending on "contractors to deliver aid programmes" doubled from £0.6bn to £1.2 billion between 2008 and 2014. USAID increased contracting commissions by 700% in the period 2000–08 to over US$14 billion.

Faced with this projected funding environment there is general consensus in the recent research and commentaries on the future challenges facing CSOs, and that development NGOs will have to adapt and change. This is reflected in analysis of the future of aid and the new aid architecture (Kharas and Rogerson 2012; Heiner 2014; Financial Times 2015; Baobob 2015), and the new models and practices that CSOs and INGOs will have to adopt (Edwards 2014; Hailey 2014; ICSC 2014; Bond 2015b; Gnarig 2015; Green 2015). The conclusion of such analysis is that CSOs and development non-profits of all kinds will face an increasingly challenging and competitive funding environment, and that they will have to evolve new ways of working and funding if they are to survive or be viable and sustainable.

New routes to CSO sustainability

As suggested above, reliance on either personal giving or official aid is a relatively high-risk strategy. Analysis of the CSO Sustainability Index highlights that financial viability as the weakest dimension of sustainability (USAID 2014). Analysis by the US non-profit resource organisation, Bridgespan, suggests that this lack of overhead funding will threaten the viability of many non-profits and jeopardise their ability to go to scale. In this increasingly competitive and challenging environment there is a growing imperative to find alternative models and strategies to ensure the viability and sustainability of development CSOs. Among these new routes to financial stability and sustainability there is growing interest across civil society in the way to fund development work through social investment and funds generated by social enterprises and the creation of new value-driven enterprises (Financial Times 2015; Hailey 2014).

Social investment

Social investment is the use of repayable finance to deliver social impact as well as financial return. A simple example could be taking a loan for a CSO to start a new social enterprise, service, or venture. However, social investment is not appropriate for all civil society activities as it relies on income generation to pay back investment finance. Social investment is therefore not business as normal, as capital must be paid back. Consequently, CSOs will have to adapt their business models to take advantage of such new forms of funding. Despite such challenges, social investment is seen as an important new medium for funding the work of the sector. In the UK, for example, many non-profits are starting to look to this as a potential way to change their funding models and this is leading to rapid growth in social investment of some 38% per annum. This is backed by significant government funding channelled through specialist institutions, such as Big Society Capital or DFID's Impact Fund managed by CDC, both of whom work with co-investors to promote investment that generates social and financial returns.

Social investment brings a new finance to civil society. It does so in a way that provides sustainability and the proper funding of overheads. It can be used to fill financing gaps for innovation and growth. It also allows CSOs to become more autonomous and financially independent. Typically, organisations' social investment funds are used to purchase assets such as a property or buildings, fund new social enterprises, or other value-driven ventures that generate additional income. Some more entrepreneurial non-profits use social investment funds to establish new fundraising platforms or expand existing fundraising campaigns.

The characteristics of those non-profits that have successfully engaged with a social investment model include: having an operational strategy and funding model that allows for the repayable finance; having a culture that embraces such a model and the associated risks; staff who have the skills and willingness to engage with and manage social investment and associated enterprises; having appropriate systems that generate suitable impact data and can track investment finance; and finally, and possibly most important, having senior managers and board members committed to engaging with such new business models and working with the opportunities and risks involved.

One of the main challenges for CSOs to engage with social investment relates to the need to change attitudes and culture so that they are more aligned with potential investors and their perception of what payback they will receive for their investment – either in terms of repayment of the investment funds or evidence of impact. There is still much to be done in terms of changing the mindset of key decision-makers in CSOs. For example, research suggests that a great majority of non-profits (over 70%) see social investment as a valuable way of accessing new funds, but that a minority of board members (less than a third) have a favourable view on repayable finance (CAF 2014b). As such unless there is a significant change in attitudes and culture it may take considerable time for managers and their trustees to access social investment or incorporate it into their fundraising strategies. Other barriers are the due diligence time and cost it takes to undertake an investment decision, the transaction costs in setting up special social investment platforms or legal entities, as well as generating the impact data to meet the demands of social investors.

Increasingly official aid donors are exploring how best to provide social investment funds, rather than just make donations. For example, DFID's new Impact Fund aims to direct investment capital towards sectors or pro-poor businesses that are otherwise unable to attract commercial investment in sub-Saharan Africa and South Asia. There are also a number of local social investment initiatives supported by official donors. For example, in Peru, GTZ, the German technical assistance agency, rewards forest dwellers who protect their timber resources from illegal logging by offering them access to a range of social investment funds. Schemes such as this community forest conservation project are a useful example of the way donors can link community sustainability to the wider demands of environmental sustainability. Philanthropic foundations are also exploring ways to use social investment as a way of levering up their financial resources and recycling capital for onward investment in a range of social, pro-poor initiatives (Financial Times 2015). Foundations, such as the Omidyar Foundation, provide a mix of grants and social investment funds to start and grow ventures that generate both social and financial returns. The scale of such a "blended" investment portfolio can be seen in the way that Omidyar made investments of US$400m alongside grants of US $479m between 2004 and 2014.

Recent research in the UK suggests that over the next five years a growing number of non-profits will adopt new business models that incorporate social investment. The research highlights a 12–15% shift towards social investment and away from grant provision. What is striking about these findings is that international NGOs were more open to embracing social investment models than domestic non-profits (Salway 2015). This trend is supported by new and innovative crowd-funding platforms, peer-to-peer lending, and new social impact investment institutions.

Such social investment is not just impact and/or results-focused but also potentially gives communities and a new generation of responsible investors a stake in developing more effective and viable CSOs. Peer-to-peer lending and crowd-funding is growing more rapidly than social investment, and CARE International's LendWithCare.Org initiative is a good example of how an INGO can use a crowd-funding platform to access loans to support its development work. It has raised and lent over £7 million since its inception in 2010. Christian Aid leads a consortium of other INGOs that has established Access to Capital for Rural Enterprises (ACRE). It aims to promote impact-first investment in rural enterprises in developing markets. Through their access to an extensive range of projects and programmes, ACRE have identified a range of viable rural enterprises and use a syndicated financing platform to link them with potential investors.

There are also a number of specialist investment management firms that focus on promoting social investments in developing countries. These include Blue Orchard, the Triodos Bank, Worthstone, and Vital Capital. For example, Truestone, a social impact investor whose portfolio of work includes levering up investment funds to support the work of local social enterprises or CSOs, is currently working with two Kenyan CSOs, the Kenyan Students' Christian Fellowship and CMS-Africa, to develop land they own in Nairobi which will generate rental income to support their education work in Kenya.

Another example is SpringHill Equity's investment in Bridge International Academies, which is the largest provider of low-cost private education in Africa and offers affordable high-quality primary education for poor families. By the end of 2014 Bridge had opened over 350 schools serving 100,000 pupils in Kenya, and is opening new schools in Uganda, Nigeria, and India. This rapid growth is based on the way it rolls out and franchises its "school-in-a-box" model and its ability to access social investment funds. Springhill see that the "market" for such affordable high-quality education in low-income communities is immense and continue to seek new investment funds for such high-impact social investments.

Enterprise supported CSOs

A growing number of development INGOs generate a proportion of their income from enterprises or commercial ventures that they own and run. These can either be self-standing commercial enterprises with clear profit-based business goals, as exemplified by the subsidiary companies created to support BRAC, the major Bangladesh-based INGO; or complementary for-profit enterprises that also have developmental goals, such as Oxfam's high street shops. In the UK charity sector an estimated 20% of income now comes from trading activities.

Typically, enterprise-supported INGOs rely on a mix of gift and aid income, and profits from their subsidiary enterprises make up only a relatively small proportion of total income. Such enterprises are commonly either direct trading activities such as Oxfam's shops or Practical Action's publishing business. In some cases, an INGO has established new service provision ventures through which it sells a particular expertise. For example, Marie Stopes International created Options in 1992 to provide specialist consulting support to enhance access to reproductive and sexual health services;

Transparency International offers anti-bribery training through its training and advisory services; and Practical Action provides a consulting service in the area of sustainable or alternative technologies.

Some CSOs have ambitious targets for enterprise-derived income, with the Bangladeshi INGO BRAC being the most commonly cited example. In 2013 a third of its annual expenditure of US $545 million came from official donors, and much of the rest was generated by the different enterprises it owns. These include a bank, internet and mobile phone companies, printing businesses, feed mills, tea companies, fisheries, dairy production, and so on. All of these operate commercially and their profits are used to support BRAC's development activities.

A crucial element of the enterprise-supported strategies of such ventures is that they commonly incorporate a developmental purpose with a profit-generating goal. For instance, Oxfam is a major trading presence in the UK. It is one of the top-ten high street retailers with 700 shops across the country and a significant online shopping presence. While these shops are expected to generate income they also have a developmental role in terms of selling fair-trade goods or handicrafts that benefit local producers, as well as a wider educational role.

Practical Action has two wholly owned subsidiary companies with a commercial and developmental remit. One, Practical Action Publishing, comprises book and journal publishing, and book retailing via mail order and the internet, geared to the needs of development professionals and academics worldwide. The other is Practical Action Consulting, which provides independent research and professional advice to a range of clients around issues of technology and development and enterprise development. While these subsidiaries are expected to be profitable it is clear by the way they operate that their wider societal and development remit is a key determinant of the strategies they pursue and the operational decisions made. Other European INGOs, such as ICCO in the Netherlands, Helvitas in Switzerland, or the Bristol-based Development Initiatives are in the process of developing similar value-based for-profit consulting subsidiaries.

A variation on this is the contracted INGO. In other words, those NGOs which rely on contracts and commissions that are awarded by a range of donors – either multilateral or bilateral donors, government departments, or foundations. There is a growing trend by official donors to contracting and NGOs have responded accordingly. For example, in the South many local NGOs depend on such contracts from local government to run their projects or programmes, while in the North we have seen a growing number of contract-dependent INGOs.

This is reflected in the business model adopted by those organisations which operate in a way akin to value-based consultancies. They bid for projects in the development marketplace, and differ from for-profit consultancies because of their particular developmental values, the way they build long-term partnerships, or have particular relationships with civil society. Examples of this include INTRAC (which works to support and strengthen civil society through training, consultancy, and research); Action on Poverty (APT works with partners to develop small enterprises and promote economic empowerment); or the Washington-based Technoserve, which helps entrepreneurial men and women in the developing world capitalise on business opportunities that create jobs and income for poor people. Technoserve works with a range of public- and private-sector partners (including USAID, the Coca-Cola Company, and JP Morgan), and in keeping with their private enterprise approach evaluate their performance using business metrics.

In practice, this is a relatively rare model and in most cases enterprise-funded INGOs receive only a small proportion of their income from such ventures. Experience also suggests these subsidiary enterprises have high start-up costs and can be a significant management burden and as a result carry high transaction costs. The trend is for CSOs to develop and support investment in a new range of social enterprises.

Evolving social enterprises

A small, but significant, trend is where a CSO evolves (or incubates) an autonomous social enterprise, or where a business, donor, and CSO work together to form new collaborative enterprises. This model has attracted much interest internationally – particularly because CSOs see them as a source of potential income. There has been a rapid growth in the number of social enterprises and new social franchise models established internationally.

Individuals and CSOs have moved to develop a range of new social enterprises and donors have contributed significant funds to support this trend. Donors are attracted to investing in such social enterprises despite the obvious risks because they are seen as innovative and more willing to adopt new approaches or techniques, able to access a range of difficult to reach markets and so seen as being more inclusive, and as such better able to overcome market failure than other initiatives (Rogerson et al. 2014).

This trend is well-reflected in the range of new entities being created by different NGOs across the world. These ventures are either traditional for-profit businesses or new social enterprise models. In Bangladesh, BRAC has actively created a range of social enterprises which in 2013 had a combined turnover of US$165 million. The Grameen Bank's social enterprise affiliate Grameen Shakti provides a range of solar-powered products. Another trend is the development of new social franchising models. This is seen in the success of Marie Stope's global network of BlueStar clinics, and in Basic Need's franchise model designed to provide mental health support in the poorest communities.

An example of an INGO incubating a franchise-based local social enterprise is FarmAfrica's evolving relationship with Sidai Africa. While Sidai still operates as an autonomous social enterprise which provides quality and affordable veterinary and other livestock services through a network of 150 branded franchises, each franchise is owned and staffed by qualified veterinarians, livestock technicians, and other professionals. Sidai operates as registered company in Kenya, and had a turnover of £1.6 million in 2013. Its goal is to be financially sustainable while also revolutionising the way that livestock and veterinary services are offered to pastoralists and farmers in Kenya.

There are also a number of recent cases where an existing CSO has transformed itself into a viable, market-driven social enterprise. Their ambition is that future income will come from selling products or services rather than relying on donor income or commissions. Examples of this include SolarAid's development of SunnyMoney and SNV's proposed strategic evolution to a social enterprise. This evolution is partly driven by the desire for greater economic and market sustainability, and partly increasing dissatisfaction with the constraints imposed by official aid donors.

SolarAid has evolved from a traditional gift-based INGO promoting the use of solar power in Africa to a development enterprise selling high-quality solar lighting across Africa. This new business model is run through a newly registered social enterprise (SunnyMoney) which is now working in four African countries to promote solar lighting, with the intention of eradicating the use of kerosene lamps while becoming financial sustainable. In 2008, SolarAid created SunnyMoney to run its operations in Africa. SunnyMoney uses an innovative distribution model to sell solar lights in rural off-grid communities dependent on costly, toxic kerosene for lighting. By building a sustainable market for solar products, SolarAid and SunnyMoney aim to eradicate the kerosene lamp from Africa by 2020. The well-established Dutch INGO SNV has also adopted an evolving strategy towards becoming a hybrid social enterprise. In an effort to move away from its dependence on official aid funding it intends to generate income by providing advice and capacity building support. Working with its existing local partners it will support local communities, businesses, and organisations to increase their incomes and become sustainable themselves.

Social enterprise: overcoming the risks

Despite this move to develop a range of new social enterprises experience and research suggests that they face considerable constraints and challenges – particularly developing sufficient capacity and attracting resources to go to scale and having enough turnover to generate a surplus and/or profit (Smith and Darko 2014). There are significant transaction costs for the host CSO in terms of management time and resources, strategic drift, and conflict of interest.

Unless they go to scale the social enterprise model is not a panacea for CSO sustainability. As a result, many CSOs are looking to share the risks by developing collaborative partnerships with established businesses. Examples of such collaborative social enterprises include Grameen Banks co-venture with the French multinational Danone, launched in 2006 to supply nutritious food to the poor in Bangladesh. Major INGOs, CARE and Plan International, have worked in partnership with Barclays Bank to develop their Banking-on-Change Programme intended to enhance access by the poor to basic banking services in eleven countries. CleanTeam Ghana, a social enterprise created by WSUP (Water and Sanitation for the Urban Poor) in conjunction with UniLever, uses a market-lead approach providing domestic toilets to the urban poor in Ghana. Other examples include Vodafone's partnership with AMREF in Kenya, or Digicel's relationships with the Irish INGO, Concern. A variation on this is where an NGO social enterprise collaborates with multinational companies, such as the way that Galvmed works in partnership with major pharmaceutical companies like Pfizer or Merial. Galvmed is a non-profit global alliance that makes affordable livestock vaccines, medicines, and diagnostics accessible to farmers across the developing world.

An alternative hybrid model is where a corporation works in collaboration with an official donor to support the development of a specialist INGO. Girl Hub, for example, was a strategic collaboration between DFID and the Nike Foundation (the philanthropic arm of the multinational sports company). Girl Hub was a British-registered NGO, with operations in Ethiopia, Rwanda, and Nigeria. It helped decision-makers and donors to address the needs and rights of adolescent girls. Girl Hub's strategy was to combine DFID's development expertise and global reach with Nike's experience and expertise – particularly in communication, business planning, and innovation, and the experience of the Nike Foundation's international work to empower adolescent girls. Another example is the collaborative support provided by Coca-Cola and USAID to support the Water and Development Alliance (WADA) and its programmes across sub-Saharan Africa.

Conclusion

This article is concerned with the alternative strategies for CSO sustainability. Clearly there is an appetite to explore new routes to financial sustainability, whether it is digital crowd-funding platforms, new models of accessing social investment, or developing new types of value-driven, market-driven, financially viable social enterprises. While the great majority of INGOs still rely on voluntary donations and fully aided-NGOs are a rarity, all the evidence suggests that there is growing interest in developing alternative enterprise-based models that reduce dependence on gift incomes and official aid.

It is recognised that there are challenges associated with this trend that CSOs need to address. There are concerns that the drive for profitability or need to repay investments inherent in such ventures undermines their humanitarian values and identity. Many believe that the way that social enterprises work is fundamentally different from the way CSOs work with their different values, goals, and resourcing strategies, importantly needing a different "entrepreneurial" mindset to operate them successfully. The theory of change that underpins the work of social enterprises is also seen as distinct from those of many CSOs. Social enterprises operate in the expectation that they will continue to grow, and work on the premise that they can attract sufficient investment to ensure continuity and develop their position in a social marketplace. In contrast, many CSOs expect that at some point in the future they will "do themselves out of a job" because their work will be sufficiently effective to remove poverty and suffering in the communities with which they work.

Despite these concerns and challenges there is clearly a momentum around the evolution of these new market-based models. The evidence is that a growing number of CSOs are looking to provide loan capital of their own to develop social enterprise models in the communities they serve. This not only proactively creates new ventures but also demonstrates a first loss position against which others use as evidence of viable investment. There is also a new breed of social business development professionals who help find potential investors, and facilitate links with established entrepreneurs. CSOs may also encourage their staff to promote new social ventures models as "intra-preneurs" (innovators and entrepreneurs working within their own organisations).

The trend seems to be one of greater independence through diversified income sources and a willingness to explore more entrepreneurial routes to financial sustainability. These trends have major consequences on management in terms of time invested and skills needed, as well as impli-cations for the existing culture and values inherent in CSOs. Arguably if the sector is to benefit from these alternative models they need to learn new skills, adopt new thinking, and embrace new strategies. This is not about instant returns on new investment but a capacity building process that will take time to become embedded; one that will lead to greater resilience and oppor-tunities for innovation.

Disclosure statement

No potential conflict of interest was reported by the authors.

References

Baobab. 2015. *"Civil Society Aid Trends." Baobab Briefing Paper 3*. Oxford: Baobab.

Benton, A. and A. Monroy. 2004. *Business Approaches for the Reproductive Health NGOs*. Washington, DC.: CMS and USAID.

Birin, D. 2015. *The Philanthropic Outlook*. Lyndhurst: Lily School of Philanthropy and Marts and Lundy.

Bond. 2015a. *Tomorrows World: How Might Mega-Trends in Development Affect the Future Role of UK-Based INGOs*. London: Bond.

Bond. 2015b. *Fast Forward: Changing Role of UK-Based NGOs*. London: Bond.

CAF. 2014a. *Future World Giving*. London: Charities Aid Foundation.

CAF. 2014b. *In Demand: The Changing Need for Charity Finance in the Charity Sector*. London: Charities Aid Foundation.

CIVICUS. 2014. *State of Civil Society Report*. Johannesburg: CIVICUS.

Development Initiatives. 2014a. *Measuring Private Development Assistance: Emerging Trends and Challenges*. Bristol: Development Initiatives.

Development Initiatives. 2014b. *NGO Resources for Development*. Bristol: Development Initiatives.

Edwards, M. 2014. *Civil Society*. London: Polity Press.

Financial Times. 2015. *Investing for Global Impact*. London: Financial Times.

Gnarig, B. 2015. *The Hedgehog and the Beetle: Disruption and Innovation in the Civil Society Sector*. Berlin: ICSC.

Green, D. 2015. *Fit for the Future: Development Trends and the Role of INGOs*. Oxford: Oxfam.

Hailey, J. 2014a. *Models of INGO Sustainability*. Policy Briefing Paper No.41. Oxford: INTRAC.

Hailey, J. 2014b. *EveryChild's Journey to a New Model: Transitioning from an INGO to a Network*. London: EveryChild.

Hamschmidt, J., and M. Pirson. 2011. *Case Studies in Social Entrepreneurship and Sustainability*. Sheffield: Greenleaf.

Heiner, J. 2014. *"Beyond Aid and the Future of Development Cooperation."* German Development Institute Briefing Paper 6. Bonn.

ICSC. 2014. *Diversify, Adapt and Innovate: Changing ICSO Business Models*. Berlin: ICSC.

Kharas, H., and A. Rogerson. 2012. *Horizon 2025: Creative Destruction in the Aid Industry*. London: ODI.

Mango. 2015. *Financial Sustainability Guide*. Oxford: Mango.

Rogerson, R. 2014. *Why and How are Donors Supporting Social Enterprise?* London: ODI.

Salway, M. 2015. *"Social Investment Trends: The Feedback."* Presentation to the Social Investment Symposium, Cass Business School, City University, London.

Smith, W., and E. Darko. 2014. *Social Enterprise: Constraints and Opportunities*. London: ODI.

Spalling, H., G. Brouwer, and J. Njoka. 2014. *"Factors Affecting the Sustainability of a Community Water Supply Project in Kenya." Development in Practice* 24 (7): 797–811.

USAID. 2015a. *The 2014 CSO Sustainability Index for Sub-Saharan Africa*. Washington, DC: USAID.

USAID. 2015b. *The 2014 CSO Sustainability Index for Central and Eastern Europe and Eurasia*. Washington, DC: USAID.

WACSI. 2015. *The State of CSO Sustainability in Ghana*. Accra: West African Civil Society Institute.

Wilson, J., J. Pryke, and S. Howes. 2015. "Running faster to stand still: Australian development NGO fundraising costs." Accessed January 12, 2016. http://devpolicy.org/running-faster-to-stand-still-australian-development-ngo-fundraising-expenditures-20151126

Civil society organisations and the fight for rights in Brazil: analysis of an evolving context and future challenges

Patricia Mendonça, Mário Aquino Alves, and Fernando Nogueira

ABSTRACT

The operational environment of civil society organisations (CSOs) in Brazil has undergone several changes since the 1990s that deepened in the last decade, especially for a group of organisations that are the focus of this study: CSOs working for the promotion and defence of rights (AHRCSOs – advocacy and human rights CSOs). This article examines these recent changes, detailing the main limitations and conditions imposed on AHRCSOs by analysing their organisational and cultural characteristics. The organisational field of AHRCSOs is fluid and dispersed, and several organisations perform different activities. The article traces the history of these organisations and the foundations that led them to build their shared identity project. It then discusses AHRCSOs' organisational features and culture, in relation to the changes faced by the field and the challenges to be met. The closing remarks point to the need for changes in the culture and operations of these organisations in order to guarantee their sustainability of funding, as well as their capacity for social dialogue and intervention.

L'environnement opérationnel des organisations de la société civile (OSC) au Brésil a connu plusieurs changements depuis les années 1990, changements qui se sont intensifiés durant les dix dernières années, en particulier pour le groupe d'organisations sur lequel se penche cette étude : les OSC qui se consacrent à la promotion et à la défense des droits (OSC de plaidoyer et de défense des droits de l'homme — OSCPDDH). Cet article examine ces changements récents, présentant de manière détaillée les principales limites et conditions imposées aux OSCPDDH en analysant leurs caractéristiques organisationnelles et culturelles. Le terrain organisationnel des OSCPDDH est fluide et dispersé, et plusieurs organisations effectuent des activités différentes. Cet article retrace l'histoire de ces organisations et les fondations qui les ont amenées à bâtir leur projet commun d'identité. Il traite ensuite des caractéristiques organisationnelles et de la culture des OSCPDDH, par rapport aux changements auxquels est confronté le terrain et aux défis à relever. Les remarques finales indiquent la nécessité d'effectuer des changements au niveau de la culture et des opérations de ces organisations afin de garantir leur durabilité sur le plan du financement, ainsi que leur capacité de dialogue et d'intervention sociaux.

Desde 1990, el ambiente operativo de las organizaciones de la sociedad civil (OSC) de Brasil ha experimentado diversas transformaciones que se profundizaron durante la última década, especialmente en el caso del grupo de organizaciones que constituye el centro del presente estudio: las OSC que trabajan para promover y defender los derechos (OSCIDH, es decir, OSC de incidencia y derechos humanos). En este sentido, a partir del análisis de las características organizacionales y culturales de éstas, el artículo examina los cambios recientes, detallando las principales limitaciones y las condiciones impuestas a las OSCIDH. Resulta evidente que el ámbito organizacional de las OSCIDH es cambiante y disperso, a lo cual se agrega el hecho de que varias organizaciones realizan distintas actividades. El artículo revisa la historia de estas organizaciones y los preceptos que les permitieron construir su proyecto de identidad compartida. Asimismo, considera los rasgos y la cultura organizacionales de las OSCIDH en relación con los cambios enfrentados en este ámbito y los retos que deberán afrontar. El último apartado señala la necesidad de impulsar cambios en la cultura y el aspecto operativo de estas organizaciones, en aras de asegurar su sostenibilidad financiera y su capacidad para el diálogo y la intervención sociales.

Introduction

Since the early 1990s there has been a growing academic interest in civil society organisations (CSOs). The CSO field includes organisations with widely different operations, structures, and funding models; among others, it includes religious organisations, local organisations, professional NGOs, corporate-based organisations (corporate associations or foundations), and solidarity-based production cooperatives.

CSOs exist largely to promote their causes and to change their field and environment, but at the same time, they are also strongly affected by this environment. The operational environment of CSOs in Brazil has been dramatically changing in waves since the 1980s. The first wave of changes was linked to the re-democratisation processes after the military regime, when most CSOs became legal and formal, and created bridges to the state to formulate and implement policies. CSOs played a critical role in consolidating Brazilian democracy, acting as key players in the extension of social rights in Brazil.

The second wave of changes was connected to the transformation of funding trends in the 2000s. At the international level, changes of priorities of the international development cooperation (IDC) donors resulted in decreasing funds for Brazilian CSOs. At the national level, the closer links between CSOs and the state to implement public policies, and with the corporate philanthropy sector to implement social projects, moved CSOs to become more project-oriented and dependent on these restricted funds. More recently, there has been the emergence of significant ongoing innovations related to CSOs' funding such as social business and crowdfunding (Biekart 2013; Dora and Pannunzio 2013; Durão 2013; Milani 2013). This second wave of changes has impacted a particular group of CSOs, those working for the promotion and defence of rights, advocacy, and human rights CSOs (AHRCSOs). Due to their particular causes and agenda – fighting for the most vulnerable and deprived peoples – Brazilian AHRCSOs have been the most affected by this second wave of changes, as most of their traditional donors faded away and the appeal of their causes have not been strong enough to mobilise national donors.

This is especially relevant as AHRCSOs have represented important social forces in the fight for democracy and rights in the history of Brazil (Landim 2002). It is important to acknowledge their new role in a society that has been redefining the engagement of citizens with the state, companies, and CSOs. In recent years, this new setting evolved alongside the expansion of consumption and increasing complexities of markets, which raised Brazil to the position of a middle-income nation, joining other countries of the BRICS group. Over the past decade, Brazil has undergone significant economic and social advancements; however, these improvements contrast with persistent inequality, where many citizens have their basic rights denied, against a backdrop of frequent reports of human rights violations (Mendonça 2014; Nader 2013).

This paradoxical scenario demands a strong civil society, where the role of AHRCSOs is central to sustain these recent developments. Moreover, recent political developments in Latin America and in Brazil show that this development model is fading out. Consequently, defending the social justice project from a developing reactionary movement, which carries a potentially harmful agenda for the citizenship, demands stronger AHRCSOs (*The Guardian* 2016; *The New York Times* 2016).

This article examines these recent changes, seeking to detail the main limitations and conditions imposed on AHRCSOs by analysing their organisational and cultural characteristics. We first seek to establish a definition of AHRCSOs in Brazil. While official definitions of CSOs don't explicitly cover AHRCSOs, field activists define themselves and their organisations based on the construction of a shared identity (Iorio 2002; Landim 1988; Romano and Antunes 2002). Despite this apparent disconnection between official definitions and activists' understandings of AHRCSOs, official figures point to a decline in the number of AHRCSOs (IBGE 2012), while other research also reports a low level of renewal in the field (Nogueira 2014). These figures demonstrate the struggles AHRCSOs face to survive in a context of shortage of resources.

We then discuss some of the features of AHRCSOs: their history and path, organisational features and culture. The field of human rights and advocacy in Brazil and the emergence of AHRCSOs in the 1970s and 1980s were tightly connected to IDC funding. These links enabled the creation of a modest number of organisations; however, these organisations performed a large representative voice, generating visible political effects, especially during the democratisation period (Landim 2002). AHRCSOs' organisation model reflected their links to the IDC donors: outright grant funding of all the activities, precarious working contracts and conditions, and fragile structures to support the implementation of projects (Fernandes and Piquet Carneiro 1991; Landim 2002; Mendes 1999).

These difficulties persist during the first and second waves of changes. Particularly during the 2000s, the insufficiency of the organisational model based on international grants highlighted AHRCSOs' challenges to maintaining their own goals and strategies (Nogueira 2014). The shifting relations with the state, the private sector, and other societal actors created new challenges that had to be confronted. Moreover, the actual meaning of defending rights in a diverse institutional democratic context defies old assumptions that are embedded in the AHRCSOs' organisational cultures and identities.

The closing remarks point to the need for changes in the culture and operations of these organisations in order to guarantee their sustainability of funding, as well as their capacity for social dialogue and intervention.

CSOs: key definitions and classifications

In the last 40 years, the literature on development has used a plethora of acronyms and designations to identify non-profit organisations that work in the field. Apart from the terms used, the problems of classification and differentiation of the enormous diversity of organisations remain (Salomon and Anheier 1992; Vakil 1997), and the adoption of each term reflects complex relationships and the organisation's identity.

In Latin America, "NGO" was originally used to refer to organisations established among the social movements and the fight against the dictatorships that took power in the continent during the 1960s and 1970s (Fernandes 1994; Landim 1988). Many NGOs were established with an agenda of defending rights and promoting democracy (Landim 2002). Some NGOs also set goals related to economic, social, and community development; the defence and preservation of the environment; social assistance to marginalised populations; health and education, and so on. In the 1990s, especially in the aftermath of the Rio-92 Conference, NGOs were positively celebrated. For a significant period, the term was used in Brazil as an umbrella term, which included a range of organisations from grassroots social movement organisations to philanthropic and charitable organisations (Alves 2002). As a result, different organisations such as foundations, non-profits, social organisations, associations, and NGOs started to be treated as synonyms.

This positive image of NGOs changed in the 2000s. Between 2007 and 2010, complaints involving the transfer of federal funds to non-profit organisations led to the establishment of a Parliamentary Commission of Inquiry (Comissão Parlamentar de Inquérito – CPI) in the Brazilian Senate, called "NGOs CPI". In spite of the fact that only a few organisations were actually involved in the complaints,

Table 1. FASFIL classification by area of operation.

Area	Total	Share %
Religion	82,853	28.5
Trade and professional associations	44,939	15.5
Promotion and defence of rights	42,463	14.6
Culture and leisure	36,921	12.7
Social assistance	30,414	10.5
Education and research	17,664	6.1
Health	6029	2.1
Environment and animal protection	2242	0.8
Housing	292	0.1
Others	26,875	9.2

Source: IBGE-FASFIL 2012.

the large media coverage contributed to taint the image of the whole sector and stigmatise the term "NGOs" (Mendonça and Falcão 2016).

At this point, and following the trend of multilateral institutions, both government and civil society circles adopted the acronym civil society organisations (CSOs) instead of NGOs. We use the term AHRCSOs as we felt the need for more precision, as CSO encompasses many different kinds of organisations.

In Brazilian law there is no specific qualification for most types of CSOs. The law recognises civil non-profit associations or foundations, which may share features of different types of CSOs, such as local organisations, social movement organisations, assistance organisations, and organisations that provide community services, among others. Although the law pertaining to non-profit organisations in Brazil has recently been altered twice, the objective naming and classification of CSOs has not yet been properly settled, and the monikers civil non-profit associations or foundations are still used as general identifiers.

Due to how diverse CSOs are and how difficult it is to objectively classify them, there is insufficient research that provides accurate figures on CSOs overall. The most widely acknowledged research is the IBGE survey called FASFIL (Non-Profit Foundations and Associations). Three FASFIL surveys have been published: in 2002, based on data up to 1998; in 2008, using data up to 2005; and in 2012, using data up to 2010. The FASFIL report is based on the operational framework of the International Classification of Non-profit Organisations, recommended by the Handbook on Non-profit Institutions in the System of National Accounts of the United Nations, developed by Johns Hopkins University researchers in the 1990s.

This methodology establishes that, when assessing the number of CSOs, we should consider those formal organisations that are: private, independent from the structure of the state; established as a legal entity; not seeking profit; self-managed, voluntary, freely established.[1] FASFIL, albeit with its questionable criteria to classify organisations based on its formal designation, is the most comprehensive survey of CSOs in Brazil and the only survey that can present an accurate outlook of this universe of organisations. The 2012 FASFIL reported 290,692 CSOs, which were classified according to their area of operation as shown in Table 1.

The 2012 survey reported a slowing in the growth of CSOs compared to previous surveys. In 2006–10 growth was 8.8%, while in 2002–05 growth was 22.6%. Religious organisations showed the highest growth, accounting for 47.8% of all new CSOs created in the latest survey period. It is worth noting that the promotion and defence of rights category, which covers Brazilian AHRCSOs, presented an inverse trend compared to the general picture. The number of organisations in the promotion and defence of rights category decreased by 1.7% between 2006 and 2010.

CSOs and defence of rights: who are we talking about?

In general, when we talk about rights defence organisations, especially in the field of IDC and social movements, we refer to the rights-based approach (RBA). To understand how AHRCSOs evolved in

Brazil, it is also important to understand the development of RBA in the global field and how it was adapted to these organisations.

There is no definitive agreement on the meaning of RBA (UNHCR 2002), but we can safely say that it is a broad concept based on the fight for human rights and gender equality (Harris-Curtis 2003) and on the fight for freedom (Sen 2000). Sen highlights the intrinsic importance of human beings, their role and consequence in economic development, and their role in building values and priorities. Kindornay, Ron, and Carpenter (2012) provide an extensive survey of the entire IDC system and how it relates to RBA.

RBA emerged in the 1990s as a new paradigm for development and practical guidance for organisations involved in development cooperation: bi- and multilateral organisations, NGOs, development agencies, and consultants and advisors. Its main contribution was to match the development agenda to the human rights agenda by joining internationally recognised principles of human rights and strategies to reduce poverty.

As well as the application of human rights principles to the design of plans, programmes, and projects, the RBA guidelines also call for participatory practice, strengthening of accountability tools, focus on processes and results, and most of all, engaging local and international agents in efforts to promote the rights of the most vulnerable groups. As a result, strategies have been designed to mobilise local and international groups for global advocacy campaigns.

Romano and Antunes (2002) discuss the relationship between the empowerment approach and RBA, emphasising that the latter strategy is more frequently found in those CSOs that have promoted alternative development and the fight against poverty since the 1970s. RBA is also the subject of discussions in public policy, social movements, and the academic world in general, due to the increasing importance of analysis on the fight for citizenship and construction of social rights (Spink 2000). On the other hand, discussions focusing on empowerment are at an early stage, and are associated with proposals from cooperation agencies and multilateral bodies such as the World Bank. As a result, there is some concern among parts of society and the academic world regarding this approach.

An increasing number of CSOs have embraced RBA to promote the fight for the recognition and promotion of human rights (social, political, economic, and cultural). An example is Oxfam, which has developed a rights-based approach that references key aspects of several international treaties on human rights. Its strategic action plan, developed by 12 organisations of the Oxfam network in 2012, is acknowledged as one of the pioneers in RBA. The Oxfam approach, which is shared by several other CSOs (especially NGOs and international private foundations) and prioritises the human rights agenda, makes constant references to treaties, agreements, and other international documents that frequently shape their actions. Iorio (2002) points out that RBA attempts to connect different rights; equality, equity, accountability in its broad meaning, empowerment, participation, and non-discrimination and caring for vulnerable groups.

Until the 1990s, human rights organisations could be considered as "pure" advocacy organisations. After the advent of RBA, CSOs of different operations and sizes began using different advocacy strategies by matching their operations to the defence of rights. The approach of CSOs and international foundations, as well as local organisations and social movements focusing on the defence and promotion of rights, reflects modern development practices that emphasise the need for a fairer globalisation process, in opposition to neo-liberal ideas.

AHRCSOs are strongly influenced by RBA values and practices, but they also reflect Brazil's history and specific challenges. For Diniz and Mattos (2002), some of the key references for AHRCSOs in Brazil are:

(a) strong ideology associated with concepts of welfare state, civil participation and the defence of democratic values
(b) religious motivation, specially associated to the Catholic Church and evangelical churches; some key ideas were taken from liberation theology

Table 2. Organisations for the defence of rights within FASFIL in 2012.

Kind of organisation	Total
Neighbourhood associations	13,101
Community centres and associations	20,071
Rural development	1522
Employment and training	507
Defence of rights for groups and minorities	5129
Other forms of promotion and defence of rights	2133
Total	42,463

Source: IBGE (2012).

(c) developmentalist ideas based on the development model promoted by international cooperation, in which social transformation or transformative development are tools for social change

(d) voluntary work

(e) informal action

(f) independent from the state and the market; equality and democratic participation in management

(g) focus on demanding rights and reporting abuses, criticising and proposing improvements for public policies and government efforts.

In practice, how many AHRCSOs are there in Brazil? The FASFIL survey (see Table 2) includes a group of 43,211 organisations for the defence of rights (IBGE 2012). But not all these organisations can be considered AHRCSOs, as many are broader groups such as neighbourhood associations, or employment and training centres.

The "defence of rights for groups and minorities" group has been considered representative of AHRCSOs in Brazil by the people working in the field. However, this classification is far from being a consensus for delimiting this field. According to the official definition from IBGE (2012), these organisations include associations created to promote social causes, such as the defence of human rights, defence of the environment, defence of ethnic minorities, and excluding organisations that provide social assistance in shared or private homes or social assistance services without housing.

Sector insiders often point out that the organisations belonging to the ABONG (Brazilian Association of NGOs) network account for a significant share of AHRCSOs in Brazil. ABONG attempts to represent member organisations as "pure" organisations in the field of defence of rights. Lately ABONG has adopted the designation of "organisations for the defence of rights and promotion of common good". We focus our description and analysis on this group of AHRCSOs over the next sections, as we can consider them good representatives for the field of AHRCSOs as a whole (Landim 2002; Nogueira 2014).

The challenges Brazilian AHRCSOs face

Basis for creation, sustaining, and changes in the international setting

Nogueira's (2014) review of the history of ABONG highlights that it has been marked from its inception by ideological orientations focusing on demands for rights, making demands from the state, and establishing a dialogue with government on public policies and the extension of citizenship. Since the beginning, ABONG has tried to differentiate itself from other sectors of civil society, such as philanthropy associations, which historically focused on providing services in education, health, and social assistance, as well as corporate-based organisations that first emerged from the 1990s onwards.

As of its founding ABONG excluded from the definition of NGOs "representation associations" such as labour unions, neighbourhood associations, and professional associations, demanding that member organisations maintain independence from the state, political parties, churches, and popular movements. Criteria for network membership were *"a commitment to building a democratic society"* and *"a commitment to strengthening social movements"* (Mendes 1999).

Since its establishment ABONG has never had more than 300 members, a small number when compared to the 5,000 organisations in the sector, even though accurate figures have never been provided. Nevertheless, several authors remark on how representative the ABONG voice is in the AHRCSOs sector in Brazil (Mendes 1999; Nogueira 2014). Such representativeness stems from its history, including the history of its members, its leadership, and relations to universities, to international cooperation, and to several government and media fora. This is why it is so important to understand ABONG and its members when talking about AHRCSOs in Brazil. In addition, as Nogueira (2014) argues, as a meta-organisation (an organisation whose members are themselves organisations), ABONG incorporated the culture, values, and practices of its members. Discussing ABONG's governance and structure is thus a valid proxy to debate the Brazilian field of AHRCSOs.

To understand the background of ABONG, we need to go back to before its establishment in 1991, looking at the context and history of ABONG members. The work of Mendes (1999) provides a good foundation by analysing three organisations that have been ABONG members since the beginning: FASE (Federation of Organs for Social and Educational Assistance), CEDAC (Centre for Community Action), and IBASE (Brazilian Institute for Social and Economic Analysis). Mendes points out that all three organisations share the dedication of their founders and a decisive link to the Catholic Church and international CSO networks, specially organisations associated with churches, independent foundations, and development agencies from Europe, Canada, and United States. Between the 1960s and 1980s, Brazilian informal groups and CSOs for the defence of rights had strong ties to the international cooperation network. Landim (2002) points out that, between 1960 and 1980, there was a 68% increase in external aid for developing countries from non-governmental agencies in Europe, Canada, and United States, rising from US$2.8 billion to US$4.7 billion. A significant part of this funding helped to create and organise AHRCSOs in Brazil and had an impact in creating the field of defence of rights in Brazil (Mendonça et al, 2009).

In terms of access to resources for CSOs in the ABONG network (Mendonça et al. 2009), in 1993 around 75% of the funding for ABONG members came from IDC. This dropped to 40% by late 2003. By the late 1990s, Mendes (1999) pointed out that Brazilian AHRCSOs recognised that they should deal with the challenges posed by their strong dependence on funding from international cooperation as well as the diffuse nature of the movement for the defence of rights. Indeed, those challenges previously identified became a harsh reality in the early 2000s. The global context for IDC underwent dramatic changes, with these intensifying in the past few years (ABONG 2012; Biekart 2013; Milani 2013).

As a result, the convergence of a crisis, of restructuring of programme and geographical priorities, and the focus on efficiency have led to an environment that is clearly different from the one AHRCSOs experienced for decades, with significant impact on their funding. This change hit AHRCSOs much harder than other kinds of CSOs in Brazil, who generally counted on corporations or the government for their funds.

As we show below, the organisational structure and operational models of AHRCSOs have led to slow changes as they have difficulty in dealing with the new context of funding, establishing relationships with new players in IDC, and meeting the needs for organisational restructuring.

Organisational features and the challenges of transparency and efficiency

The organisational features of AHRCSOs include a strong focus, since their establishment, on their mission and organisational goals, which is reflected in organisational models that bring together an organic and a functional structure. Mendes (1999) points out that these organisations self-identified as popular education and development organisations, since education-related efforts were the mainstay of their activities.

These organisations have legally required statutes and bylaws, but despite frequent changes, these documents have not become a reference for the routine work performed at these institutions. The formal registry cannot keep pace with the changes happening in the daily routine.

In his 2014 study of ABONG, Nogueira reached a similar conclusion, remarking that the key focus is on internal democracy, respecting the values of member organisations. While formal structures such as general meetings, board of directors, executive management, and financial board are in place, regional directories and direct democracy play a key role.

As in the three organisations analysed by Mendes (1999), in ABONG formal structures do not keep pace with changes in internal practices and decision-making processes, since the approval of internal rules requires convening a general meeting according to ABONG statutes, something that is difficult to achieve due to members' schedules and the associated expenses.

Mendes (1999) noted that informality prevails, especially in the practices used in internal processes of leadership and decision-making, and in accountability hierarchies, but this informality can also be found in the relationship with outside partners, internal processes, and people management. Throughout their inception and development, AHRCSOs have developed internal reports and controls poorly, except when required by sponsors. The entire accountability system was developed according to rules defined by each national or international sponsoring agency. As a result, Brazilian AHRCSOs have not developed broader accountability processes or internal culture.

This is one of the key challenges that AHRCSOs in Brazil must face. In 2014 Eduardo Pannunzio wrote a newspaper article called "Can we trust civil society?", where he mentioned reports of wrongdoing involving the transfer of government funds to CSOs. In the federal government, three congressional committees were established to investigate the issue in 1993, 2002, and 2008. After another scandal surfaced in 2011, President Dilma Rousseff ordered the suspension of the transfer of funds to CSOs in partnership with the federal government. It was clear that these scandals involved extremely few organisations, none of them with significant weight and social representativeness.

As Mendes (1999) pointed out, even though they deal with considerable resources, there has been no case of a Brazilian AHRCSOs official becoming rich, which has secured these organisations the trust of international sponsors. However, the reports of wrongdoing have contributed to a general feeling of distrust of the sector, leading to a scenario where these organisations are criminalised and where CSOs that perform political work, such as AHRCSOs, are hit the hardest.

Pannunzio (2014) pointed out that CSOs are not only victims of this situation but are also part of the problem: "society doesn't know what the CSOs do, doesn't know how they are managed, and cannot tell the good organizations from the bad". A lack of transparency is prevalent not only in organisations but also in the overall sector, as indicated by the lack of information on these organisations, their activities, and their impact (Mendonça et al. 2009).

Even though reports on the results of their work were being published, as Mendes (1999) points out, AHRCSOs were not publicising this information in a way that would strengthen their own image because it was "inappropriate to make a name for yourself", maintaining the underground image from the years of the military dictatorship.

These challenges are related to the overall cultures of CSOs, which have not developed a broader information exchange with society, government, and companies – on the contrary, the prevailing posture was a combative one. The external relationship and networks of Brazilian AHRCSOs were always built with a focus on their agenda and on increasing their intervention on civil society in processes that demanded denouncement, control, and participation (Nogueira 2014), reflecting their advocacy work. While such relations are still critical, the changes in the field of the defence of rights have demanded other relations, especially those promoting the production and publication of information and broader communication with society. In order to meet the challenge of transparency, in 2012 ABONG created the Observatório da Sociedade Civil (Civil Society Observatory), a platform to "attract new partners, increase their activities, and provide a reference in the relationship between Civil Society Organizations and the public" (ABONG 2014).

However, organisational structures and processes are not designed to provide information, data, documents, and reports to the general public, as they focus on providing the information required by external sponsors. Thus, transparency is also an organisational challenge.

Throughout the 1990s several organisations had to adapt to a first period of institutional crisis reflected in their flow of funds (Mendes 1999), due particularly to the currency exchange parity of the Real Plan. AHRCSOs needed to downsize their workforce and review missions, strategies, and programmes, while also rethinking the role of associates, governance, and methods and scope of operation. This led to changes in the workforce that resulted in an increasingly professional workforce for core activities, with little change in support activities. Organisations have also moved away from their initial paths that were strongly tied to their founding leaders – a process not without its conflicts and identity crises. The adopted changes have led to smaller structures with more flexibility, greater decentralisation, and wider local networks.

Working through projects was from the start the primary work mode of AHRCSOs, something that remained unchanged in the following years. Projects provided the means, albeit precariously, for international sponsors to track the application of resources and the activities of the organisations they were funding. For AHRCSOs, projects have turned into a powerful tool for securing resources: they must reflect the goals and contents of sponsors. During the project, several reviews may be needed to meet demands that often diverge from the initial proposition of the AHRCSOs (Krause 2014). In the early stages of the relationship with international agents, these projects could cover several maintenance and development activities of the organisation. As time moved on and funds diminished, projects increasingly became more focused and relied on methods and standards for the content and frequency of reports, among other things (Carvalho 2000).

As mentioned by Fernandes and Piquet Carneiro (1991, 22): "NGOs have learned the 'project' language and make this their main tool of institutional reproduction." While pointing out concerns over this pragmatic culture from activists, the authors acknowledge that this working model has streamlined AHRCSOs to a great degree.

Nevertheless, the culture of working through projects has presented many problems to organisations, especially the following two. First, this streamlined model is limited to the core activities associated with sponsors, mixed with more organic models especially when it comes to decision-making processes. There is no overall streamlining of the entire organisational activity. The second problem is that this operational model perpetuates poor working conditions. Most of the staff in these organisations work as occasional contractors tied to each project – a paradox for AHRCSOs that defend labour rights and decent working conditions as one of their key goals.

Representative of the organisational changes experienced in the first crisis in the 1990s is the adoption of the regular creation of plans and programmes and the use of strategic planning. ABONG created the Institutional Development Program (PDI) in order to provide institutional strengthening to member organisations through debates, courses, and literature. PDI is designed to keep the focus and mission of AHRCSOs by creating a systemic concept in order to bring together the socio-political and the management sides. The organisations acknowledge how important the management side is, but they point out that management must act in service to the development of political capability and social intervention.

Among the changes that took place in the 1990s, little attention was given to internal controls and reports, focusing instead on what sponsors demanded (Mendes 1999; Nogueira 2014). Political orientation is still marked by negative reactions and strong resistance to an association with the state. AHRCSOs did not wish to be seen as taking over roles and responsibilities from the state when, at the same time, they were pointing out the lack of public policies to guide the social activities in which they engaged (Mendes 1999). There is, however, a wide variety of relationships with local governments, which has led to fruitful, cooperative experiences in some cases.

The 2002 election, which brought Lula and the Workers' Party to power, caused some changes to this scenario. At first, many AHRCSOs that were part of ABONG's network supported the new government and sought informal and formal partnerships to influence and implement public policies.

However, after a couple of years, the enthusiasm faded, due to two main reasons. First, many activists felt that it was important to maintain their independence and critical voice to the government, thus lessening the risk of real or perceived co-optation. Second, some criticised many government policies, when they felt that the reality didn't meet the expectations (Nogueira 2014).

New operational methods and models

In the past decade, the changes that began in the 1990s have been ongoing, and some challenges have become bigger as organisations in the field are still providing unsatisfactory answers. The issue of how to achieve sustainability despite diminishing resources from IDC remains (Armani 2004; Mendonça et al. 2013). As the corporate philanthropy movement grew and became institutionalised in the 1990s, AHRCSOs started talking to the business world, albeit still timidly. In the same timid way, AHRCSOs were forced to consider securing resources locally and becoming project sponsors or intermediates (Armani 2004).

The biggest impact from changes in IDC was first experienced in the 2000s, and some key facts have contributed to these developments (Biekart 2013; Lewis 2014; Milani 2013):

- Improvement of social indicators and consolidation of democracy in Brazil.
- Change in IDC focus after the September 11 attacks, prioritising several security strategies, and a stronger focus on efficiency and efficacy after the Paris Declaration of 2005.
- Concentration of support in Africa, Eastern Europe, and Asia.
- Decreasing resources available for IDC after the 2008 financial crisis.

We also highlight the presence of new agents in ICD – large corporate foundations such as the Bill and Melinda Gates Foundation – new funds and tools, such as GAVI (Global Fund Against AIDS), UNITAID (established in 2006 to fight the spread of HIV/AIDS, malaria, and tuberculosis), and new emerging donors focusing on South-South cooperation. The setting is now more complex and multi-faceted (Milani 2013). These new agents bring new agendas and new operational methods.

Locally, these changes drive the need for AHRCSOs to move closer to these new agents, especially the corporate sector. According to some authors, this need is driven by pressure from international sponsors still active in Brazil, which are themselves under similar pressure to diversify their source of resources and establish new connections (Aragão 2012). Despite this pressure and the efforts from some AHRCSOs, the connection to the corporate sector, whether directly or via their philanthropy arms, is still delicate. Corporate organisations in Brazil have yet to develop an understanding on issues related to rights, but they are showing an increasing interest on subjects like equality and the inclusion of minorities. These subjects, in general, are also not consolidated among corporate investors outside Brazil, although companies are increasingly involved in global social justice issues and working on transnational perspectives (Desai and Kharas 2010).

Pelliano (2013) points out that, although companies find it difficult to incorporate concepts and debates related to the defence of rights in their routine work, companies have started embracing a perspective of defence and demand of rights in their practices, especially in fields such as education and culture.

On the other hand, Degenszajn (2013) comments that corporate social investment is strongly marked by branding efforts, leading to the additional challenge of how to deal with "non-hegemonic" or non-consensual agendas. In general, a rights agenda is seen as a liability and not as a strategy to make society stronger. At the same time, data from the 2012 GIFE (Group of Institutes, Foundations, and Companies) survey show a significant increase in the number of organisations investing in the defence of rights, especially women's rights and diversity and inclusion.

The need to seek instructional resources used for maintenance and not tied to projects – and therefore free to be allocated anywhere – has led some AHRCSOs to seek new strategies and models for their operations and for securing resources.

A new model being tried is that of the independent civil society funds, which have provided financial resources to small- and medium-sized groups and social organisations that contribute to social transformation, promotion of social justice, and empowerment of populations who have been denied their rights in several regions of Brazil. These funds and other initiatives have been dubbed independent social investments by GIFE (2014), which is itself acting as a new agent in the field of rights and as promoter of new AHRCSOs (Lessa and Hopstein 2013). According to GIFE (2014, 13):

> "By supporting widely different types of organizations in all regions of the country, these institutions support autonomous social protagonists at the base of society … this group of civil society institutions and funds that take on the mission of supporting social protagonists of citizenship, human rights, and democracy is so important. They work on strengthening and refreshing the conditions that sustain the democratic society."

However, such initiatives are still in an experimental stage, and they demand that leaders and organisations in the field of rights acquire skills that they traditionally had not mastered, such as expertise on how to manage equity funds, how to improve tools to assess their impact, and how to design more sophisticated indicators.

Management requirements are now stronger and closer to the mindset found in corporate activity. Embracing these management models, even when they are not associated with immediate closer ties with companies, still raises concerns among operators in the field of rights.

Closing remarks

Despite improvements in the past few years, Brazil remains an unequal country, with many questions on how to extend citizenship, and therefore it is critical that society play its role in rethinking the continuities and discontinuities in Brazil's development process (Durão 2013; Mendonça 2014; Nader 2014).

As we have argued, AHRCSOs play a key role in answering the question of how best to harmonise recent developments with the social justice agenda, since these organisations have historically represented important social forces in the fight for democracy and rights (Araújo 2013; Armani 2013; Landim 2002; Nogueira 2014). Therefore, it is important to understand their new role in a society that is redefining the engagement of citizens with the state, companies, and CSOs themselves. This new setting brings together the expansion of consumption and the market, thus raising Brazil to the position of a middle-income nation that now joins other countries of the so-called BRICS group, a development model that leaves deep internal social contradictions unsolved while at the same time raising these countries' position in international agendas of South-South development. We should note that this model already shows signs of fading out both in Brazil and in other countries in Latin America.

These changes have led to a redefinition of the concept of rights itself by changing citizens' expectations, while also restructuring the scope of AHRCSOs' activities by redefining the flow of resources and driving the emergence of new agents in the IDC agenda. Therefore, it is important to analyse these changes and their impact on AHRCSOs. One of the first challenges when analysing these organisations is defining what they are and what they do. The existing legal structures and formal definitions are not sufficient to do this.

This article demonstrated how fluid and dispersed this field is, in which several organisations undertake different activities – despite showing a strong sense of unified identity. There are scarce data and information available on the sector, so in order to understand who these organisations are we need to map their history (Diniz and Mattos 2002; Fernandes 1994; Fernandes and Piquet Carneiro 1991; Landim 1988; Mendes 1999). Their identity was built primarily during the military dictatorship, which leads these organisations to share a common ideology while also defining their structure through the influence of external financing.

This foundation shapes their formats and organisational culture. An analysis of research and cases providing detailed reports on the many organisational elements of AHRCSOs shows that their history makes it more difficult to meet the challenges created by the changing scenario. They need to create professional structures that enable processing, producing, and publicising information on the field of rights, themselves, and their activities. It is only by facing this fundamental challenge that AHRCSOs will be able to meet demands for transparency, showing the public what makes them singular among CSOs at large. These new structures must also prepare these organisations to design and consolidate new strategies for securing resources.

A second challenge is related to cultural issues. How will AHRCSOs move from a unified identify that resonates internally in their field to a unified identity that resonates externally, that allows these organisations to start new conversations, and that takes into account the rapidly deepening changes in their environment?

Despite adversities and challenges, some developments are encouraging for the field of the defence of rights in Brazil. New types of organisations and new ways to secure resources are being better explored. In their relationship to corporate donors, there are signs of possible common ground on specific issues. What impact these changes will have on AHRCSOs depends on how effectively these dialogues can produce new synergy, and how capable these organisations are at influencing discussions over the development model in Brazil in relation to the social justice agenda.

Note

1. For the FASFIL survey, besides the ICNPO criteria 10 other non-profit organisation groups from the CEMPRE (Central Companies Registry) list were excluded, which included for-profit and not-for-profit organisations registered with the Brazilian Federal Revenue (school budget committees; political parties; labour unions and associations; homeowner associations; public notary's offices; S System; mediation and arbitration organisations; settlement commissions; municipal councils, funds, and consortiums; cemeteries and funeral homes).

Disclosure statement

No potential conflict of interest was reported by the authors.

References

ABONG (Brazilian Association of NGOs). 2012. "Estudo Acesso das organizações de defesa de direitos e bens comuns aos Fundos Públicos Federais. Relatório de Consultoria." Accessed December 2, 2014. www.abong.org.br/final/download/fprelatoriofinal.pdf

Alves, M. A. 2002. "Terceiro setor: as origens do conceito." *Anais do ENANPAD–Encontro anual da Anpad, 26*. Rio de Janeiro: ANPAD.

Aragão, D. M. 2012. "O controle global da solidariedade: transnacionalização e privatização na adaptação estratégica de ONGs britânicas no Brasil." *Cadernos CRH* 25 (65): 269–283. www.scielo.br/scielo.php?script=sci_arttextandpid=S0103-49792012000200006andlng=enandnrm=iso

Araújo, A. 2013. "Human Rights Funding in Brazil." Open Democracy, 12 November. Accessed August 5, 2015. www.opendemocracy.net/openglobalrights/ana-valC3A9ria-araC3BAjo/human-rights-funding-in-brazil.

Armani, D. 2004. "Sustentabilidade: Desafio democrático." In *Sustentabilidade: Aids e Sociedade Civil em Debate*, 9–14. Brasília: Ministério da Saúde.

Armani, D. 2013. "Considerações Finais: Sustentabilidade das OSCs: a difícil arquitetura da autonomia." In *Arquitetura Institucional de Apoio às Organizações da Sociedade Civil no Brasil*, edited by M. A. Alves, P. M. E. Mendonça, and F. A. Nogueira, 241–249. São Paulo: Editora Programa Gestão Pública e Cidadania.

Biekart, K. 2013. "Novos desafios para os atores da sociedade civil brasileira em um contexto de mudanças na cooperação internacional." In *Arquitetura Institucional de Apoio às Organizações da Sociedade Civil no Brasil*, edited by M. A. Alves, P. M. E. Mendonça, and F. A. Nogueira, 81–97. São Paulo: Editora Programa Gestão Pública e Cidadania.

Carvalho, C. A. P. 2000. "A transformação organizacional das ONGs no Brasil: um processo de isomorfismo com as ONGs do norte." *Anais Encontro de Estudos Organizacionais, 1*, 1–13. Curitiba: ANPAD.

Degenszajn, A. 2013. "Características e desafios do investimento social no Brasil: uma conversa com André Degenszajn." In *Arquitetura Institucional de Apoio às Organizações da Sociedade Civil no Brasil*, edited by M. A. Alves, P. M. E. Mendonça, and F. A. Nogueira, 233–239. São Paulo: Editora Programa Gestão Pública e Cidadania.

Desai, R. M., and H. Kharas. 2010. "Democratizing Foreign Aid: Online Philanthropy and International Development Assistance." *International Law and Politics* 42: 1111–1142.

Diniz, J. H., and P. L. Mattos. 2002. "Organizações não governamentais e gestão estratégica: desfiguração do seu caráter institucional original?" *Anais do Encontro Nacional da Associação de Pós Graduação em Administração, 26*. Salvador.

Dora, D., and E. Pannunzio. 2013. "Marco Regulatório das Organizações da Sociedade Civil: cenário Atual e Estratégias de Avanço." *Análise CPJA*, Direito FGV. http://cpja.fgv.br/sites/cpja.fgv.br/files/marco_regulatorio_das_oscs.pdf.

Durão, J. 2013. "Prefácio." In *Arquitetura Institucional de Apoio às Organizações da Sociedade Civil no Brasil*, edited by M. A. Alves, P. M. E. Mendonça, and F. A. Nogueira, 11–16. São Paulo: Editora Programa Gestão Pública e Cidadania.

Durão, J. 2014. "O novo marco legal das OSC: avanço a se comemorar ou vitória de Pirro?" Notícias ABONG, 17 November. Accessed December 5, 2014. www.abong.org.br/noticias.php?id = 7658.

Fernandes, R. C. 1994. *Privado porém Público*. Rio de Janeiro: Relume Dumará.

Fernandes, R. C., and L. Piquet Carneiro. 1991. *ONGs Anos 90: a opinião dos dirigentes brasileiros*. Rio: ISER, Núcleo de Pesquisa.

GIFE (Grupo de Institutos, Fundações e Empresas). 2014. *Investimento Social Independente para o Fortalecimento das Organizações da Sociedade Civil*. São Paulo: GIFE. Accessed December 5, 2014. www.gife.org.br/arquivos/publicacoes/36/Investimento%20Social%20Privado.pdf

Harris-Curtis, E. 2003. "Rights-based Approaches – Issues for NGOs." *Development in Practice* 13 (5): 558–563.

IBGE (Instituto Brasileiro de Geografia e Estatística). 2012. "As Fundações Privadas e Associações sem fins Lucrativos (FASFIL)." *Série IBGE Estudos and Pesquisas*: Informação Econômica N° 20. Acessed December 5, 2014. ftp://ftp.ibge.gov.br/Fundacoes_Privadas_e_Associacoes/2010/fasfil.pdf.

Iorio, C. 2002. "Algumas considerações sobre estratégias de empoderamento e de direitos." *Empoderamento e Direitos no Combate à Pobreza*. Rio de Janeiro: ActionAid Brasil.

Kindornay, S., J. Ron, and C. Carpenter. 2012. "Rights-Based Approaches to Development: Implications for NGOs." *Human Rights Quarterly* 34 (2): 472–506.

Krause, M. 2014. *The Good Project: Humanitarian Relief NGOs and the Fragmentation of Reason*. Chicago: University of Chicago Press.

Landim, L. 1988. *As Organizações Não-Governamentais no Brasil*. Rio de Janeiro: ISER.

Landim, L. 2002. "Experiência militante: histórias das assim chamadas ONGs." In *Les organisations non gouvernementales en lusophonie: terrains et débats*, 215–239. Paris: Karthala.

Lessa, C., and G. Hopstein. 2013. "Transformando a filantropia no Brasil: o fenômeno da Rede de Fundos Independentes para a Justiça Social." In *Arquitetura Institucional de Apoio às Organizações da Sociedade Civil no Brasil*, edited by M. A. Alves, P. M. E. Mendonça, and F. A. Nogueira, 131–143. São Paulo: Editora Programa Gestão Pública e Cidadania.

Lewis, D. 2014. *Non-governmental Organizations, Management and Development*. London: Routledge.

Mendes, L. C. A. 1999. "Visitando o Terceiro Setor (ou parte dele)." *IPEA, Texto para Discussão n° 647*. Brasília. Acessed May 5, 2015. http://repositorio.ipea.gov.br/bitstream/11058/2618/1/td_0647.pdf

Mendonça, P. 2014. "Enquanto os olhos do mundo se voltam para o Brasil, os grupos locais de direitos humanos devem aproveitar o dia." Open Democracy, 29 May. Accessed December 5, 2014. www.opendemocracy.net/openglobalrights/patricia-mendon%C3%A7a/enquanto-os-olhos-do-mundo-se-voltam-para-o-brasil-os-grupos-loca.

Mendonça, P., and D. Falcão. 2016. "Novo Marco Regulatório para a realização de parcerias entre o Estado e as OSCs - Organizações da Sociedade Civil: inovação ou peso do passado?" *Cadernos Gestão Pública e Cidadania* 21 (68): 44–62.

Mendonça, P., A. Teodósio, F. Alvim, and E. Araújo. 2009. "Desafios e Dilemas das ONGs na Cooperação Internacional: Uma analise da realidade brasileira." *Gestão.Org. Revista Eletrônica de Gestão Organizacional* 7: 69–83.

Milani, C. R. S. 2013. "Cooperação internacional para o desenvolvimento e ONGs brasileiras: financiamento e autonomia política." In *Arquitetura Institucional de Apoio às Organizações da Sociedade Civil no Brasil*, edited by M. A. Alves, P. M. E. Mendonça, and F. A. Nogueira, 67–79. São Paulo: Editora Programa Gestão Pública e Cidadania.

Nader, L. 2013. "Mismatch: Why are Human Rights NGOs in Emerging Powers not Emerging?" Open Democracy, 15 November. Accessed December 5, 2014. www.opendemocracy.net/openglobalrights/lucia-nader/mismatch-why-are-human-rights-ngos-in-emerging-powers-not-emerging

Nogueira, F. A. 2014. "Gestão de Membresia: A relação entre associação e associados em três casos brasileiros." PhD thesis, Programa de Administração Pública e Governo, Fundação Getúlio Vargas.

Pannunzio, E. 2014. "Dá para confiar na Sociedade Civil?" *Brasil Post*. www.brasilpost.com.br/eduardo-pannunzio/da-para-confiar-na-sociedade-civil_b_5153273.html.

Pelliano, A. M. 2013. "Modismo ou tendência? Uma conversa sobre investimento social com Anna Maria Peliano." In *Arquitetura Institucional de Apoio às Organizações da Sociedade Civil no Brasil*, edited by M. A. Alves, P. M. E. Mendonça, and F. A. Nogueira, 223–231. São Paulo: Editora Programa Gestão Pública e Cidadania.

Romano, J., and M. Antunes. 2002. "Introdução ao debate sobre empoderamento e direitos no combate à pobreza." In *Empoderamento e Direitos no Combate à Pobreza*, edited by J. Romano and M. Antunes, 5–8. Rio de Janeiro: ActionAid Brasil. Accessed October 1, 2014. http://187.45.205.122/Portals/0/Docs/empoderamento.pdf.

Salomon, L.; Anheier, H. 1992. "In Search of the Non-profit Sector II: The Problem of Classification." *Voluntas: International Journal of Voluntary and Nonprofit Organizations* 3 (3): 267–309.

Sen, A. 2000. *Development as Freedom*. Oxford: Oxford University Press.

Spink, P. 2000. "The Rights Approach to Local Public Management: Experiences from Brazil." *RAE - Revista de Administração de Empresas* 40 (3): 45–65.

The Guardian. 2016. "The Guardian View on Dilma Rousseff's Impeachment: A Tragedy and a Scandal. Editorial." Accessed May 5, 2016. www.theguardian.com/commentisfree/2016/apr/18/the-guardian-view-on-dilma-rousseffs-impeachment-a-tragedy-and-a-scandal.

The New York Times. 2016. "Facing Impeachment, Dilma Rousseff Fights for Political Survival. Editorial." 18 April, 2016. Accessed May 5, 2016. http://mobile.nytimes.com/2016/04/19/opinion/dilma-rousseffs-fight-for-political-survival.html?rref=collection%2Ftimestopic%2FRousseff%2C%20Dilmaandaction=clickandcontentCollection=timestopics.

UNHCR (UN Office of the High Commissioner for Human Rights). 2002. "Draft Guidelines: A Human Rights Approach to Poverty Reduction Strategies." Accessed November 3, 2012. www.unhcr.org/refworld/docid/3f8298544.html.

Vakil, A. C. 1997. "Confronting the Classification Problem: Toward a Taxonomy of NGOs." *World Development* 25 (12): 2057–2070.

The sustainability of Latin American CSOs: historical patterns and new funding sources

Inés M. Pousadela and Anabel Cruz

ABSTRACT

As an increasingly consolidated middle-income region, Latin America's position within the international aid architecture has shifted. Funding for civil society has decreased as a result of economic growth, crises affecting bilateral donors, and operational and financial restrictions stemming from political polarisation and increasing government hostility in various countries. Based on a current and historical literature review as well as informal consultations with CSO sources, this article summarises the results of a research project focused on civil society's funding mechanisms in Latin America and accounts for recent CSO efforts to explore novel funding alternatives.

La position de l'Amérique latine, en tant que région s'imposant de plus en plus comme une région à revenu intermédiaire, au sein de l'architecture internationale de l'aide a évolué. Les financements destinés à la société civile ont diminué suite à la croissance économique, aux crises touchant les bailleurs de fonds bilatéraux et aux restrictions opérationnelles et financières dues à la polarisation politique et à l'hostilité croissante des gouvernements dans divers pays. Sur la base d'une revue documentaire actuelle et historique, ainsi que de consultations informelles avec des OSC sources, cet article résume les résultats d'un projet de recherche axé sur les mécanismes de financement de la société civile en Amérique latine et présente un compte rendu des efforts récents des OSC pour examiner des alternatives de financement originales.

A medida que América Latina se consolida como una región de ingresos medios, su situación en el ámbito de la ayuda internacional se ha modificado. Debido al crecimiento económico, a las crisis que han incidido en los donantes bilaterales, a las restricciones operativas y financieras provocadas por la polarización política y a la creciente hostilidad gubernamental en varios países, se redujo el financiamiento para la sociedad civil. A partir de una revisión de estudios actuales e históricos, así como de consultas informales a varias OSC, el presente artículo sintetiza los resultados de un proyecto de investigación centrado en los mecanismos de financiación utilizados por la sociedad civil en América Latina, dando cuenta de los recientes esfuerzos de las OSC por explorar nuevas alternativas en este sentido.

Introduction

As an increasingly consolidated middle-income region, Latin America's position has shifted within the international aid architecture.[1] Along with the crises and recessions that have severely hit many traditional bilateral donors, this has increased funding restrictions for civil society (OECD 2012). The impact has been especially hard on a subset of countries that are highly dependent on foreign aid and where international cooperation has played a prominent role in civil society's growth in post-conflict and/or post-transitional contexts. Additionally, civil society organisations (CSOs) in some countries are currently experiencing further restrictions, both operational and financial, as a result of political polarisation and increasing government hostility against CSOs in general, and against those focused on democratic governance, human rights, citizen participation, and government accountability in particular.[2]

This article summarises the results of a research project focused on civil society's funding mechanisms in Latin America and the ongoing efforts of CSOs in the region to secure new funding sources. It is based on a current and historical literature review, the analysis of the latest available information on international cooperation fluxes produced by international organisations and donor countries' cooperation agencies, and the systematisation of the findings yielded by three recent sub-regional reports on CSO funding covering eighteen Latin American countries (Sinergia 2014; ICD 2014a; ICD 2014b; Morales López 2014).

After briefly discussing the methodology, the article assesses the various national and international funding sources currently available to CSOs in Latin America. It then identifies the three (unequal) angles of the funding triangle – international cooperation, the state, and the private sector – and describes the most recent changes undergone by each, as well as the restrictions and challenges that CSOs face as a result.

On the basis of country-level data, three prevalent funding patterns are identified: persistently high dependence on international cooperation funds; growing reliance on government contracts; and mixed funding with growing – but still minority – private sector participation (Stoianova 2013). The consequences of the consolidation of these funding patterns are explored in terms of internal civil society role differentiation, fragmentation, and CSO lifespan and rotation; differential impact on organisations focused on advocacy and service delivery; and the potential erosion of CSO autonomy and advocacy capacity. The article also accounts for recent CSO efforts to turn challenges into opportunities by exploring and experimenting with novel funding alternatives.

Methodology

This article is based on secondary sources, including statistical databases, press releases, and qualitative studies, as well as on primary data from an online CSO survey administered in one of the sub-regions and a series of semi-structured interviews and informal consultations with key civil society informants throughout the region. These included, but were not limited to, leaders of national NGO associations, members of regional networks and collective platforms, and several advocacy CSOs. While the interviews do not provide systematic data at a macro level, they contribute to corroborate some of the outlined trends.

Our main secondary sources are three sub-regional reports on funding mechanisms in Central America and Mexico (Morales López 2014), the Andes (Sinergia 2014), and the Southern Cone (ICD 2014a), commissioned in 2013 by Mesa de Articulación, a coordinating body for national NGO organisations and regional networks in Latin America and the Caribbean. An earlier version of this article was published by the Instituto de Comunicación y Desarrollo (Institute for Communication and Development) as a regional report (ICD 2014b). Overall, 18 Latin American countries are covered in these reports: Argentina, Belize, Bolivia, Brazil, Chile, Colombia, Costa Rica, Ecuador, El Salvador, Guatemala, Honduras, Mexico, Nicaragua, Panama, Paraguay, Peru, Uruguay, and Venezuela.

In putting together the three documents' findings, we aim at identifying common features and distinctive patterns and challenges within and across sub-regions in order to contribute to the ongoing discussion regarding Latin American CSOs' quest for fresh funding allowing them to fulfil their missions within rapidly changing and increasingly complex environments. The main shortcoming to be acknowledged concerns the reports' limited comparative potential, which did not allow us to safely move beyond pointing to broad trends and into the realm of hard quantitative evidence of the relative dimension and weight of the described phenomena.

Civil society and Latin America's dual transition

Latin America and the Caribbean is a middle-income region, and most of its countries fall into the middle-income category.[3] It is, however, highly heterogeneous, with countries ranging from the Western Hemisphere's only low-income country, Haiti, to high-income economies such as Chile; from heavily indebted countries such as Bolivia or Nicaragua, to rising powers like Brazil, the world's seventh largest economy. Most countries, including those with the highest incomes, are also internally heterogeneous and highly unequal.[4] In fact, despite over the past decade experiencing its highest economic growth rates since the 1960s and achieving impressive declines in poverty and significant declines in inequality, the region is still the most unequal – although by no means the poorest – in the world (López-Calva and Lustig 2010; UNDP 2014).

All the countries under study regularly hold reasonably free and fair elections. Many, however, still bear the marks of the chronic political stability endured throughout the twentieth century, and are burdened by the legacy of authoritarian regimes (typically led by the military) that ruled them in the 1960s and 1970s (and in some cases, well into the 1990s). The region took part in the so-called "third wave" of democratic transitions (Huntington 1991), with countries (re)democratising as early as 1979 (Ecuador) and as late as 1993 (Paraguay) and 2000 (Mexico). Despite a few short-lived interruptions over the decades that followed, democracy has eventually prevailed in the region, with CSOs and social movements playing prominent roles in the opposition to several dictatorships and the subsequent restoration of democracies (Domike 2008).

Partially overlapping with the democratic transition processes, since the late 1980s and early 1990s the region also experienced a transition towards market economies, guided by the principles of the so-called Washington Consensus. Democracy, therefore, has survived in environments typically characterised by deep social inequalities disproportionately affecting women, youth, indigenous peoples, rural populations, and Afro-descendants; high social conflict; and mounting citizen security issues. As a result, fear of authoritarian reversals has been largely replaced with concern with the quality of democratic governance (Diamond and Morlino 2005; Levine and Molina 2011). The democratic experience has fallen short of citizens' expectations and human rights violations have persisted even in democratic contexts, as a result of actions by both state agents (the military and police) and private entities (criminal organisations and paramilitary groups) (Méndez, Pinheiro, and O'Donnell 1999; Brinks and Botero 2010).

Throughout the region, CSOs have played relevant roles within this dual transition process and in the flawed democratic contexts that ensued, both as human rights advocates and promoters of better democratic practices (transparency, accountability, citizen participation, gender equality, and so on), and by complementing state action and even stepping in when the state retracted in key areas, notably health, education, poverty reduction, and community and rural development (Risley 2015). Regardless of the widely differing baselines, relative sizes, and levels of dynamism, the so-called non-profit, civil society, or third sector (named and defined differently from one country to the next) has notably increased in size and complexity in every country in the region. Reliable numbers are difficult to come by, but civil society mapping efforts are currently being undertaken in a number of Latin American countries, and their results all point to the same direction. In Chile, for instance, more than 240,000 CSOs were counted in the most recent survey (Centro UC 2016). Having more than doubled in size in the past decade, Chile's not-for-profit sector has become one of the biggest relative to the country's population (although various analyses appear to show declines in advocacy capacity). This is by no means an exception in the region, although it is possibly one of the most extreme manifestations of a phenomenon resulting from recent shifts in funding patterns for the sector. In Brazil, there were more than 290,000 not-for-profit organisations in 2010, including religious organisations (28.5%), trade and professional associations

(15.5%), and advocacy CSOs (14.6%). More than 54,000 were active in the fields of health, education, research, and social services. The sector grew by 8.8% between 2006 and 2010, but its expansion appears to have decelerated in recent years (IBGE 2012).

Shifts in international cooperation

Overall, official development aid (ODA) from OECD to the countries of Latin America and the Caribbean (LAC) has increased exponentially in absolute terms since the 1960s, although its growth seems to be currently decelerating. In relative terms, the region's share of global aid has decreased from 20.6% in 1960 to 12.2% in 2011 (after reaching its lowest point in the 1980s and somewhat increasing in the 1990s).[5] As elsewhere, the bulk of international cooperation funds in LAC flow towards governments; an extremely small proportion goes directly to domestic CSOs. The situation is no different within newer forms of development cooperation, including South-South initiatives.

According to a number of civil society sources, international cooperation funds allocated directly to CSOs are usually small, involve complex procedures, and tend to lack continuity. Whenever bigger amounts are involved, they are typically concentrated in a handful of organisations that are not necessarily representative of the wider spectrum of CSOs. During the 1980s and 1990s much of the aid was channelled through INGOs located in OECD countries; today many INGOs manage their own programmes in recipient countries, consequently reducing access to funding by local CSOs. In fact, approximately 150 such INGOs operate in the Andean sub-region alone (Sinergia 2014). In other cases, particularly in the Southern Cone, international cooperation funds are increasingly channelled through local and federal governments, which in turn sub-contract with CSOs to deliver social programmes (ICD 2014b).

International funding typically takes the form of projects supported by donor countries' embassies or government agencies (such as the Spanish AECID, Japanese JICA, Swedish SIDA, and American USAID), foundations from donor countries (sometimes linked to political parties), and special programmes funded by multilateral organisations (the United Nations system, the European Union, the Inter-American Development Bank, and the World Bank). Faith-based organisations are also supported by their international affiliates, the Catholic Church and US-based religious networks being two of the most common sources. Although each cooperation agency follows their own procedures and has its own thematic (as well as geographic) funding targets, much of the available resources end up being directed towards service delivery and emergency assistance for poor populations, as well as capacity development for local actors.

CSOs in many LAC countries have recently experienced discontinuities in funding due to both structural processes and critical junctures. First and foremost, the region has grown and, despite maintaining huge inequalities, many of its countries are now treated as a middle – or even high – income, with funds disproportionately flowing towards the remaining low and lower middle-income countries. Second, many OECD countries, such as the Nordic ones, are starting to prioritise funding to other regions of the developing world and therefore designing exit strategies from countries such as Nicaragua, El Salvador, and Guatemala (Castán 2011).[6] Third, the economic recession that recently hit some important bilateral donors, especially Spain, has also resulted in the closure of operations in several countries and decreased transfers towards the rest (Daguerre et al. 2012). Reductions in European bilateral aid have had a particularly strong impact on CSOs and networks promoting human rights and democratisation. Last but not least, whatever funding is still directed towards the third sector in the region, the number of CSOs currently pushing for their share is many times higher than it used to be just a couple of decades ago, accounting for what various CSO sources describe as merciless competition for scarce resources.

Not surprisingly, many CSOs, particularly in upper middle- and high-income countries, reveal that while they used to receive most funding from international cooperation agencies, they currently depend to about the same extent on state funding. Although international cooperation continues to be the main source of funding for civil society in the region as a whole, levels of dependence appear to be lowest in the Southern Cone and highest in the Andes, Central America, and parts of the Caribbean. As analysed below, Latin American CSOs have also increasingly become recipients of domestic government funds – a portion of which comes from international aid sources as well – a trend that seems to be deepest in countries where international cooperation has traditionally been lowest. CSOs in Latin America are also funded in small but increasing proportions by contributions from private companies and corporate foundations, both international and domestic (Villar Gómez 2015). National legal frameworks, however, differ widely regarding the provision of incentives for private donations – as does the readiness of CSOs to request and receive contributions from the private sector.

Patterns of CSO funding

Shifts in funding are currently a major cause of concern for CSOs in Latin America. Despite the fact that international cooperation remains the main source of funding overall, distinct sub-regional patterns have emerged depending on the relative weight of foreign assistance, government funds, and private donors on CSO resources.

Privileged relationships with the state

While state funds still represent a small contribution to CSO resources in countries that retain priority status for international cooperation agencies, they have become a major source of income for CSOs in the Southern Cone, particularly in Chile and Uruguay, which receive the lowest proportions of international cooperation funds. Unlike traditional international cooperation, domestic states tend to focus their links with CSOs on social services delivery. Typically, the trend towards the delegation of basic state functions on CSOs started decades ago, when cooperation agencies resorted to CSOs to implement social projects in view of states' failures in that regard; nowadays, paradoxically, the process has deepened as a result of the retraction of international cooperation (ICD 2014b).

The trend is probably strongest in Chile, where it began more than two decades ago, when international cooperation agencies started redirecting funding towards the government as the country transitioned to democracy. As a result, early on CSOs started partnering with the public sector to implement social programmes. According to available estimates, Chilean CSOs now receive about 70% their funding from the national, regional, or municipal governments, mostly for their contribution to government projects, 20% from international donors, and a meagre 10% from private companies (Morales López 2014, 111). Most government funding is earmarked for social projects in the areas of health or poverty alleviation, and/or targeted at children, youth, or women. The situation is similar in Uruguay, where the decrease in foreign cooperation has been countered by an increase in government funds, especially in the form of contracts to implement public policies in social areas. This trend has deepened since 2005, as the newly elected left-wing coalition national government implemented new social programmes and established novel mechanisms for civil society participation in public policy (ICD 2014b).

The relationship with the state not as a donor but as provider of opportunities for consultancy, technical advice, and policy implementation has a number of consequences. First, it tends to reward CSOs that adjust their roles to provide social services and implement public policy (typically without having a say in its conception and design) to the detriment of more vocal advocacy CSOs and networks. Second, this sort of link is usually based on ad hoc contracts that (as was also the case with international cooperation funds) rarely include resources for institutional strengthening and capacity building. As a result, the phenomenon of poor organisations managing rich projects is relatively common. Third, this relationship exposes CSOs to some of the state's worst vices: cumbersome procedures, opaque allocation criteria, and ideological discrimination. Fourth, delegation of functions on CSOs puts the state in the position of a controller, a role that it frequently has no adequate tools to perform, and that it tends to focus on the fulfilment of formal and financial requirements rather than on the evaluation of results and impacts, therefore distorting CSOs' use of their institutional resources. Fifth, excessive administrative requirements result in the concentration of funding on organisations that are bigger, more experienced, and better connected, as well as in the spread of suspicion regarding the will and ability of the sector to perform in a transparent and accountable way. Sixth, increased dependence on state funds makes CSOs more vulnerable to changes in the country's political climate, as CSO–government relationships usually fluctuate in both magnitude and format as the government changes. In short, dependence on the state as a funding source tends to reduce the autonomy of civil society to play its vital role of advocating for rights and criticising, denouncing, and forcing the powerful to account for their actions, either because CSOs tend to align ideologically with the hand that feeds them (or are overlooked if they do not), or because they are driven to unilaterally emphasise technical knowhow and compete for government contracts with other CSOs (and even with private companies).

Reliance on international funding

Most countries in Central America and the Andes, as well as Paraguay in the Southern Cone, still receive considerable international cooperation funds, some of which are channelled through local CSOs. By some estimates, about 95% of CSOs in the sub-region of Central America plus Mexico have some access to international funding (Morales López 2014, 144). According to a survey of 48 NGOs in five Andean countries, 70% have access to funding from INGOs, accounting for 20% of their budget, while 43% receive aid from multilateral donors and 33% do so from bilateral ones. Overall, international funding accounts for 44% of CSO budgets, while domestic funding – including self-generated income – accounts for 56%. Seventy per cent of surveyed NGOs produce some kind of income, amounting to 21% of their budgets, while 48% receive funding from the government (14% of budgets) and 65% declare some sort of contribution by private domestic companies (19% of budgets). There is no claim, however, that these numbers are representative of the civil society landscape in the Andes (Sinergia 2014, 39).

Along with the United Nations and international financial institutions, the European Commission offers the most opportunities to CSOs in Central America, particularly benefitting CSOs in Nicaragua, Honduras, Guatemala, and El Salvador, which retain priority status. Funding applies mostly to projects on democratic governance, human rights, food security, emergency response, poverty alleviation, education, health, and the environment.[7] According to CSOs in those countries, however, the process to obtain such funding is complex and involves technical, administrative, and financial requirements that many do not meet. Spanish aid used to stand out among bilateral cooperation funds in the 2000s, but recently dropped by 70–75% in only three years (compared to its 2008–09 levels) due to the country's deep recession. Northern European cooperation agencies also began to reduce their operations a few years ago, mostly as a result of priority changes.

With the notable exceptions of Colombia (until the 1990s) and Venezuela (until today), international funding has also been key for the development of civil society in the Andean countries, where CSOs are still highly dependent on it. Interviewed representatives of local CSOs, however, state either that those funds are already declining (given that although a very high proportion of CSOs still have access to them, they nonetheless make up a declining fraction of their budgets) or that they predict that they will in the near future. They also note that international cooperation funds have for some time now been channelled towards narrower social areas, harming CSOs with broader aims that had to either downsize or shut their operations, and benefiting those that run the specific kind of health, education, and social promotion programmes favoured by international cooperation agencies.

Bolivia, the biggest per capita development aid recipient in the Andes, provides a good illustration of the ongoing changes. Bolivian CSOs were historically highly dependent on foreign aid, and they mushroomed – and their dependence increased – in the 1980s, when neo-liberal reforms reduced the role of government in social service delivery, which came to be supplemented by CSOs (Arellano

López and Petras 1994). Administrative decentralisation in the 1990s and the promotion of social participation by a newly elected leftist government in the 2000s provided further opportunities for civil society involvement, but rapid political and administrative change also resulted in high CSO turnover, translating in an unusually high proportion of young organisations (Freiberg 2011). Although the country, South America's poorest, retains priority status with international cooperation agencies, Bolivian CSOs do not necessarily enjoy priority treatment. On the contrary, as the Bolivian government obtained international aid to implement its National Development Plan in 2008, many bilateral cooperation resources that used to flow directly towards CSOs began instead to be channelled through the central government (Sinergia 2014).

In Paraguay, the Southern Cone country where CSO–government links are newest and weakest (partly due to its late transition to democracy), civil society gets most funding from international sources. Funding sources, however, vary widely: while advocacy CSOs and those working on democracy and development issues receive most funding from international cooperation agencies, a growing number of CSOs focused on social service delivery – particularly in health and education, where they virtually replace the state – subsist mostly on government allocations (ICD 2014a).

Generally speaking, international cooperation agencies fund CSO activities in areas that domestic states do not, and its concentration on fewer issues – including democratic governance, rights advocacy, and rural development – translates into high impact. Cooperation agencies also tend to support CSOs that do not have any access to government funds because their governments either ideologically discriminate against them or view them as competitors for international funding rather than potential allies. However, excessive reliance on international flows makes CSOs dependent on increasingly fluctuating and unpredictable sources, as seen in the aftermath of the recent European crisis and recession. Sudden reductions of financial support by traditional cooperating agencies are currently threatening the survival of the civil society institutional framework built around international aid flows.

Hybrid scenarios and the private sector

The call for private collaboration to fund development had a global milestone in the 2000 launch of the United Nations' Global Compact, further strengthened by the G20 decision to enlist corporate social responsibility (CSR) towards the achievement of the Millennium Development Goals. By 2009 more than 6,200 private companies and 400 corporate associations in 135 countries were part of the Global Compact initiative, focused on four areas: human rights, labour, anticorruption, and the environment.[8] Since then, collaboration between CSOs and private companies has increased, and it has not been uncommon, even in Latin America, for CSOs to promote the adoption of CSR codes among private companies. This development is striking in view of the region's history of reciprocal mistrust, and particularly of civil society hostility towards private companies, whose predatory practices many CSOs have long systematically denounced. It is however a budding process, as suspicions persist and many CSOs maintain a critical position and only under very specific conditions accept the idea of corporate funding.

The penetration of private funding of CSOs is highly uneven in the region. It is generally still very low, with the exception of a few countries like Colombia and Venezuela, where foreign funding has traditionally been very limited and domestic funding from private sources was established earlier. In Ecuador, for example, only 7% of CSR initiatives are implemented by CSOs, while 42% are managed directly by the donors themselves and 10% are channelled through churches (Torresano 2012, 47).

The situation is different in Colombia and Venezuela, where only a very small minority of CSOs do not maintain any link at all with private companies or corporate foundations. In Colombia, civil society grew slowly and late as a result of scarce foreign aid, which also made CSOs more dependent on domestic funding, originated in both the government and the private sector. Several corporate foundations were established in the country as early as the 1960s, when international cooperation was under US$3 per capita and reached a limited number of CSOs (but was significant for organisations that opposed the government and were therefore denied public funding). Although they began with a markedly philanthropic orientation, they later turned their attention to areas such as job training, education, microcredit, the promotion of family businesses, and the establishment of not-for-profit social enterprises offering health, recreation, and housing services. Volunteerism has also increased since the 1960s. The density of corporate foundations in Colombia is currently among the highest in the region: according to a study by the Ford Foundation, there are 97 such entities, compared with 50 in Argentina, 28 in Chile, and 10 in Peru. Many run their own social and economic development programmes, including several focused on supporting micro-enterprises (Rojas 2000; Gutiérrez et al. 2006). In other areas, such as peacebuilding, many Colombian organisations receive private sector support. The steep increase in official development aid that took place since 1999, which quadrupled previous amounts, has not substantially altered the scenario described above. Indeed, most of the new flow of international funds went straight to the Plan Colombia, overwhelmingly focused on spraying coca and opium crops and fighting drug-trafficking guerrillas (Shifter 2012).

In turn, the history of Venezuelan CSOs is linked to the development of the oil economy, particularly since 1973–74, when the increase in crude prices and the nationalisation of oil companies turned the state into the main (but not necessarily the more efficient) economic actor and the country into a rich (albeit not more integrated) country. CSOs took the lead in subsequent poverty alleviation efforts in a country that, given its high per capita GDP, barely received any development aid. Today, international cooperation in Venezuela is still relatively small and concentrates on just a few issues, such as human rights, gender, and the environment. CSOs were therefore driven to seek either government contracts or private sector donations to fund their activities. The first federation of corporate entities and several corporate philanthropic foundations were established earlier than 1950, and before 1960 the country was home to several domestic as well as foreign corporate foundations. After the guerrillas made their appearance in the 1960s and human rights organisations multiplied, the corporate perspective shifted from charity towards social development, leading to involvement with, and funding of, community participation, popular housing, and education initiatives. Private companies currently perform their development aid duty within the CSR framework; the amount of their contribution, however, has decreased as industry took a hard blow and the number of active companies in the country abruptly dropped. Interviewed organisations claim that the situation is increasingly difficult for the non-profit sector as private donations have diminished and the government actively discriminates against independent CSOs (Sinergia 2014).

Lastly, in countries like Argentina, Brazil, and Mexico, CSO funding is more mixed. In the latter, for example, CSOs have long acquired experience in collaborating with the state, aided by a legal framework that grants them some role in policy-making. They also maintain ties with several corporate foundations both foreign (and especially from the United States) and domestic (such as those established by Carlos Slim, Telmex, Televisa, and Azteca). Similar entities have been established by big companies in the services and agricultural exporting sectors in Guatemala, El Salvador, Honduras, and Nicaragua; they differ from Mexico's however in that the relative weight of their contributions is incommensurate with that of international cooperation in those countries (Morales López 2014).

In Brazil, the funding situation is harder to elucidate. According to the Brazilian Institute of Geography and Statistics, only about 10,000 of the country's private foundations and CSOs in the country receive funds from the federal government (IBGE 2012). Nevertheless, as noted by the Centre of Studies on Information and Communication Technologies (CETIC), in 2012 66% had access to some sort of government funds, either at the local, state, or federal level, and these were the main source of income for 24% of 3,546 surveyed organisations (ICD 2014a). Government funding, however, is not prevalent, as members' contributions are the main resource for about one-fourth of surveyed CSOs, and corporate funding is also relevant and growing, fuelled by several recently established foundations (Banco Itaú, Gerdau, Vale, Roberto Marinho, and Odebrecht, among others). Nevertheless, according to the most recent study by Brazil's Grupo de Institutos, Fundações e Empresas (GIFE 2015), only 18% of the surveyed organisations were donors (defined as organisations that donate more than 90% of their resources) and they contributed a meagre 7% to the total amount of social investment in 2014, while 37% were executing organisations (defined as those that invest more than 90% on their own projects), and 45% were hybrid ones. Hybrid and executing organisations accounted for 45% and 50% of the invested funds, respectively. In short, donations to third parties are a key investment strategy for just a small minority of private foundations and companies in Brazil.

Private funding is also on the rise, but still lower, in neighbouring Argentina. For instance, even though 72% of the 89 organisations that make up the HelpArgentina network declare support by private companies and corporate foundations, for 35% of them such contributions represent less than 20% of their budget, and for one-fourth it represents between 20 and 40% (RACI 2010).

Closing reflections on CSO sustainability in Latin America

Interviews and informal consultations throughout the region support the notion that financial sustainability is currently one of, if not *the* main challenge facing civil society in Latin America. Traditional funding sources – bilateral and multilateral North–South cooperation agencies, as well as domestic governments that not only sub-contract with CSOs but also manage the bulk of international cooperation funds – are undergoing processes of change. CSO feelings of vulnerability increase at the sight of the withdrawal of cooperation agencies that played relevant roles in their countries' democratic transitions or peace processes. Ironically, the ensuing struggle for survival takes place while CSOs are for the first time ever officially recognised as relevant development actors and are therefore subject to growing demands in terms of efficiency, transparency, and accountability.

Broadly speaking, one classic source of CSO funding – foreign bilateral and multilateral donors – is currently receding in the region as a whole, while two other sources, government agencies at every level, and private companies and corporate foundations, appear to be on the rise. Although ODA has exponentially grown in absolute terms during the past decades, Latin America's share has decreased, some countries in the region have "graduated" as aid recipients, bilateral donors have undergone crises and recessions and, more fundamentally, their priorities have shifted. In addition, most funding keeps flowing toward governments rather than CSOs, and whatever trickles down to civil society is to be allocated among a swelling number of organisations. Lack of proportion between supply and demand of funding is apparent in the exceedingly low approval rates of the typical call for projects (3% for the World Bank's Global Partnership for Social Accountability in 2013–14, with only 10% of all approved projects allocated to Latin American CSOs) (ICD 2014a). Actual or feared reductions of international CSO funding are leading CSOs to explore new sources that were practically unthinkable in several countries a few years back, including but not limited to the establishment of relationships with governments and the private sector.

Changes in funding patterns are causing further role differentiation within civil society. Where state funding is prevalent or on the rise as the government is stepping in to supplement or replace shrunken international cooperation resources, many CSOs are morphing into (or being created as) service providers and therefore foregoing advocacy work. In other contexts where the market appears more promising than the state as a source of income, many CSOs start following the social enterprise model or microfinance. Either way, they risk relegating the non-market aspects of their activities and losing sight of the mission and character that used to make them distinct from for-profit entities.

As well as causing sudden and uncontrollable changes in resource flows that can seal the fate of a CSO, reliance on specific funding sources appears to draw CSOs towards specific roles. Indeed, while governments tend to earmark funding for service provision, corporate foundations tend to focus on social venture projects, and bilateral and multilateral internationals are increasingly moving towards service provision in areas such as health, education, and housing while still supporting – in some countries more than others – the advancement of rights, political participation, and democratic governance. As a result, advocacy CSOs – typically organisations that are more politically vulnerable and have less access to domestic funding – are reliant on a faltering source of support, namely North–

South international cooperation. Meanwhile, countless CSOs dedicated to service delivery prosper by establishing links with local, provincial, or federal state agencies (which are usually the ones handling the bulk of international cooperation money).

While the complexities of CSO–state relationships are better known and have already been referred to, there are also downsides to the other main alternative, namely the search for funding from private companies and corporate foundations. First, such funding is difficult to obtain; problems may reside not just in the conditions and constraints resulting from such links, but also in the inability to establish them in the first place. Indeed, the surge of CSR initiatives has not necessarily resulted in a stronger flow of private funds towards CSOs. Regardless of each country's density of private or corporate foundations and their involvement in social development projects, it is relatively common across the region for private foundations to run their own programmes and projects, sometimes in partnership with governments, other companies, or even community organisations, rather than funding CSO activities and structures.

Interviewed CSO leaders across the region speculate that this may be due to the fact that businesses have low confidence in CSOs' abilities to efficiently carry out their missions; companies' and corporate foundations' preference for aligning their social investment with their or their respective companies' businesses; and/or the fact that investors have better access to information to decide on and control their investments when they place them into their own rather than third parties' projects (see also ABONG 2013). It follows that it is to a great extent up to CSOs to change prevailing perceptions, encourage priority changes, and promote a better understanding with the private sector.

When corporate foundations do make their social investment by funding CSO activities, one shortcoming that interviewed CSO actors frequently point out is that they tend to concentrate donations – not necessarily in cash but also in kind – in narrow areas depending on their company's priorities (which is also one reason they often prefer to operate their own projects). They also tend to favour direct social aid to the detriment of long-term development projects. Additionally, not unlike much of international cooperation funding, they are unlikely to devote resources to institutional strengthening or collective learning processes.

Differential access to funding is increasing civil society fragmentation beyond the already mentioned differentiation between advocacy CSOs and service providers, or between organisations that rely on the commitment of activists and those that depend on voluntary work. CSOs that are slower to adapt to environmental change experience more drastic reductions in staff and coverage, while those more open to partnerships with a wider variety of private and public, domestic and international actors, and to modify their structure in response to environmental restrictions, are more able to funnel the resources they need to grow. Diversified organisational formats ensue: as described in Sinergia (2014) for the Andean region, the new landscape comprises compact organisations (small, with limited scope and reach, whose directors are also members of their work teams); organisations with centralised leadership and operational regionalisation; decentralised CSOs with a "mother" organisation that establishes regional offices and thematic programmes that eventually become separate organisations under a shared institutional umbrella, or creates new organisations, including for-profit ones to support the work related to the main organisation's original mission; franchised organisations that replicate successful models of social entrepreneurship in a way that is very similar to that of commercial franchises; networks aimed at extending the capacities of member organisations; and CSOs that function as the local chapters of international organisations. Efforts to adapt to funding fluctuations have also produced a new species that a Colombian CSO key informant defined as *"accordions that expand or retract depending on project funding"*. As a result, labour relations usually become sensitive, inasmuch as CSOs resort to more flexible contracts and reorganise themselves as a series of concentric circles, with a small core of permanent staff surrounded by layers of volunteers and employees hired for short-term projects. This not only results in friction with organised labour but also negatively affects CSOs' ability to capitalise on accumulated experience and institutional memory.

Surveyed CSOs throughout the region agree that funding sources should be as diverse as possible in order to offset the disadvantages of each funding alternative, protect them against contingencies, and preserve their autonomy to dissent and their watchdog role (a particularly pressing issue wherever the state has become too prevalent a funding source). Accordingly, CSO informants typically state that no potential source – international donations, including the novel South-South cooperation model, state contracts, and alliances with private companies and corporate foundations – should be overlooked. They also recognise the need to strengthen and modernise management structures, promote volunteer work, establish alliances with institutions such as universities, and develop fundraising activities among the wider public, including the use of online tools. Additionally, many CSOs even contemplate the possibility of offering professional services and undertaking other for-profit activities to generate independent income.

Beyond the issue of the origin of the resources, CSOs typically express preference for any funding form that preserves their ability to set the course of action rather than turning them into passive aid recipients. In contexts where CSOs with government contracts have specialised in service delivery and social policy implementation, for instance, this means negotiating a seat at the table where the programmes that they contribute to implement are designed and evaluated. It also means, for the sake of future sustainability, seeking stability beyond partisan change with the public administration and securing funding that covers not just programme activities but also operational costs and investment on institutional development.

Discussion of any such strategy needs to take place within a broader framework. Debate regarding where much-needed additional or alternative funding could come from should not overshadow the more fundamental discussion regarding the reasons why civil society organisations of all actors should be on the receiving end of such flow. In other words, beyond discussion of the amount of resources civil society needs, serious conversations need to take place regarding what civil society needs those resources for, and what the world would look like if poorly equipped civil society actors were unable to do their job. It is at this point that other, non-financial dimensions of both CSO sustainability and civil society endeavours – the quality of the surrounding civic space, transparency and accountability practices and the trust they elicit among their fellow citizens, to name just a few – need to be brought into the equation.

Notes

1. The expression "international aid architecture" refers to *"a system of institutions, rules, norms, and practices that govern the transfer of concessional resources for development"* (Bräutigam 2010, 8).
2. See "Foreign Funding of NGOS – Donors: Keep Out", *The Economist*, 13 September 2014: www.economist.com/news/international/21616969-more-and-more-autocrats-are-stifling-criticism-barring-non-governmental-organisations.
3. Average annual GDP per capita for Latin America and the Caribbean is US$9846. See ECLAC, CEPALSTAT: Databases and Statistical Publications, http://statistics.eclac.org.
4. According to the World Bank classification, six of the countries included in this study – Bolivia, El Salvador, Guatemala, Honduras, Nicaragua, and Paraguay – are lower middle-income economies, while nine –Argentina, Brazil, Colombia, Costa Rica, Ecuador, Mexico, Panama, Peru, and Venezuela – are upper middle-income economies. The remaining two (Chile and Uruguay) are high-income economies.
5. See http://datos.bancomundial.org.
6. See also "Exit Project Nicaragua, background": www.exitonicaragua.net/es/content/exit-project-nicaragua-background-english.
7. See https://ec.europa.eu/europeaid/node/7432.
8. See www.unglobalcompact.org.

Disclosure statement

No potential conflict of interest was reported by the authors.

References

ABONG. 2013. "O dinheiro das ONGs: Como as Organizações da Sociedade Civil sustentam suas atividades - e porque isso é fundamental para o Brasil." www.abong.org.br.

Arellano López, S., and J. F. Petras. 1994. "Non-Governmental Organizations and Poverty Alleviation in Bolivia." *Development and Change* 25 (3): 555–568.

Bräutigam, D. 2010. *China, Africa and the International Aid Architecture*. Working Paper No. 107. African Development Bank Group, Tunis.

Brinks, D. M., and S. Botero. 2010. "Inequality and the Rule of Law: Ineffective Rights in Latin American Democracies." Paper presented at the APSA Anual Meeting, Washington, DC.

Castán, J. M. 2011. "Nicaragua: Concerns about the New Course of International Cooperation." *Envío* 54. Managua, Nicaragua. www.envio.org.ni/articulo/4298.

Centro UC. 2016. "Mapa de las organizaciones de la sociedad civil 2015." Accessed March 1, 2016. www.sociedadenaccion.cl/wp-content/uploads/2016/01/PDF-Brochure-Mapa-de-las-Organizaciones.pdf.

Daguerre, J. A., M. Fittipaldi Freire, and C. López Burian. 2012. "Los impactos de la crisis en la cooperación española: desafíos y oportunidades. Reflexiones desde América Latina." *Tiempo de Paz* 105. Madrid, Spain.

Diamond, L., and L. Morlino, eds. 2005. *Assessing the Quality of Democracy*. Baltimore: The Johns Hopkins University Press.

Domike, A., ed. 2008. *Sociedad civil y movimientos sociales. Construyendo democracias sostenibles en América Latina*. Washington, DC: IADB.

Freiberg, D. von. 2011. "Las ONG bolivianas: análisis de su evolución y dimensión financier." *Tinkazos* 30: 79–103. La Paz, Bolivia.

GIFE. 2015. *Censo GIFE 2014*. São Paulo: Grupo de Institutos Fundações e Empresas.

Gutiérrez, R., et al. 2006. *Aportes y Desafíos de la Responsabilidad Social Empresarial en Colombia*. Bogota: Corona Foundation.

Huntington, S. 1991. *The Third Wave: Democratization in the Late Twentieth Century*. Norman: University of Oklahoma Press.

IBGE. 2012. "As Fundações Privadas e Associações sem Fins Lucrativos no Brasil 2010." Accessed March 1, 2016. http://biblioteca.ibge.gov.br/visualizacao/livros/liv62841.pdf.

ICD. 2014a. *Aporte a la generación de propuestas de mecanismos de financiamiento de las ONG en el Cono Sur y Brasil*. Montevideo: ICD.

ICD. 2014b. *Estudio regional sobre los mecanismos de financiamiento de las organizaciones de la sociedad civil en América Latina*. Montevideo: ICD.

Levine, D. H., and J. E. Molina, eds. 2011. *The Quality of Democracy in Latin America*. Boulder: Lynne Rienner Publishers.

López-Calva, L. F., and N. Lustig, eds. 2010. *Declining Inequality in Latin America. A Decade of Progress?* Baltimore: Brookings Institution Press.

Méndez, J. E., P. S. Pinheiro, and G. O'Donnell, eds. 1999. *The (Un)Rule of Law & the Underprivileged in Latin America*. Notre Dame: University of Notre Dame Press.

Morales López, H. 2014. *Financiación de las ONG: Retos y desafíos*. Guatemala: Mesa de Articulación.

OECD. 2012. "Development: Aid to Developing Countries Falls because of Global Recession." Accessed March 1, 2016. www.oecd.org/newsroom/developmentaidtodevelopingcountriesfallsbecauseofglobalrecession.htm.

RACI. 2010. *Mapas y prioridades estratégicas de la Cooperación Internacional*. Buenos Aires: RACI.

Risley, A. 2015. *Civil Society Organizations, Advocacy, and Policy Making in Latin American Democracies*. New York: Palgrave Macmillan.

Rojas, M. C. 2000. "Corporate Philatrophy and Democratic Governance in Colombia." Paper presented at the LASA International Congress, Miami, Florida.

Shifter, M. 2012. "Plan Colombia: A Retrospective." *Americas Quarterly* 6 (3): 36–42.

Sinergia. 2014. *Evolución de la ayuda al desarrollo y estrategias exitosas de sostenibilidad financiera en la Región Andina*. Caracas: Sinergia.

Stoianova, V. 2013. *Private Funding for Humanitarian Assistance. Filling the gap?* Bristol: Global Humanitarian Assistance.

Torresano, M. 2012. "Estudio de Responsabilidad Social de Empresas en Ecuador." AVINA, GIZ, IDE. Accessed March 1, 2016. http://responsabilidadsocialquito.com.ec/wp-content/uploads/2015/09/Estudio-de-RS-de-empresas-del-Ecuador-2012.pdf.

UNDP. 2014. "Perfil de estratos sociales en América Latina: pobres, vulnerables y clases medias." Accessed March 1, 2016. www.sv.undp.org/content/dam/el_salvador/docs/vih-sida/Grupos_sociales_AL.pdf.

Villar Gómez, R. 2015. *Recursos privados para la transformación social. Filantropía e inversion social privada en América Latina hoy.* Bogotá: GDFE at al.

Action for Children: a model for stimulating local fundraising in low- and middle-income countries

Robert Wiggers

ABSTRACT

This practical note reflects on the conclusions and learning from an evaluation of the Action for Children programme in four countries: Brazil, India, Kenya, and South Africa. Action for Children was developed by Wilde Ganzen to enhance diversity in funding and organisational sustainability through increased local resource mobilisation and, more specifically, local fundraising. The note looks at the challenges the programme sought to address, and examines the findings from the evaluation, plus the long-term prospects of sustainability for the local partners.

Cette note pratique présente une réflexion sur les conclusions et les enseignements d'une évaluation du programme *Action for Children* (Action pour les enfants) dans quatre pays : Brésil, Inde, Kenya et Afrique du Sud. Action for Children a été mis au point par Wilde Ganzen pour améliorer la diversité sur le plan du financement et de la durabilité organisationnelle grâce à une mobilisation accrue des ressources locales et, plus précisément, de la mobilisation de fonds au niveau local. Cette note examine le défi que le programme a cherché à relever et examine les conclusions de l'évaluation, ainsi que les perspectives à long terme de la durabilité pour les partenaires locaux.

Esta nota práctica analiza las conclusiones y los aprendizajes surgidos de una evaluación realizada al programa Action for Children en cuatro países: Brasil, India, Kenia y Sudáfrica. Esta organización fue fundada por Wilde Ganzen, con el propósito de ampliar la diversidad del ámbito de la financiación y la sostenibilidad organizacional mediante la mayor movilización de recursos locales, específicamente, a través de la recaudación de fondos a nivel local. Asimismo, la nota examina el reto que pretende enfrentar el programa, los resultados provenientes de la evaluación y la perspectiva de sostenibilidad a largo plazo para las contrapartes locales.

Introduction: Action for Children and the importance of local fundraising

In the early years of the new millennium, as international aid for some countries was decreasing and many other countries began to explore channels other than local community based organisations (CBOs) and NGOs, Wilde Ganzen (in English, Wild Geese Foundation; hereinafter WGF) felt local fundraising was increasingly important to keep the work of such local CBOs and NGOs going. More recently, it has become clear that local fundraising is also important because it decreases the dependency of local CBOs and NGOs on their national government. This is even more important as many governments decrease the possibilities for civil society organisations to function as independent development actors and to receive foreign aid (see, for example, Hodenfield and Pegus 2013).

Local fundraising contributes to the financial sustainability of an organisation and spreads financial risks: with different sources of income an organisation can cope better with donors that withdraw, or other setbacks. In addition, it provides a better guarantee that local priorities, instead of those of donors, prevail: research has shown that all too often, donors' priorities dictate where the money goes and thus, which problems are solved and which not. Local fundraising also contributes to organisations being better embedded in the local community: it increases the need to involve all, not only as beneficiaries, but also as active citizens, such as fundraisers, potential donors, or volunteers. And it gives legitimacy: the broader an organisation's support base, the stronger its right to voice the interests and concerns of the community it serves.[1]

Based on these insights, WGF developed the Action for Children (AfC) programme which is described in this practical note. AfC helps CBOs and NGOs in four countries in the Global South to increase their income and strengthen their legitimacy by building a strong indigenous support base and becoming less dependent on foreign aid. In this way, AfC contributes to civil society sustainability.

The challenge: pro-poor income redistribution

Worldwide, the face of poverty has changed: some 20 years ago more than 90% of the poor lived in low-income countries. Nowadays, according to the World Bank definition of poverty (a person living on less than US$1.25 per day) more than two-thirds of the poor live in low (with per capita income between GNI US$1046 and $4125) and high middle-income countries (with a per capita income between GNI US$4126 and $12745). The number of low-income countries (LICs) in the past decade has decreased to 52, while the number of lower and higher middle-income countries (MICs) has increased to 95 (OECD 2014).

These figures look promising, but deserve critical reflection. According to the Dutch Advisory Council on International Affairs, for instance, the image of poverty shifting to MICs requires some qualification. It is only because a limited number of large countries are now classified as MICs, that more than two-thirds of the world's poor now live in such countries. The reduction in global poverty from 1.7 billion people in 1990 to 1.3 billion in 2008 can be attributed almost entirely to the fall in the number of poor in China. Also, both LICs and MICs are relatively heterogeneous groups. Some MICs have a sound socio-economic basis and reasonably functioning institutions, while others are fragile states or states in conflict (Advisory Council on International Affairs 2012).

In many countries, large sections of the population either do not or hardly receive a share of the benefits of economic growth and remain poor. In most countries in Africa and Latin America, income inequality is among the highest in the world. More so than in the past, poverty has become a distribution issue. One can disagree on the sustainability of the perceived growth of the middle class in the Global South. But even if that growth were to slow down, there is an enormous potential for securing donations and voluntary time from individuals. The Charities Aid Foundation, in a summary on the key findings of its World Giving Index 2015, found that *some of the world's most generous countries are among the most deprived. The G-20, which represents the world's largest economies, accounts for only 5 of the top 20 countries* [on the WGI 2015 list]" (Charities Aid Foundation 2015).

There are two key challenges. The first is to stimulate pro-poor income redistribution enforced by the state, through taxation, subsidies, scholarship schemes, participatory budgeting, and so on. The second challenge is to increase voluntary giving to poverty alleviation activities, stimulated by civil society organisations.

Promoting a culture of local philanthropy and increased self-sufficiency in cooperation with strong national partner organisations

Based on the insights and trends described above, the Dutch *stichting* Wilde Ganzen took up the second challenge. It started the Action for Children programme (AfC) using a subsidy from the

Dutch government under its co-financing scheme and its own private funding. The government subsidy covered the period from 1 January 2007 to 31 December 2015.

By means of an innovative mix of funding, training activities, exchanges, and coaching, AfC strengthened national partner organisations in Brazil, India, Kenya, and South Africa to:

(a) Raise money at the national level for the functioning of their own organisation and the funding of the projects supported by it.
(b) Bring attention to child rights and the Millennium Development Goals.
(c) Train CBOs and small NGOs to raise 50% of the funds needed for their own projects themselves, in their own project areas.
(d) Match (double) the funds that CBOs and small NGOs raised locally.

In their evaluation report on AfC, the external evaluators (a team of consultants from INTRAC) developed a Theory of Change for the programme (Figure 1).

The matching funding was provided by a combination of a Dutch government subsidy, a contribution from Wilde Ganzen, and money the national partner organisations raised at the national level, from companies and the middle class.

At the core of the design was the presumption that over the course of the programme, the Dutch government subsidy and WGF's contribution would decrease while the contribution of the national partner organisation would increase. Thus, foreign funding would be gradually replaced by domestic funding. At the start of the programme, in 2006, it was estimated that 10 to 12 years would be needed for the programme to attain full independence from foreign funding. At the start of the second phase, in 2010, this was adjusted to between 12 and 15 years.

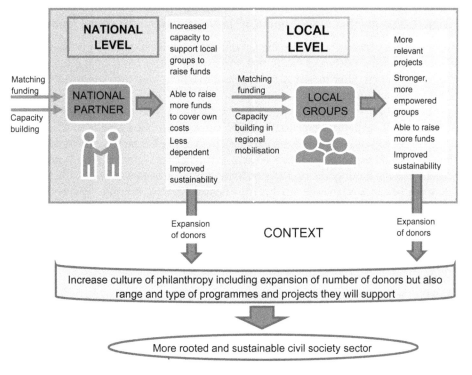

Figure 1. Theory of Change.

To help achieve this, WGF needed partner organisations with experience in different fields. They needed to be strong or potentially strong in fundraising and communication – given that they had to secure a continuously increasing contribution from domestic funding; be experts in delivering capacity strengthening to smaller organisations; and have experience with re-granting. Local and international consultants were invited to make a long list of potential partner organisations for three of the four selected partner countries. Based on secondary research and telephone interviews, they subsequently produced a short list of 10 organisations. In each country, face-to-face interviews were then held with five of the shortlisted organisations. Based on these interviews, the organisation that seemed most promising was selected. In Brazil, WGF were already in partnership with one of the only two or three networks with a rich experience in re-granting that were still in existence after the withdrawal of many foreign donors in the early 2000s.

Promising growth in numbers of projects supported, funds raised locally, and degree of self-sufficiency

AfC started in 2007 in Brazil with CESE, in 2008 in India with Smile Foundation, and in 2009 in South Africa with Soul City Institute, as the national partner organisations of WGF. In the second phase of programme, it was expanded to Kenya, with the Kenya Community Development Foundation (KCDF) as the national partner. One of the roles of these national partners was to grant-fund the projects of local CBOs and NGOs.

During the first phase of the programme (2006–09), the first three national partner organisations used different criteria to calculate the number of projects supported and the funds raised at the local level. In the second phase, covering 2011–15, this was remedied to consistent criteria. The methodological changes between the first and the second phase make it difficult to present figures that are comparable. Therefore, the statistics that follow are for the second phase only.

A yearly increasing number of CBO and NGO projects successfully raised funds locally

In the second phase of the programme, the national partner organisations approved a total of 903 local projects from local CBOs and NGOs that successfully raised funds at the local level. Only a handful of organisations, after receiving training and coaching, were not successful in raising their share of the necessary funds.

Table 1 shows the trend in the number of local CBO and NGO projects selected, trained, and coached by the national partner organisations that successfully raised their 50% share of funding.

The number of projects increased every year, except for 2015. The fact that the results for 2015 are lower than one would expect is a consequence of the principles underlying the Dutch government subsidy that made the programme possible. All funds had to be disbursed before the end of the year and could solely be allocated to activities that were finalised before year end. Experience showed that it takes time for CBOs and small local NGOs to raise funds after their proposal has been received and approved, and that it is not certain when exactly they will have reached their fundraising target. As a result, in order to avoid any risk of committing matching funds that could not be paid from the subsidy and therefore entering into commitments that could become a financial risk for themselves,

Table 1. Number of local projects, 2011–15.

Partner and country/year	2011	2012	2013	2014	2015	Total
CESE, Brazil	33	57	69	112	27	298
Smile Foundation, India	50	50	61	64	88	313
Soul City Institute, South Africa	20	45	57	51	83	256
KCDF, Kenya	0	4	11	10	11	36
Total number of local projects approved and disbursed	103	156	198	237	209	903

Table 2. Domestic funds raised locally and nationally for projects, 2011–15 (in €).

All four countries together	2011	2012	2013	2014	2015	Total
Results of local fundraising actions by CBOs and small NGOs	211,915	288,074	396,523	534,313	406,456	1,837,281
Matching funds raised at national level by national partner organisation	98,239	166,346	217,396	244,701	300,526	1,027,208
Local action + own contribution premium	310,154	454,420	613,919	779,014	706,982	2,864,489

CESE in Brazil decided not to approve any projects after June 2015, while KCDF in Kenya decided to consolidate the number of approved projects. This influenced the overall results for 2015.

Taking this into consideration, from Table 1 it becomes clear that organisations who started earlier are ahead of those who started later, although South Africa was a very strong runner up in the last year of the programme. The overall and steady increase in numbers indicates that there is potential for further growth.

An increasing amount of funds raised in country for local projects

Usually, CBOs and small NGOs, after training on local fundraising given by the national partner organisations, were able to raise half of the funds they needed for their projects. When they finished their fundraising activities, the national partner organisations provided the matching grant. In some cases, like for a limited number of projects in Brazil where another domestic donor became involved that insisted on contributing 60% to the overall costs of the local projects instead of 50%, the local contribution was less than 50%. In other cases, a national partner organisation put in more domestic funding of its own if a local organisation had good reasons for being unable to raise its full share. This happened in India, for instance. On the other hand, sometimes the results of a local fundraising action by CBOs were higher than expected. The surplus did not always receive matching funds as available funding was limited (see Table 2).

The lower results for 2015 can be explained by the same reasons as for Table 1. Aside from this, the number of projects supported, and the amount raised for projects at the local and at the national level, increased every year, more or less confirming what was anticipated at the planning stage. This could be taken as an indicator of the aim to contribute to improvements in the culture of local philanthropy. This, however, would be too simple a conclusion (see later section).

An increasing amount of funds raised in country for the functioning of the overall programme

In order to make the programme fully independent from foreign aid after 12 to 15 years, the national partner organisations were to contribute a gradually increasing share of their own implementation costs for the programme. These included, for instance, the salary costs of their staff, overheads, domestic travel, investments in their communications and marketing – needed to improve their own fundraising – and costs of training and coaching local CBOs and NGOs.

The growth rate for the contribution of the national partner organisations is comparable to the one that applies for the projects, although the take off started later. It is more difficult to raise funds for these types of interventions as potencional donors, be they middle-class individuals or companies, like elsewhere in world, prefer to donate to concrete projects and programmes. It takes time to gain their trust and to convince them to also donate to cover the costs that come with any development activity, and especially for a model that involves a large amount of capacity

Table 3. Contribution of national partner organisations towards programme costs, 2011–15 (in €).

	2011	2012	2013	2014	2015	Total
All countries	100,038	132,089	201,775	309,917	401,538	1,145,357

Table 4. Comparison of external financial inputs and domestic financial results, 2011–15 (in €).

External contributions	2011	2012	2013	2014	2015	Total
Total Dutch government subsidy spent in the four countries	701,897	653,748	811,714	876,490	512,907	3,556,756
WGF contribution	84,082	140,990	279,023	346,665	278,984	1,129,744
Total external inputs	785,979	794,738	1,090,737	1,223,155	791,891	4,686,500
As part of overall costs	66%	58%	57%	53%	42%	
Domestic contributions						
Local fundraising actions + matching funds national partner organisations (Table 3)	310,154	454,420	613,919	779,014	706,982	2,864,489
National partner organisations (Table 4)	100,038	132,089	201,775	309,917	401,538	1,145,357
Total domestic contributions	410,192	586,509	815,694	1,088,931	1,108,520	4,009,846
As part of overall costs	34%	42%	43%	47%	58%	

strengthening. The results in Table 3 indicate, however, that this is possible. Unlike for the local projects, the own contribution continued to grow in 2015. Here, there were no barriers caused by the subsidy rules.

Decreasing investments and growing returns

The data given in Tables 1 to 3 need to be compared with the investments made, in order to see whether the premises of the programme are correct (Table 4).

The assumption that the subsidy would gradually decrease was, in absolute terms, at first counteracted by the growth of the subsidy in the first four years. This was caused by the fact that some of the national partner organisations had difficulties designing suitable fundraising activities and thus postponed investing the money that was available. However, the amount of domestic funds raised grew continuously and the percentage of the Dutch government subsidy plus the contribution of Wilde Ganzen decreased every year as domestic contributions and the percentage of overall costs they covered consistently grew. In 2015, the results of domestic fundraising exceeded external financial inputs for the first time, and by quite a substantial amount.

In 2011, foreign contributions were still almost twice as much as the funds raised domestically in the four countries. In 2015, external financial inputs covered only 42% of the overall cost of the local projects supported and the programme's running costs. It is safe to presume that if the programme had continued as planned, from 2016 increasingly more money would have been raised domestically in these four countries, and the return on investment on the decreasing subsidy given would have rapidly grown. Unfortunately, the span of commitment of most institutional donors is much shorter than 12 to 15 years. Based on the above, WGF decided to continue the programme with private funding of its own, although at a smaller scale.

Challenges encountered

There were many challenges that had to be overcome in the course of the nine years of the programme. Some challenges were common to all four countries, while others were more country specific.

The time needed to achieve full self-sufficiency

The main common challenge was that in 2006, when the subsidy request was submitted to the Dutch Ministry of Foreign Affairs for the first phase of AfC (2007–10), no one knew how much time it would take to make a programme like this self-sufficient. There were a few estimates, like the minimum and maximum amounts a local organisation with little to no experience of local fundraising could raise, after training, within a time span of six months; and the growth in fundraising a national partner organisation could achieve at the national level if certain investments in its fundraising capacity were made. Based on these assumptions, it was estimated that 10 to 12 years would be sufficient to make the programme fully independent from foreign aid, and that after this period domestic fundraising would continue to grow.

This proved to be overly optimistic: in the first four years, most partner organisations consistently lagged behind the targets set. Based on the experiences from the first phase, in the application for the second phase of the project, the estimated period needed to achieve full self-sufficiency was adjusted to 12 to 15 years: 12 for Smile Foundation in India, 15 for CESE in Brazil and Soul City Institute in South Africa, and somewhere between 12 and 15 for KCDF in Kenya.

In 2012, after five years' participation in AfC, Simile Foundation had reached the breakeven point where the funds raised domestically at least equalled the external contributions. This is an indication that the adjusted estimated periods may be correct (Frerks et al. 2014, 11). So too is the fact that targets were far more consistently reached in the second phase than in the first. This was achieved with the aid of more peer-to-peer learning between national partner organisations; taking a more flexible approach as to the exact percentage of local funding achieved – not always precisely 50%; and the growing experience of the national partner organisations on how to raise the necessary funds for their own contribution at the national level, and closer monitoring of local fundraising actions of CBOs and NGOs.

Internal resistance and child-related projects

Results sometimes lagged behind because of the nature and philosophy of the selected partner organisation. In Brazil, for instance, CESE as a human rights organisation had done a great job on nationwide advocacy programmes and on funding and building the capacity of small local projects concerning the rights of women, the landless, indigenous people, and the black community. However, it had rarely previously worked on children's issues. Nevertheless, WGF selected it as its national partner organisation because it knew CESE from previous work, and CESE was one of the only two or three national NGOs in Brazil still working with delegated funds for small projects.

Through AfC CESE became part of a programme that concentrated on child-related projects, as WGF assumed that in countries were local philanthropy was only nascent, individual donors could probably be more easily persuaded to donate if their donation was for children. Within CESE, there was strong internal resistance to what several staff considered to be a "donor-driven" move. It took years, two additional visits by WGF, and exposure visits to the other national partner organisations, for the organisation to overcome this internal resistance. It would be interesting to do further research on to what extent CESE's legitimacy has been affected by the tension between adjusting to WGF's requirements as a donor and remaining true to its original cause, in terms of how it is perceived by other actors in its context and especially by its constituency.

In the second phase of the programme (2010–15), the focus on children's projects was dropped, but by then the national partner organisations had already embraced the approach. According to the 2014 evaluation, the focus on fundraising for child-related development projects was in itself useful, especially in South Africa and India, but was almost secondary to the issue of transition from a situation where development activities were funded by external donors to one in which external donors have withdrawn. What was also more important was that the national partner organisations learnt how to assist local civil society cope with this transition: "Other sectoral areas (water, health, small business support, social research) would or could also have gained from the introduction of a similar alternative resourcing strategy" (Pratt 2014, 4).

Limited experience with one or more of the fields of expertise required

National partner organisations for a programme like AfC ideally need to be experts in delegated project funding and everything that this entails, like attracting applications, project selection, PME, and so on; capacity strengthening of local CBOs and small NGOs; advocacy; communication and PR, including the media; and local fundraising with different types of donors (corporate, middle-class individuals, local government). None of the organisations WGF selected were able to fit all criteria equally well, and this led to country specific hurdles. Where a national partner had some previous experience it was easier for them to engage with the AfC model. KCDF and Smile, for example, already had experience in local fundraising. CESE had a great deal of experience in grant management, but little experience in local fundraising. Both of these skills were relatively new for Soul City. Staff and managers had to learn new skills in communication, marketing, and branding. The partner organisations had to learn how to use a different set of networking styles and how to run fundraising events. They had to start dealing with celebrities, the press, and local and national businesses. This took time and resources, and the development of an understanding and commitment to work in a new and different way (Pratt 2014, 5).

The AfC programme invested in exchange visits between the national partners, to allow for peer-to-peer learning: those excelling in project funding advising those with less experience in this, while those excelling in marketing and fundraising advised those with little experience in this domain. In addition, partners were given funds to attract experienced staff, hire consultants, invest in training of staff, and participate in national and international congresses. This helped organisations to improve their performance, but in some cases it took time. If WGF were to expand AfC to new countries, the selection process should pay more attention to the various forms of expertise a partner organisation needs. Investing more money in the start-up phase to address identified weaknesses would seem wise.

Fundraising in remote areas versus fundraising at the national level

There is evidence that fundraising is more difficult in remote areas, but that even there, resources can be mobilised. KCDF in Kenya discovered that, in the absence of a local middle class and local businesses, in isolated rural areas the model of local fundraising can be very difficult. Soul City in South Africa saw marked differences between the successes of schools in urban areas compared to those in isolated rural areas. Yet, as the evaluation says: *"The programme has shown that even in relatively poor areas resources do exist and can be obtained for local initiatives"* (Pratt 2014, 4). Fundraising in poorer areas needs more time and thus it takes longer before the projects can start. In such areas one could explore if quicker results could be obtained if contributions in kind were matched with grants in cash. Partner organisations continued to press for this, but WGF felt it would be too much of a challenge to measure results achieved in an objective way. Looking back, it would have been good to experiment.

The greatest difficulty, or better, challenge, according to all three evaluations that took place in 2014, lies in mobilising funds from the national middle class. In societies where most of the funding for poverty alleviation used to come from abroad, the perceived need to donate was low. In all four countries fundraising at the local level was more successful than the attempts to mobilise resources for the national partners themselves. KCDF in Kenya and Smile Foundation in India have had more success in this field than the partner organisations in Brazil and South Africa. There is no doubt that this should be attributed to their greater experience with marketing and fundraising. But *"even where fundraising targets were not achieved there has on the whole been slow steady progress over the period reviewed"* (Pratt 2014, 4).

Conclusion: prospects and potential for long-term sustainability

Back in 2010, the Free University Amsterdam concluded in an evaluation on the period 2007–09 that the AfC project had the potential to function as an inspiring example for future international development projects, which could be replicated elsewhere by others. Better linkages with national and state government agencies could make it reach an even larger target group and achieve many more results (Schuyt et al. 2010, ii). Four years later, INTRAC concluded that the AfC programme has provided an important alternative answer to the question of how to help NGOs/CSOs transition from a dependence on external funds to a sustainable future based on local resource mobilisation. In four very different countries it has *"carved out an interesting and valuable alternative model using co-funding to develop several different levels of domestic action for civil society"* (Pratt 2014, 4–5).

The success of the programme goes beyond local fundraising. The film "I am Kalam", for example, that addresses the wish of a child to access education and was produced by Smile Foundation in India, with the voluntary participation of popular Bollywood producers and actors, was partly funded with a small seed money contribution from AfC. In 2012 and 2013 the film won many awards, both within India and at renowned international film festivals. It is a good example of how the right to education can be promoted through non-conventional means. It also contributed greatly to the brand awareness by companies in India, who started to see Smile as a highly professional development organisation worth being associated with.

From a more political perspective, a programme like AfC can also pay off. In May 2014, national partner organisation CESE received an award from the federal government of Brazil and UNDP for the contribution of AfC to the realisation of the Millennium Development Goals in Brazil. When receiving the award from President Dilma Rousseff, CESE's head of projects and training, Dimas Galvao, used the opportunity to lobby for the introduction of a regulatory framework drafted by Brazilian NGOs to regulate cooperation between state and civil society: an issue already discussed in the early stages of AfC and on which CESE had become one of a select number of NGOs that led the lobby campaign. That same day, the President tweeted that she backed the framework, and a few months later she signed it.

Both the statistics and the more qualitative data indicate that the methodology developed can be a useful tool for enhancing local resource mobilisation and increasing the legitimacy of civil society organisations. It requires a rather limited amount of extra funding and some more years to continue the exercise to its end: a fully independent, 100% locally funded mechanism to raise funds both at the local and the national level in low- and middle-income countries. However, expanding the model to other countries is a far bigger challenge: even with the experience gained, WGF feels it would cost around a million euros per country to repeat the programme in a series of other countries where it could be successful. Such funding is not readily available, unless a major donor decides to become involved.

If funds for a further expansion were available, there is still the challenge of involving the middle class better, stimulating it to donate to pro-poor poverty alleviation and human rights projects. This was the area where AfC was least successful. There are political and cultural barriers to overcome, and understanding these better might require more academic research. There are also practical obstacles to overcome, such as an absence of laws and regulations that help create an enabling environment for donating, such as tax exemptions. Successfully inviting middle-class individuals to donate or to donate more perhaps also requires more training in the different fundraising techniques that exist worldwide than AfC was able to provide.

Ten years after the start of the AfC programme, it is becoming ever more evident that civil society organisations not only need to improve their financial sustainability, but must also increase their legitimacy. Many governments tend to restrict space for civil society and make it more difficult for civil society groups to receive foreign funding. Strong local organisations are needed that work on the basis of local priorities, can prove that they have the backing of a large number of volunteers and members, receive a good number of individual and corporate donations, are independent from foreign donors, both financially and in terms of choosing their own priorities, and are well-equipped to hold duty-bearers responsible for what they are supposed to deliver.

These broader needs led WGF and its national partner organisations to develop the Change the Game Academy (CtGA). CtGA is both a supplement to, and an alternative for, AfC. It is based on the lessons learnt, and the good practices and training content and methodologies developed under AfC in the areas of domestic resource mobilisation and advocacy. CtGA offers a powerful cocktail of: feeding the results of research into national legislation and regulations; organising face-to-face training workshops; offering e-learning courses, modules, and toolkits on organisational capacity, local fundraising, and lobby and advocacy; building databases with successful examples; sharing an annotated library with relevant publications; and, in the near future, offering communities for discussions, sharing, and learning.

Therefore, any organisation in low- and middle-income countries can benefit from the results of the investments in AfC made by the Dutch government, the individual donors of Wilde Ganzen, the national partner organisations (CESE, KCDF, Smile Foundation, and Soul City Institute) and their donors, and the efforts of those local CBOs and NGOs who participated and contributed their lessons learnt. The platform has been open since 26 January 2016 and is accessible to anybody in the world who would like to learn about local fundraising, and lobby and advocacy. It is available at www.changethegameacademy.org

Note

1. These considerations can be found in an international e-learning tool developed by WGF: www. changethegameacademy.org/about/about-raising-funds.

Disclosure statement

No potential conflict of interest was reported by the author.

References

Advisory Council on International Affairs. 2012. "Unequal Worlds. Poverty, Growth, Inequality and the Role of International Cooperation." Report No. 80. The Hague: Advisory Council on International Affairs.
Charities Aid Foundation. 2015. "World Giving Index 2015." Accessed March 5, 2016. www.cafonline.org/about-us/publications/2015-publications/world-giving-index-2015.
Frerks, G., et al. 2014. "Endline Report MFS II Joint Evaluations, 2014."
Hodenfield, T., and C-M. Pegus. 2013. *Global Trends on Civil Society Restrictions. Mounting Restrictions on Civil Society: The Gap between Rhetoric and Reality*. Johannesburg: CIVICUS.
OECD. 2014. "DAC list of ODA Recipients 2014." Accessed March 5, 2016. www.oecd.org/dac/stats/documentupload/DAC%20List%20of%20ODA%20Recipients%202014%20final.pdf.
Pratt, B. 2014. *Overview Report for Action for Children*. Oxford: INTRAC.
Schuyt, Th. N. M., et al. 2010. *Evaluation Action for Children Program 2007–2010. Promoting National Fundraising for (Child) Poverty Alleviation and Child Rights*. Amsterdam: Vrije Universiteit.

Gender, diversity, and sustainable civil society strengthening: lessons from Ethiopia

Elsa L. Dawson

ABSTRACT

This practical note explores how an awareness of gender and diversity issues can enable work in strengthening civil society to achieve lasting impact on the lives of women and men living in poverty. Understanding that people are poor because of their gender or diversity identity enables CSOs to be relevant. If work to strengthen civil society is to contribute to long-term social inclusion and greater social justice and equality, it must start from an analysis of who is excluded and why; here gender and diversity contextual analysis is indispensable, as is action on how civil society initiatives can help to level the playing field.

Cette note pratique examine la manière dont une prise de conscience des questions de genre et de diversité peut permettre un travail de renforcement de la société civile afin d'avoir un impact durable sur la vie des femmes et des hommes en situation de pauvreté. Si elles comprennent que les gens sont pauvres en raison de leur sexe ou de leur identité dans le contexte de la diversité, les OSC peuvent être pertinentes. Si l'on veut que le travail de renforcement de la société civile contribue à l'inclusion sociale à long terme et à une justice et une égalité sociales accrues, il faut commencer par mener une analyse des personnes qui sont exclues et des raisons de cet état de fait ; ici, l'analyse contextuelle du genre et de la diversité est indispensable, à l'instar de l'action sur la manière dont les initiatives de la société civile peuvent contribuer à uniformiser les règles du jeu.

La presente nota práctica examina el grado en que el conocimiento sobre cuestiones de género y diversidad puede facilitar el trabajo orientado a fortalecer a la sociedad civil, de manera de lograr un impacto duradero en la vida de las mujeres y los hombres empobrecidos. Comprender que la gente está empobrecida debido a su identidad, basada en su género o su diversidad, permite que el trabajo de las OSC se adecúe a estas circunstancias. Si el trabajo destinado a fortalecer a la sociedad civil se encamina a lograr la inclusión social a largo plazo y a alcanzar mayor justicia social e igualdad, debe comenzar determinando quién está excluido y por qué lo está; en este empeño, resulta indispensable realizar un análisis contextual sobre género y diversidad, así como sobre la forma en que las iniciativas de la sociedad civil pueden establecer condiciones de igualdad.

Introduction

Gender and diversity sensitivity is indispensable to achieving sustainability in civil society strengthening, if sustainability is understood to include a concern for the equal distribution of resources. An awareness of gender and diversity issues and equality enables work on strengthening civil society to achieve in-depth and lasting impact on the lives of women and men living in poverty, and especially the poorest of the poor. Understanding that people are poor because of their gender or diversity identity enables civil society organisations (CSOs) to be relevant to those who most need their support.

If work to strengthen civil society is to contribute to long-term social inclusion and greater social justice and equality, it must start from an analysis of who is excluded and why. This is where gender and diversity contextual analysis is of fundamental importance, as is action based on addressing how and which civil society initiatives can help level the playing field and include the excluded. What kind of civil society initiatives will be prioritised is the crucial question. CSOs effectively supporting the interests of given identity groups play a crucial part in gaining greater social equality. What this might mean in practice is demonstrated by examples from the Civil Society Support Programme (CSSP) in Ethiopia, currently managed by a consortium including INTRAC on behalf of a pool of donors.

The author was asked to support the designers of CSSP with ways of mainstreaming gender and social diversity. The success of the strategy followed is most notable in the Tigray programme. Organisations focusing on support for groups marginalised on the basis of their identity are likely to have less capacity and resources. Given this, how can their sustainability both in terms of their own organisation and their work best be supported? The Tigray cases included below show ways in which this has successfully been done.

Sustainability and civil society

This practical note will look at five different dimensions of sustainable civil society development identified by INTRAC (2014) and how each relates to gender and diversity in terms of the capacity of CSOs:

(1) Clarity of purpose, mission, vision, and values.
(2) Internal capacity for programme and financial management.
(3) Funding models.
(4) Legitimacy and accountability.
(5) Institutional and legislative aspects.

Consideration should be given to how each of these dimensions relates to the achievement of substantive equality for all, especially the first dimension. Purpose, mission, vision, and values could all contain explicit statements regarding the centrality of social equality to the essential motivation of a given CSO. Capacity in terms of staff skills and experience, information, and understanding, are all essential in terms of the contextual situation with regard to differing social groups, their needs and aspirations, and how these can best be addressed. More support with financial management may be required by incipient organisations emerging to support such groups in achieving greater equality and social justice. The funding models they require may also be different according to their context and the resources available for their activities, which are likely to be restricted. They may be in the early stages of developing clear legitimacy among their proposed constituents and effective systems of accountability. Finally, their insertion in institutional and legislative frameworks may be particularly hampered by discriminatory attitudes embedded in a given society, and therefore carefully targeted support may be needed in terms of policy influence at a wider level.

The question of whether CSOs and their interventions are sustainable or not, should be viewed in terms of their ability to work towards and create substantive equality. Whereas equality itself is now enshrined in the legislation of most countries in the world, and has been given new prominence in the Sustainable Development Goals (SDGs), the reality lived by millions remains untouched by such principles. What is now required is the achievement of substantive equality, where such legislation is realised in practice. UN Women's latest report defines substantive equality as being:

"concerned with the results and outcomes of (laws and policies that treat women equally), ensuring that they do not maintain, but rather alleviate, the inherent disadvantage that particular groups experience. Achieving substantive equality is broken down into three areas: redressing women's socio-economic disadvantage; addressing stereotyping, stigma and violence; and strengthening women's agency, voice and participation." (UN Women 2015, 12–13)

The principle of social justice requires that substantive equality forms an essential part of what constitutes the sustainability of development interventions aimed at the eradication of poverty.

The civil society support programme in Ethiopia

This programme provides examples which show how these concepts can be translated into practical action on behalf of vulnerable groups. It is funded by a consortium of Canada, Danida, DFID, the Dutch Ministry of Foreign Affairs, Irish Aid, NORAD, and SIDA. The goal is to support CSOs and associations or membership organisations representing potential beneficiaries by providing grants and capacity building to contribute to reducing the poverty of people who are "hard to reach". At the author's suggestion, it was decided that what might make people "hard to reach" was not just the geographic remoteness or inaccessibility of their homes, but also their gender and/or other forms of diverse identity. Gender and social inclusion were seamlessly integrated into the heart of the guiding focus of this programme. This gender equality and social inclusion approach contributed crucially to the likely sustainability (in the sense proposed by this note) of the interventions funded, and of the agencies responsible for implementing the interventions.

The region where this approach seemed to have been carried out most effectively was Tigray Regional State, where nearly every funded project addressed a crucial issue related to the gender or diversity based exclusion of the target beneficiaries, leading to the likelihood of significant change in the lives of the poorest. This region was the subject of a results review covering the whole programme, and most of the information below regarding the CSSP is taken from this (Kassa, Kelkilachew, and Hailu 2015). The review was based on extensive consultations with key stakeholders, including project implementing partners and project target groups, who provide convincing evidence of likely future impact.

According to the review, all the projects in the Tigray region represented innovative ways of tackling important issues relating to aspects of poverty, gender and diversity, and the intersection between them, using minimal funding. They took on issues related to such extreme cases of hardship as people living with leprosy, disabled children lacking any form of education, and girls dropping out of school owing to being unable to relieve themselves during school hours. Many represented practical ways of ensuring that future power relations would be less unequal, and already demonstrate signs of future impact. However, gender equality within the staff of the partners lags behind, showing there is still work to be done in terms of gendered power relations.

Kassa provided many examples of early signs of impact, four of which are described below.

The women's association of Tigray

A WAT project funded in Adi Daero resulted in communities becoming more aware that violence against women and girls was unjust, and that power relationships between women and men should be balanced and beneficial to both. Practical approaches served to reduce violence against women and girls through an understanding that silence perpetuated the problem, and of the link between violence and the spread of HIV/AIDS. The Kebelle where this project was carried out has seen a reduction in early marriage, the abduction of girls, and FGM. The project has achieved local community commitment to more balanced power relations between women and men, the achievement of which is key to sustainable impact in terms of greater gender equality. The work has already led to an increase in women seeking legal aid services and confidently presenting claims in the social court, and this has contributed to enhanced governance, justice, and improved protection mechanisms.

Ethiopian legislation restricts NGOs from directly addressing women's rights, so this project used the SASA! method (a community mobilisation methodology developed by the organisation Raising Voices in Uganda), to address power relations through the empowerment of the community organisation around issues of violence against women and girls. Sixty local activists trained and worked with 1,000 women.

The women involved have also undertaken initiatives to strengthen their economic situation by engaging in local microfinance systems called "lqub", where members contribute a monthly amount, and by starting sheep breeding and petty trading with this money.[1] Such economic empowerment, which the reviewers felt could have been stronger, could potentially enable women to have more equal power relationships with men in the future.

These activities have been enthusiastically supported by local Woreda government offices, which see the project as exemplary in tackling a known problem in a more effective way. A Woreda Steering Committee has been established and is helping coordinate and oversee implementation. People from neighbouring communities are requesting that the Woreda launch similar programmes for their benefit.

Kunama girls' education

The dropout rate of girl students from the Kunama hunter gatherer people was reduced by 10.12% in a school by the work of Operation Rescue Ethiopia (ORE). Dedicated female toilets were constructed at the opposite side of the school from ones used by male students, which meant girls did not have to go home during the school day if they needed to use the toilet. Considerable changes in awareness have already been achieved among the Kunama, for whom it had been seen as shameful for girls to be seen by men so much as entering a latrine, or even in locations where people might assume they were going to relieve themselves.

However, the service is not yet complete due to the lack of water, which if not provided will constitute a serious limitation on sustainability. It was also noted that there was limited participation of the Kunama community owing to their geographical locations. This points to another serious challenge to working on sustainable change for the hardest to reach and most unequal – how to ensure their active participation in conceptualising, managing, and reviewing the results of an intervention.

Income generation for people living with leprosy

The work of the Tigray Branch of the Ethiopian National Association of People Affected by Leprosy (ENAPAL) has enabled 150 people affected by leprosy to become economically self-reliant and to support their children. Six income-generation schemes are currently operational in irrigation, poultry, weaving, dairy production, and beekeeping. Their products are now purchased by people outside their group, unlikely to have happened previously especially in the case of food, due to cultural beliefs. The psychological and social impact on members, who previously faced a lifetime of begging as social outcasts, has been significant.

Their initiatives are now supported by government resources, adding to their likely sustainability. The dairy production group received a 250-square metre piece of land on which to construct a shade. The communities living nearby have realised that people affected by leprosy can work and be productive with appropriate support.

Enabling centre for the blind

Students at the centre were empowered thanks to computer training using JAWS software, braille literacy, and mobility orientation, provided by ORE. The centre is equipped with computers with the software and a braille printer, and each student has a voice recorder. The most important change achieved was the psychological impact on students, whose confidence and self-esteem was significantly enhanced. The project demonstrated that these students were equally as capable as those without visual impairments as long as they had the right equipment.

The reliance on sophisticated equipment is a risk in terms of sustainability, although the impact on the lives of these students in particular cannot be denied. The CSSP reviewers felt that regional education, labour, and social affairs bureaus should be able to ensure that at least the equipment in this centre will be maintained. The Bureau of Education had already bought 70 computers with JAWS software and distributed 60 to schools attended by students with visual impairments, so the government is increasing the sustainability of this work. It is also training visually impaired teachers in the use of JAWS software, and working on accessibility in schools by stipulating that new schools must have ramps and accessible toilet facilities.

Gender, diversity, and the five dimensions of sustainability

The CSSP promoted the capacity of their partners in terms of the key attributes they require for sustainability, both of their work and themselves as organisations. This section examines how the five dimensions of sustainability outlined above were handled in relation to gender and diversity by the two tiers of CSOs the CSSP partnered: community based membership associations, and implementing agencies or CSOs.

Clarity of purpose, mission, vision, and values

If CSOs and community based associations working to support those who are excluded are to survive in the long term, it is essential that they are formally committed to achieving sustainable impact in terms of poverty reduction and equality. As explained above, this needs to be clearly articulated both in written public statements of purpose, mission, vision, and/or values and within the discourse of their leaders and staff. To work effectively on inequalities based on gender and diversity based exclusion, this aim must be conceptually integrated into these statements. Staff rarely pay attention to a separate gender or diversity strategy.

An effective way of developing such conceptual clarity is to invite groups of staff to draw visual images of their visions of what their organisation's purpose or mission is. The ideas resulting from such an exercise often produce inspiring results which would have been unlikely to emerge from a purely verbal discussion, as it helps participants to draw on the creative and emotive side of their brains.

By funding their work, CSSP has empowered partner organisations responsible for achievements such as those described above to develop their purpose and mission to make lasting changes in the lives of their members and target beneficiaries. ORE, for example, had previously only worked on the issue of orphan children, but thanks to CSSP support now designs and delivers projects targeting women, men, girls and boys, and those living with disability.

Internal capacity for project and financial management

While the ability to effectively design and manage projects is essential to an organisation's ability to create lasting impact in the lives of members or beneficiaries, integrating a concern for gender and diversity issues into the way it manages the project cycle will system with a strong focus on people centred design, enable it to ensure that the needs of excluded groups are addressed.

CSSP partners received training in participatory project cycle management which was widely seen to have enhanced their abilities to produce proposals for gaining new funding. It enabled partners to develop the skills of designing participatory projects targeting urgent issues faced by hard-to-reach people through community based approaches. A number of partners developed new manuals and systems for project design and delivery, and carried out baseline studies to identify the top priority needs of hard-to-reach people. CSSP provided seed funds for carrying out these studies. This was a crucial contribution as the contextual analysis stage enables a project to be firmly based in real data regarding the actual felt needs of differing identity groups, and is frequently omitted through lack of available funds prior to the approval of a project. Moreover, the fact it was done was seen by reviewers as having led to the enthusiastic involvement of beneficiaries in participating in the project (Kassa, Kelkilachew, and Hailu 2015, 40).

CSSP partner organisations identified simple ways to make a difference to the lives of severely marginalised groups that were easily replicable. The reviewers (Kassa, Kelkilachew, and Hailu 2015) found the capacity building component of CSSP to be its most successful aspect as almost all partners attributed their improved situation and even survival to CSSP support. ORE, for example, now actively involves its stakeholders (partner organisations, target groups, and government officers) throughout the cycle from project conceptualisation through to monitoring and evaluation. However, generally the reviewers felt that the involvement of beneficiaries in monitoring and evaluation was insufficient.

The CSSP also provided training in financial management, enabling partners such as ORE to update their financial manuals and systems, and keep comprehensive financial records. However, this training could have been better contextualised to the project area and partners, and the financial reporting template could have been more user-friendly.

Funding models

As observed by Hailey (2014), the financial sustainability and longevity of a CSO depends on its ability to diversify its income and to access new funds. The more different sources of funds a CSO has, the more financially self-sufficient and sustainable it will be.

The training CSSP provided to CSOs enabled them to draw up more authentic and convincing proposals which in the future are likely to enable them to diversify their funding sources. CSSP partners have already started using the programme's inputs to design similar projects to win grants from other sources. Using CSSP's proposal writing template, ORE has won a grant for a project proposal targeting HTR issues from the Geneva Global Fund.

A crucial balance needs to be developed between restricted and unrestricted income in order for an organisation to survive in the long term (INTRAC 2014). Previously, ENAPAL had existed thanks to the minimal contributions of its members, so it had existing unrestricted funds when it became a CSSP partner and received a grant for its work in promoting income-generation activities for people living with leprosy. The capacity of such organisations to continue receiving membership contributions will be a crucial factor for their long-term survival.

The problem for organisations supporting gender and diversity issues is that their work tends to cost more per beneficiary, given the fact that they are usually harder to reach and to support. An example is the high level of investment per student which was required in the project for those with visual impairments. The CSOs in Tigray tend to base themselves in and around Mekelle (the regional capital), but implement projects in the remoter parts of the region. This too has cost implications. At the same time, their membership consists of those with fewest resources. They therefore require ongoing support by either government sources or international development funds to maintain their work on behalf of their clients, and so their survival depends crucially on the relationships they can build up with such sources of funds.

Legitimacy and accountability

Claims to benefit particular groups in society should be backed up with accountability mechanisms, including transparency, participation, learning, and for the handling of complaints in ways that enable an organisation to demonstrate not only how it relates to those from whom it receives support, but also importantly those whom it claims to support (Hammer 2014). These aspects are key when considering the effectiveness of a given organisation to support the interest of identity groups such as women, people living with disabilities, ethnic groups, and so on.

In Tigray, it is mandatory for a CSO to account to the target community. The CSSP results review team concluded that promoting the participation of the wider community had facilitated trust-based community relationships. They concluded that the CSSP had managed to develop a sense of ownership among partners and beneficiaries which aided accountability (Kassa, Kelkilachew, and Hailu 2015, 41).

The best example from CSSP's programme is the SASA! project described above, where violence against women was tackled by local women and men conducting awareness-raising in social events. Local activists were directly involved in training community members. Social fora such as church masses, Iqub, and weddings were successfully used to tackle problems of underage marriage and other forms of violence.

However, as noted above, the monitoring and evaluation of the CSSP projects lacked the active involvement of beneficiary groups, and some projects for children with disabilities were seriously criticised by the community as inadequate. This active involvement is crucial for accountability, and needs to be more than a mere consultative tick-box exercise. Feedback needs to be listened to and incorporated into future plans for projects and skill enhancement.

Institutional and legislative aspects

If CSOs are to survive in the long term they need to be firmly embedded in the institutional life of a given country. Thanks to the CSSP, the organisations it supported to work on gender and social inclusion received widespread government recognition for their ability to attend to previously overlooked issues amongst neglected population groups. Such CSOs have not only survived, but increased in number as a result of the programme. The Ethiopian Government has a recent history of not appreciating the potential contribution of CSOs, in 2009 implementing a law restricting their activities, the Charities and Societies Proclamation. The number of CSOs in the country declined after this law's introduction for a number of reasons, but thanks to the CSSP the CSOs working on hard-to-reach issues are both surviving and new ones emerging.

Combining the hard-to-reach concept with gender and social inclusion revealed important social issues the Ethiopian Government had lacked the capacity to tackle effectively, and the CSSP-supported work has provided them with low-cost ways of doing so. Greater trust has been built up with senior government officials, which is already leading to interventions aimed at making a significant difference to the lives of those suffering exclusion because of their gender, disability, ethnic group, leprosy, and so on. They also recognise that in Tigray, smaller CSOs working on overlooked issues related to these groups are now emerging, thanks to improved government CSO relations, and that the government has started to see them as potential partners. CSOs are participating in sector-based policy and legislative debates on issues of health, disability, and youth affairs. A draft guideline is awaiting approval to further institutionalise such joint engagements.

CSOs supported by CSSP are now receiving government support. For example, an agency working on mental health issues has received financial and material support from the Bureau of Labour and Social Affairs to implement a mental health project. The government is even replicating some of the above interventions. For example, a similar centre to the Enabling Centre for the Blind established by ORE with CSSP support is being set up in another town, Adigrat, and 70 new computers have been installed there. This centre may become a national training centre.

Conclusion

Time will tell how well both the work undertaken for those excluded on the basis of gender or diversity and the agencies involved in the CSSP survive in Tigray. However, the indications are at present that this is likely, thanks to the conceptual integration of gender and social inclusion with the hard-to-reach concept, particularly in terms of the contextual analysis underlying both the choice of grants and the activities promoted.

Considering its short time of existence (since 2011), CSSP partners performed well in terms of the aspects of sustainable civil society explored. The impact of the projects they implemented is likely to contribute in some way to the achievement of substantive equality for some of the most socially excluded groups in Ethiopia. This contribution will be more significant where they are being used to influence government policy or being replicated by the Government. The achievements described above may make some contribution to substantive equality in terms of:

- reduced violence against women and girls
- increased income levels for those living with leprosy
- improved education levels for women and girls from hunter gatherer groups, and students with visual impairment.

The experience demonstrates practical ways in which it is possible to integrate a concern for social justice, in terms of gender and diversity of different kinds, into civil society action, and that it is in this way that such action can actually reduce poverty for those who are least equal in any given society.

However, it has to be recognised that those who are most vulnerable are also the hardest to assist in sustainable ways. More resources per head of population are generally required, as are longer time periods to effect results. Moreover, these generally are the people who have the least time and energy to devote to participating actively in interventions to improve their lives; for example, disabled people generally suffer from worse health situations in addition to their disability. Those with the most serious impairments often lack a voice at all. It is therefore crucial that only those interventions which will meaningfully address their needs are funded and implemented, and that, wherever possible, continuous support is provided.

Finally, any support to excluded groups must address unequal power relations, without which substantive equality cannot be achieved. This work is necessarily complex, context specific, and likely to take many years, requiring radical changes in social attitudes and government political will to produce real impact on people's lives.

Note

1. Iqub is an indigenous savings and loans mechanism which operates throughout both urban and rural Ethiopia, and from the very poorest groups to the most wealthy.

Disclosure statement

No potential conflict of interest was reported by the author.

References

Hailey, J. 2014. "The Sustainable NGO: Why Resourcing Matters." In *Building Sustainability of Civil Society: Beyond Resourcing, Reflections from INTRAC Staff and Associates*. Oxford: INTRAC.

Hammer, M. 2014. "Legitimacy and Sustainability of CSOs." In *Building Sustainability of Civil Society: Beyond Resourcing, Reflections from INTRAC Staff and Associates*. Oxford: INTRAC.

INTRAC. 2014. *Building Sustainability of Civil Society: Beyond Resourcing: Reflections from INTRAC Staff and Associates*. Oxford: INTRAC.

Kassa, G., A. Kelkilachew, and A. Hailu. 2015. *CSSP 2015 Results Review, Field Visit Two: Tigray*. Addis Ababa.

UN Women. 2015. *Progress of the World's Women 2015–2016: Transforming Economies, Realizing Rights*. New York: UN Women.

The state of Arab philanthropy and the case for change

Naila Farouky

ABSTRACT

The Arab Foundations Forum (AFF) has spent the past two years studying the landscape in which the forum functions. AFF, as a membership-based network of philanthropic foundations based in and/or working in the Arab region, is uniquely positioned to canvass the region's donors, grant-makers, and civil society players, and to draw conclusions about the state of the region's philanthropic sector. The overarching conclusion presented in this viewpoint is that there are many challenges, but also ways in which we can help to mitigate these challenges over time. The article points to three key ways in which the philanthropic sector is being challenged.

L'*Arab Foundations Forum* (AFF) a passé les deux dernières années à étudier le paysage au sein duquel fonctionne le forum. L'AFF, en tant que réseau formé de membres de fondations philanthropiques basées et/ou travaillant dans la région arabe, occupe une position sans pareille pour sonder les bailleurs de fonds, entités d'octroi de subventions et acteurs de la société civile de la région, et pour tirer les conclusions de ces enquêtes quant à l'état du secteur philanthropique de la région. La conclusion globale présentée dans ce point de vue est qu'il y a de nombreux défis en présence, mais qu'il y a également des manières de contribuer à atténuer ces difficultés au fil du temps. Cet article indique les trois défis clés auxquel est confronté le secteur philanthropique.

Durante los últimos dos años, el Foro de Fundaciones Árabes (FFA) ha estado estudiando el ámbito en que se desenvuelve. El FFA, una red basada en la membresía de fundaciones filantrópicas, localizadas en —o trabajando en — la región árabe, se encuentra en condiciones excepcionales para sondear a los donantes, a las agencias financiadoras y a los integrantes de la sociedad civil de la región, lo que le permite llegar a conclusiones respecto a la situación en que se encuentra este sector en esa zona. A manera de conclusión general, el artículo establece que existen muchos retos, así como maneras para que, con el pasar del tiempo, se puedan mitigar los desafíos. Al respecto, el artículo examina tres maneras importantes en que el sector filantrópico está siendo desafiado.

Introduction

There was a watershed moment in 2011, across the Arab region, when hope dared to rise. Following on the heels of the "domino uprisings" that seemed to sweep across the region – Tunisia, Egypt, Bahrain, Libya, Syria, to name a few – there was perhaps but an inkling of that hope, but it was there nonetheless.

Not the obvious hope of new beginnings and fresh starts and an end to oppressive regimes and all of that. I'm referring more to the hope of what the consequences of all that could be: the hope that maybe, finally, there would be a paradigm shift that would allow for some of the decades-old bureaucracies to at least diminish a little, the hope that maybe some of the more draconian laws restricting the freedoms of civilians would be somewhat lifted and relieved, the hope that we may finally be a region – in all its vastness and diversity and the sheer richness of our resources – that is allowed to begin building societies that can flourish and reach a modicum of the potential they promise. It was a significant moment, to say the least. And now, five years later, we take stock of where that moment has led us.

At the Arab Foundations Forum (AFF), we have spent the past two years in purposeful study of the landscape in which our forum functions – specifically the landscape of philanthropy and the players within it. AFF, as a membership-based network of philanthropic foundations based in and/or working in the Arab region, is uniquely positioned to canvass the region's donors, grant-makers, and civil society players, and to draw conclusions about the state of the region's philanthropic sector. The overarching conclusion is that there are many challenges, but also there are ways in which we can help to mitigate these challenges over time.

For focus and brevity, we can point to three key ways in which the philanthropic sector is being challenged:

(1) The political environment is generally un-enabling for philanthropy to thrive in any significant way.
(2) The lack of accountability and transparency in the sector – in fact, the lack of any expectation of either – is an impediment to the potential impact (and the measurement thereof) this sector can have.
(3) The egregious lack of comprehensive data, even in the most basic sense, on the sector and on the deployment of philanthropic capital throughout the region is arguably catastrophic or, at the very least, of huge concern.

The big picture: where does Arab philanthropy currently stand? A SWOT analysis

One way to take stock and analyse the ecosystem of philanthropy in the Arab region is to apply the SWOT analysis approach – an examination of the strengths, weaknesses, opportunities, and threats facing the region and our philanthropy ecosystem. This is also useful in providing an overview of the many pieces that make up the whole of this ecosystem.

Strengths

- The recent geo-political transition across the Arab region means there is increased awareness of the possibility of and potential for further change, as well as the awareness of the potential power of civil society and philanthropy in contributing to effective change.
- A burgeoning "youth bulge" across the region means there is a current and future generation of "change-makers" to be harnessed. The youth population (under 25 years old) in the region is estimated to be about 50% of the region's approximately 380 million people – 190 million people who are poised to contribute to the region's economy and development.
- There is wealth across the region, both in fiscal terms and human resources, which means there is abundant capital to be deployed.
- There is a long-standing tradition of giving in the region, so there is an embedded culture of giving and the will to give towards social good and change.
- Increasingly, there is awareness and readiness by players in the sector to implement more cutting-edge, innovative ways of giving – be it crowd-funding, legacy philanthropy, impact investing, etc.
- A multi-million-dollar capital market of regional philanthropy offers an advantage in light of reduced regional government spending on civil society and social issues. It can help fill the gap and will allow private sector capital to be increasingly deployed for public good.

Weaknesses

- A lack of strategic planning that goes beyond five years and a lack of a forensic accounting of crises and deep-rooted examination of the issues that lead to crises mean that impact is thwarted, interventions are short term, mitigation of those challenges is obstructed, and overall sustainability is threatened.
- Although there is wealth across the region, that wealth is unevenly distributed which decreases the opportunities for collaboration and cooperation among Arab donors.
- An egregious lack of data, knowledge-sharing, and a will to collaborate grossly diminish the potential for lasting impact.
- A weak infrastructure – be it on the government level, or other support institutions (education, banking, etc.) – means there is a lack of support for the implementation of more cutting-edge and innovative means of philanthropic giving across borders.

Opportunities

- There is renewed interest among philanthropists in the region to explore new, global trends in giving – whether strategic philanthropy, venture philanthropy, impact investing, and so on – and this allows for the opportunity to engage philanthropists in a new way.
- Access to a more global and connected platform allows for ease in sharing information and knowledge, engaging a more global audience, and is particularly useful in engaging a younger, more cyber-engaged population across the region.
- Shared interest – both regionally and globally – in combating the current rise in radicalisation means there is an opportunity to collaborate and engage in innovative ways to provide alternatives to the Arab region's youth and to create more long-term, sustainable models of giving and impact.
- There is a small, but rapid, growth community around social enterprise that some actors the region are nurturing, embracing, and connecting to youth. The future of Arab philanthropy, given the size of the youth demographic, may not be in more foundations but instead may appear in the form of a youth population with a sense of social purpose and the ability to create their own businesses that are both financially viable and able to resolve a social challenge at scale.
- The advent of Arab foundations adopting more progressive and high-impact models than the traditional, simply "cheque writing" grant-making foundations means there is potential to catalyse the professionalisation of the sector and instigate a paradigm shift.

Threats

- The majority of the burgeoning youth bulge in the region is disenfranchised. This has manifested in an increased sense of frustration and further inclination towards radicalisation.
- Regional governments are unreliable and inconsistent in terms of the laws and policies that govern the sector, which means that the environment in unpredictable and doesn't allow for any meaningful long-term planning and strategic development.
- The growing restrictions in the region vis-à-vis the philanthropic sector have forced many international NGOs to close down and leave. This has left many local NGOs and implementing partners on the ground with unfinished and unfunded interventions that are necessary, but have been abandoned.
- Increasingly, there is growing mistrust among regional governments, as well as growing mistrust globally vis-à-vis the region, that has halted intra-regional giving, if not rendered much of it forbidden altogether.

- Without question, the continuing threat of war and general instability in the region – Syria, Yemen, Libya, Egypt, to name a few – poses seemingly insurmountable challenges to the philanthropic sector in at least two ways:
  - Development and aid funding are being continuously diverted from long-term and sustainable programmes and activities and are going towards emergency and humanitarian relief.
  - The constant state of instability and war make it difficult for any philanthropic and development funding to move with ease across borders.

The trifecta of obstacles

When we examine the philanthropy landscape from the vantage point of its strengths, weaknesses, opportunities, and threats, we may find that the picture is somewhat bleak and leaves much to be desired. While that may be the case in some areas, there are several reasons why that may be the case, as well as some reasons for hope and a more encouraging future to strive toward.

On the whole, much of Arab philanthropy is deeply rooted in a religious tradition of giving. Whether it is the Islamic model of charitable giving, *waqf* (loosely translated as endowment); *zakat* (alms or charitable giving, which is the third pillar in Islam and is obligatory for believers); *sadaqa* (benevolence and voluntary giving, which differs from Islam in that it is not obligatory); or the Coptic Christian *oshour* (non-obligatory giving to the Church of up to 10% of wages) and *bokour* (non-obligatory donation to the Church of one's first full month salary), a high proportion of giving in the region is motivated by religion. To that end, there is also a model of anonymity as regards the giving – the more anonymous the giving, the higher the value placed on that giving. Beyond God, there is little to incentivise the average citizen to give.

The general lack of a metrics for accountability and transparency across all sectors in the region has created a culture where no expectation of either exists. Some would argue that the concepts of accountability and transparency in the context of Arab philanthropy need to be reviewed through the lens of the region and culture, rather than imposing a taxonomy that is foreign and, therefore, inapplicable. Regardless, the fact remains that, to date, we have yet to define a metrics through which these values can be applied, and this means that in many ways Arab philanthropy has struggled to measure up against a global scale because it has remained opaque.

Adding to the obfuscation of accountability and transparency in the region is the lack of data on the sector. While there are a number of reputable and well-resourced institutions across the region with the capability to collect, aggregate, analyse, and share data, we have yet to find the model by which these institutions are funded and supported in a meaningful way.

Accountability and transparency: the case for creating an Arab taxonomy

It would not be an exaggeration to say there is a lack of accountability and transparency in the Arab region overall. For the purposes of this discussion, we will focus on the philanthropic sector. There tends to be an assumption, especially in today's geo-political climate, that Arab philanthropists and NGOs are opaque because they have something to hide. And this isn't necessarily an assumption that is only being made from outside of the region looking in – by most accounts, the degree of scrutiny which non-profit entities, grantors and grantees alike, are being subjected to is indicative of a level of mistrust aimed at this sector that is quite disturbing. It all leads to that assumption that "philanthropy and terrorism" are somehow linked. The truth is this is very far from the reality. In most cases, the reasons why the philanthropic sector in the Arab region does not practise accountability and transparency with any consistency can be explained by far less sinister reasons.

Namely, there are three key reasons: (1) there is no expectation for transparency and/or accountability at any official level (government or otherwise). Unless an organisation has a requirement for this in their own internal governance, there are no defined metrics by which accountability and transparency are defined; (2) there is no incentive – and, in fact, there are many disincentives – for nonprofit and philanthropic entities to be fully transparent in any official capacity; and (3) in many cases, for players in the sector – particularly if they are visible and well-regarded – it is safer to fund and invest in the spaces that are condoned by the government in question rather than risk the consequences of trying to invest in spaces that may be deemed "threatening" or undesirable by the regime.

When we consider the case for creating a more contextualised taxonomy for the values of accountability and transparency, it bears noting that the rejection of those concepts is not mutually exclusive to the rejection of their value – it only indicates a need to present them in a way that is more applicable to the region's context in which they will serve their function. Whatever metrics will be designed need to take into account the various environmental factors of the region – the institutions and government infrastructures that govern the policies of practice around giving, the incentives (or lack thereof) that giving is channelled within, and the paradigms through which giving is perceived.

It does bear noting, however, that in certain pockets throughout the region – the Gulf Cooperation Council (GCC) region (comprising Bahrain, Kuwait, Oman, Qatar, Saudi Arabia, and the United Arab Emirates), specifically – there is a move towards re-examining the parameters of accountability and transparency, and we are witnessing a slowly emerging trend in the acknowledgment of applying metrics to these values. In the rest of the region, many corporate foundations, as well as some of the larger entities – for example, PalTel and Welfare Association in Palestine, the Hani Qaddumi Scholarship Foundation in Jordan (serving Palestinian students), the Sawiris Foundation and the CIB Foundation in Egypt, to name a few – inasmuch as they are able, without confronting penalties, have a desire and a concerted effort to publish consistent annual reports and to be more transparent about finances than in the past. However, we have yet to see the kind of transparency and openness in the sector within the region where details concerning the distribution of finances are shared. For example, while annual reports may outline overall grant-making and programme support, we are hard-pressed to find an organisation that discloses its spending on overheads and direct operational costs. The gap in this information, while making it easier to estimate giving in the aggregate, does not reveal the full picture as it does not show how that giving compares to the overall spending of an organisation: in short, how much does it cost for a foundation to do what it does and give what it gives?

Data – the big black hole

In the most basic sense, there is no data-point in the region where one can find a comprehensive view of the sector. When we think of the data we need in order to be better informed, we think in terms of the "5 Ws and the H" – the *"who, what, where, when, why and how?"* of the sector. Who is doing what? Where are they doing it? When? Why are they doing it, and with whom? And, lastly, how are they doing it? While we have some access to that information, we certainly don't have the comprehensive picture. Our position is that, in order for the sector to be formalised and informed, we should be able to at least have the answers to the "5 Ws and the H".

The data are simply not available and haven't been collected in any coordinated way by regional entities. However, the data are being gathered by external, foreign entities and it is also being analysed and reported by non-regional players. This poses a threat to the region and here's why: when we don't own our own data, we also do not own the narrative. And, in turn we do not own nor can we tell our own story. But when these data are owned by someone else, *they* are the owners of the narrative, and the message and the results are skewed and biased – unintentionally in most cases, but the fact remains that the nuances, local contexts, and local views are ultimately not accurately represented and the results of that can be less than desirable, at the very minimum.

It is worth noting, however, that there are examples more recently of local, reputable, and very capable entities and institutions taking on the issue of data and examining it, as well as contributing to it, in an impactful and meaningful way. For instance, the John D. Gerhart Center for Philanthropy and Civic Engagement at the American University in Cairo has undertaken a multi-country, regional research scan of the philanthropy landscape in three countries (Saudi Arabia, Kuwait, and the United Arab Emirates). The final results of that research are expected to be available by the end of 2016 or beginning of 2017 and will add important data to locally sourced information and knowledge on the sector in the region *by* the sector in the region.

Similarly, the Sheikh Saud bin Saqr Al Qasimi Foundation in the UAE places great value on education and research, and serves as a bridge between the research and policy-making communities – bringing attention to the public policy issues that are important to Ras Al Khaima (an Emirate of the UAE) and, in turn, disseminating research findings in order to promote innovative policy tools and models that will impact positive social change and can be replicated across the region.

Another example of a regional entity leading the charge on the conversation around data and their values is the Emirates Foundation for Youth Development in Abu Dhabi. Emirates Foundation hosts an annual conference on youth and, for 2016, the theme of the conference will focus on big data, offering the opportunity for Arab regional foundations, academic institutions, and policymakers to convene around the issue and share information and knowledge that is likely to prove to be of immense value to the sector.

These are but a few examples of the trajectory of the region's recognition of the value inherent in sound and scientific research and data, but more emphasis needs to be placed on the overall value of long-term investment in these institutions and the purposeful funding and deployment of capital toward the sustainability of the regional entities that can deliver such research and data. In some cases, the focus of organisations and governments when collecting data has been more on quantitative rather than qualitative data. While the quantitative data are useful, they do not present a comprehensive view and therefore the narrative is half-complete.

One of the ways in which locally sourced data and knowledge can be more beneficial is for there to be less of a disconnect between the producers of the knowledge and those for whom and about whom the knowledge is produced. If we agree that data are not only useful in and of themselves, but that they also help towards producing a narrative that can be made accessible to the public beyond simply those who are "in the sector", then finding ways to address this disconnect will undoubtedly increase the chances for more sustainable and impactful outcomes for the philanthropic sector.

Government – where is our enabling environment?

In the 1990s, the trend in Western foreign policy was to support civil society organisations by way of providing significant foreign aid in an attempt to promote the gradual move toward democratic change across the Arab region. Some may argue that this was naïve, particularly when viewed from the vantage point of hindsight, when we know that democratic transitions have failed to materialise in the Arab region in any meaningful way (Langohr 2005; Yom 2005).

Over time, many regional observers have all but lost faith in civil society and its importance and potential impact. Fair or not, this has brought to bear certain outcomes that leave much to be desired in the way of progress. For one thing, it has allowed governments in the region to essentially marginalise civil society and, in some cases, to go so far as to criminalise it.

More recently, the processes for receiving foreign funds and making cross-border grants in the Arab region have become increasingly challenging, leaving many non-profit entities unable to find ways to navigate these obstacles in order to get down to the business of getting things done. Many Arab foundations, for instance, are set up with headquarters in the US or Europe, with branch (or, secondary) offices based in the region. But with the growing restrictions being placed by regional, as well as global, banks it is becoming more and more difficult to receive grant funding and to make grants – in some cases, even within the country itself.

There is a growing narrative that boils down to the assumption that "philanthropy leads to terrorism". Not only is this a dangerous premise to consider, it also has dire consequences for the region's civil society and philanthropy sectors, leaving them vulnerable and exposed to threats that are difficult to reign in.

An examination of the FATF (Financial Action Task Force) recommendations as they pertain to the non-profit sector is reason enough to pay close attention to this pervasive narrative and to develop ways to counter it. FATF is *"an inter-governmental body established in Paris in 1989 by the Group of 7 (G7). It seeks to combat money laundering, terrorist financing and other threats to the international financial system. It is both a policy-making and enforcement body."*

The Task Force was initially set up to tackle the issues of money laundering and misuse of financial institutions resulting from drug trafficking in the 1990s. Initially, FAFT laid out 40 detailed recommendations on ways to mitigate this threat. In the period post-9/11, an additional eight special recommendations were added and the FATF's mandate grew to include the fight against terrorist financing. Finally, in 2004, a ninth recommendation was added (The Non-Profit Platform on the FAFT n.d.a).

Among the 40 recommendations, the one that is the most worrisome for the non-profit, NGO, and foundation sector is Recommendation 8. It states that:

"Countries should review the adequacy of laws and regulations that relate to entities that can be abused for the financing of terrorism. Non-profit organizations are particularly vulnerable, and countries should ensure that they cannot be misused:
  (a) by terrorist organizations posing as legitimate entities;
  (b) to exploit legitimate entities as conduits for terrorist financing, including for the purpose of escaping asset-freezing measures; and
  (c) to conceal or obscure the clandestine diversion of funds intended for legitimate purposes to terrorist organizations." (The Non-Profit Platform on the FAFT n.d.b)

Essentially, Recommendation 8 and its Interpretative Note require countries to review the activities, size, and any other relevant features of the NGO and NPO sector within their purview, as well as the adequacy of applicable laws and regulations. It also requires countries to gather pertinent information from the NGO and NPO sectors by reaching out to them and to subsequently take appropriate action by instigating investigations where abuse is suspected.

More recently, 123 diverse NGOs, peace builders, and other donor organisations from 46 countries have signed a letter asking FATF to revise Recommendation 8 due to some of the negative consequences and impact the recommendation has had on the charitable and development sectors.

For one thing, there is no evidence that NGOs are particularly vulnerable to financial misuse compared to other sectors and very little evidence that points to actual misuse among the NGO sector worldwide of funds – for that reason alone, the stipulations of the recommendation need to be reviewed and clarified. For another, the argument is that Recommendation 8 *"misleads governments to apply heightened measures to the entire NPO [NGO] sector that result in over-regulation of the sector and various restrictions"* (Global NPO Coalition on FATF 2016).

The implications of such sweeping generalisations about the sector – and particularly with the complete lack of any credible evidence to support them – are many. The growing restrictions across the Arab region in making or receiving any amount of grant money are jarring and, in many cases, bring about insurmountable challenges that have caused the complete paralysis of some organisations. Ask any Arab philanthropic entity how they would rate their experience – particularly in the past two years – vis-à-vis their banking and financial transaction process, and you will hear a very familiar and oft-repeated lament. Furthermore, over-regulation of the sector means that progress for many activities and programme-based foundations is impeded, and often with negative consequences.

What is next for Arab philanthropy?

The Arab region is undeniably at a crossroads. There are winds of change across all aspects of the region's societies and, on the whole, this presents a unique opportunity for the philanthropic and civil society sectors to play a role in galvanising and advocating for change. In some cases, the more aggressive and confrontational changes will have to give way to subtler and more benign approaches to achieve systemic change, but this should not deter the sector from taking the initial steps towards implementing more short-term interventions with a view towards long-term paradigm shifts. It can be argued that for any real paradigm shift to occur, one must expect to be patient to the tune of two generations, or 50 years. That may seem like a cumbersome feat, but the reality is that no change occurs in a vacuum, nor does it occur overnight. The time is now, and what follows are some of the ways in which we can instigate that change.

We need to *professionalise* the sector by putting in place some of the best practices necessary for creating a standard by which we can be measured and held accountable. If this necessitates the creation of a more culturally contextualised metric of transparency and accountability that borrows from, but does not necessarily duplicate, a non-Arab taxonomy, then so be it, but it needs to be done. We also need to raise the standards of practice for the sector and find ways in which to attract the talent and resource of the region to the sector – the argument can be made that the more professional, resource rich, and formalised the sector is, the more attractive it is to those who can contribute to it.

Advocacy can be an immensely useful tool for making the case for change and the Arab region is in no shortage of causes to advocate for. As it pertains to the sector, we need to advocate for incentives that target the average citizen beyond the high net-worth individual and the corporate/private sector. Initiatives such as signing the letter petitioning FATF to revise Recommendation 8 in order to ease some of the more cumbersome restrictions on the laws and policies governing the sector are one way to do that. Collaborating with global entities on initiatives that address global issues on a government level, such as the OECD (Organization for Economic Cooperation and Development) or UN agencies prevalent in the field, and providing context for some of the advocacy initiatives is another mechanism to be leveraged and an effective way to advocate for change in a collective and visible way, and not addressing the challenges in isolation. At the Arab Foundations Forum, for example, we are always seeking ways in which we can bring forward the different conversations that need to be had around the issues that face our sector, but we attempt to always remain mindful of the context in which we have those discussions. We've found that by creating the space for the players in the sector to convene and discuss the pressing and pertinent issues offers the opportunity for the collective to worry less about being perceived as dissenting or as the "lone voice," and more as unified and cohesive about their concerns and recommended approaches for change.

Understanding and appreciating the value of sound *research and data*, investing in the institutions that can provide that data and research, and investing in an approach that allows for a more forensic accounting of our region's challenges, will go a long way in providing a better documented, and therefore accountable, sector. This approach will lend credibility to the sector and will allow it to measure its impact and sustainability against a framework that is more global, ultimately garnering a level of respect and gravitas for the sector in the region and beyond.

Finally, and this cannot be stressed more urgently, an engagement of the region's most precious and abundant resource – its *youth* – is possibly the single most effective way in which Arab philanthropy and civil society can effect long-term change. We need to introduce policies and programmes that help encourage entrepreneurship in the social impact sphere and facilitate the process by which the region's youth can participate in this space.

At the Arab Foundations Forum we have acknowledged this opportunity and the riches it can bestow on the region and, to that end, we are partnering with a number of our youth-focused member foundations, in collaboration with the OECD's Net Forward Accelerating Impact 2030 (AI2030) campaign, to create a coalition that will address the issues of youth engagement and the creation of substantive opportunities for the region's youth with a view towards long-term impact and contribution to the sector.

The initiative, which consists of a platform where foundations and other development actors can learn, dialogue, and take action together, will enable foundations to engage together in order to achieve mutual development objectives faster and with greater impact, while helping them make resource allocation decisions into key areas that are critical to meet the Sustainable Development Goals (SDGs). The initiative is based on three key pillars, knowledge, dialogue, and partnerships, and seeks to complement existing advocacy and data-gathering efforts by creating bridges between different sets of development actors and allowing them to learn, dialogue, and implement innovative partnerships that are based on enhanced impact at scale (netFWD 2015).

Ultimately, it is the congruence of all these interventions that will help pave the way toward a more systemic shift in the ecosystem of philanthropy and civil society. With a more purposeful approach to the mitigation of our region's challenges, and particularly as they pertain to the sector, we are likely to find points and flashes of hope and success springing up along the way. The hope is that we will begin to lay the foundation for a more cohesive, informed, impactful, and sustainable sector – one that will not only aspire to effect significant change, but will achieve it.

References

Global NPO Coalition on FAFT. 2016. "Global NPO Coalition on FATF calls for revision of the FATF Recommendation 8." Accessed May 1, 2016. http://fatfplatform.org/wp-content/uploads/2016/01/Global_NPO_Coalition_on_FATF_evision_R8_letter_15012016-002.pdf.

Langohr, V. 2005. "Too Much Civil Society, Too Little Politics?" In *Authoritarianism in the Middle East*, edited by M. Pripstein Posusney, and M. Penner Angrist, 193–220. Boulder: Lynne Rienner.

netFWD. 2015. "Accelerating Impact 2030." Accessed May 1, 2016. www.oecd.org/site/netfwd/acceleratingimpact2030.htm.

The Non-Profit Platform on the FAFT. n.d.a. "What is the FAFT?" Accessed May 1, 2016. http://fatfplatform.org/what-is-the-fatf/.

The Non-Profit Platform on the FAFT. n.d.b. "Recommendation 8." Accessed May 1, 2016. http://fatfplatform.org/recommendation-8/.

Yom, S. 2005. "Civil Society and Democratization: Critical Views from the Middle East." *Middle East Review of International Affairs* 9 (4): 14–33.

Civil society versus captured state: a winning strategy for sustainable change

Orysia Lutsevych

ABSTRACT

In the West, Ukraine is known as country of wasted potential, and most recently the scene of a proxy war between the West and Russia. What is often missing in the analysis is that, internally, the country faces serious nation- and state-building challenges. These call for development of institutions, values, and behaviours that could sustain an open democratic system of governance. A strong and sustainable civil society is an integral part of such a system. In 2013 a popular uprising toppled the corrupt regime of Victor Yanukovych. This triggered the Russian annexation of Crimea and unleashed a violent separatist movement in Ukraine's industrial heartland, the Donbass. Since 2014 Ukraine has been both under external attack and simultaneously trying to reform its corrupt and captured political system.

En Occident, l'Ukraine est connue comme un pays au potentiel inexploité, et plus récemment la scène d'une guerre par procuration entre l'Occident et la Russie. Un élément souvent absent de cette analyse est le fait qu'au niveau interne, le pays se heurte à de sérieux défis sur le plan de la construction de la nation et de l'État. Ces défis exigent le développement d'institutions, de valeurs et de comportements qui pourraient soutenir un système démocratique ouvert de gouvernance. Une société civile solide et durable constitue une partie intégrale d'un tel système. En 2013, un soulèvement populaire a renversé le régime corrompu de Victor Yanukovych. Cela a déclenché l'annexion de la Crimée par la Russie et déchaîné un mouvement séparatiste violent dans le cœur industiel de l'Ukraine, le Donbass. Depuis 2014 l'Ukraine est soumise à une attaque externe tout en tentant de réformer son système politique corrompu et capturé.

En Occidente, Ucrania es reconocido como un país cuyo potencial se encuentra desaprovechado y que, en los últimos años, fue escenario de una guerra indirecta entre Occidente y Rusia. Un aspecto que no suele figurar en los análisis tiene que ver con los retos muy serios enfrentados por el país internamente en términos de construcción de la nación y el Estado. Estas tareas implican el desarrollo de instituciones, valores y comportamientos que permitan sostener un sistema de gobierno abierto y democrático. Una parte íntegra de este sistema radica en la existencia de una sociedad civil fuerte y sostenible. En 2013, un levantamiento popular derrocó al corrupto régimen de Víktor Yanukóvich, desencadenando la anexión rusa de Crimea y un movimiento separatista violento en Donbás, corazón industrial de Ucrania. Desde 2014, al mismo tiempo que experimenta embates externos, Ucrania intenta reformar su sistema político corrupto y capturado.

Introduction

In the West, Ukraine is known as a country of wasted potential, and most recently the scene of a proxy war between the West and Russia. What doesn't make the headlines is the fact that internally, the country faces serious nation- and state-building challenges. These call for development of institutions, values, and behaviours that could sustain an open democratic system of governance. A strong and sustainable civil society is an integral part of such a system.

This quest started more than two years ago with a popular uprising known as the "Revolution of Dignity", or "Euromaidan", which toppled the corrupt regime of Victor Yanukovych. This triggered the Russian annexation of Crimea and unleashed a violent separatist conflict in the industrial heartland of Ukraine, the Donbass. Since 2014 Ukraine has been under external attack, while at the same time trying to reform its corrupt and captured political system that triggered the protest in 2013.

The newly elected President Petro Poroshenko, new Parliament, and new Ukrainian government announced ambitious plans to deliver upon the expectations of Ukrainians, who waved EU flags and demanded justice, the rule of law, and war on corruption during the freezing temperatures of a Kyiv winter. The programme, called "Ukraine 2020", outlined eight reform priorities to prepare Ukraine for EU membership application in 2020. It spans across all sectors and includes 62 reforms.[1]

The Euromaidan protest led to an influx of a new generation of policymakers into old institutions. Parliament was renewed with over 50% of new members, including some from civil society. Most of the new ministers have never served in the old, corrupt, system. Many came from the private sector and held the best intentions to reform Ukraine. This influx of new faces from civil society and the private sector created hope that the old system would be destroyed and new rules of transparency, accountability, and inclusivity be established.

However, the victors of Euromaidan have inherited a deeply corrupt system with strong vested interests running across all major political parties even after the new elections. Ukraine is one of the most corrupt countries in Europe, ranking 130th globally in the Transparency International Corruption Index (Transparency International 2015). Seventy-five years of Soviet totalitarian regime, combined with almost 25 years of failed reforms, have distorted institutions, undermined trust in the state, and created informal networks that run the country. The Rule of Law Index places Ukraine at the same level as Lebanon and the Dominican Republic. Neighbouring Poland scores almost twice as highly (World Justice Project 2015).

Many, including famous philanthropist George Soros, describe the current Ukraine as a battleground between old Ukraine and new Ukraine. Losing the new Ukraine, as represented by its reformers and new generation in parliament and government, could cause an *"irreparable challenge of having unstable volatile state in the centre of Europe"* (Soros 2015). The hope for this new Ukraine to prevail comes partly from its own civil society that pushes for change and tries to contribute to reforms.

The definition of civil society used here as a: *"set of diverse non-governmental institutions, which is strong enough to counterbalance the state, and whilst not preventing the state from fulfilling the state the role of keeper of peace and arbitrator between major interests, can nevertheless prevent it from dominating and atomising the rest of society."* (Hall 1995).

The key question for this article is whether the current cohort of civil society organisations (CSOs) is up to the challenge of counterbalancing the state and pushing for reforms. How can they effectively promote systemic transformations in the country with endemic corruption, weak institutions, strong vested interests, and weak political parties? Can increased civic activism expressed during the Euromaidan and further mobilised by the war with Russia make CSOs more sustainable and reinforce their impact?

For the purpose of this analysis, the sustainability of CSOs is defined as a state which allows an organisation to perform its core mission and achieve impact. It is assumed that most organisations in Ukraine aim at bringing sustainable structural change, either at the national or regional level, and aspire to influence policy. Sustainable organisations are less volatile, more focused on achieving impact, and are in a better position to drive the development agenda. Sustainability requires a set of qualities and processes that are often linked with solid financial resources, human capital, and a firm knowledge base of problems and issues that are covered by an organisational mission.

This article is informed by various studies of the CSO sector in Ukraine. The findings are also based on empirical data, monitoring of social media, and interviews conducted by the author in 2014–15 with many think tanks, government officials, and regional human rights groups that cooperate with the United Nations Development Programme in Ukraine.

Ukrainian *indignados*

Ukrainian society has always been freedom-loving and willing to express discontent against the state at moments of direct encroachment on human and political rights. Across its modern history four large waves of popular protests threatened the state's power. At the dusk of the Soviet Union, in 1990, Ukrainian students gathered together in the first public protest on Maidan, with tents installed on the central square in Kyiv, demanded the resignation of the then Prime Minister Mosol, and protested against a new treaty to renew the Soviet Union.[2] This so-called "Revolution on Granite" was successful. In 2000, "Ukraine without Kuchma" demanded the resignation of then President Kuchma after leaked tapes implied that a famous journalist might have been killed on the orders of the president. This protest was suffocated without any success for the protesters.

Four years later in 2004, the Orange Revolution prevented election fraud and the instalment of a pro-Russian president in Victor Yanukovych. Almost 10 years later, students came to the same square in October 2013 to protest against their stolen European future, after the refusal of Yanukovych's government to sign a trade and association agreement with the EU. This triggered one of the largest, and the only bloody, protest in the history of modern Ukraine, a protest known as "Euromaidan". After four months of continued occupation of the square and over 100 deaths by sniper fire, the president fled the country and a new leadership came to power. This has put Ukraine back on the track of European integration and launched structural reforms.

In most of these cases, society was mobilised by shared values of democracy, freedom, rule of law, justice, and rejection of state violence. In 2013, Ukrainian society was also enraged by the growing corruption of the top political elite, that was preventing Ukraine's economic development. This formed a common basis for many citizens who joined the protests.

But we should be careful not to fall into the trap of equating the success of Ukraine's protest movement with the strength of its organised civil society. In fact, in 2013 91% of protesters came to Euromaidan independently (Democratic Initiatives Foundation 2013). Euromaidan, like many recent protests around the world, was a revolution by the individual that was anti-institutional, based on spontaneous, internet-centred activism independent from formal organisational thinking (Krastev 2014). The fact that people took to the streets was partially caused by the lack of more civil and non-conflictual avenues to influence public policies, including via civil society organisations.

Ukraine's frequent protests suggest a strong civic spirit that expresses itself in the times of serious encroachment or threat to political and economic liberties. It is brave and mature sign. However, what matters most for social change in Ukraine is what happens between Maidan popular protests. Are there interactions and exchanges that create the fabric of civil society that provides connections between citizens around both political and social issues? Is there public life that ensures inclusion of various citizen's views and opinions into official policy-making processes?

Civil society space

In the post-Soviet region, the civil society sector was traditionally understood as officially registered NGOs, often supported by Western donors. Twenty-five years after the collapse of the Soviet totalitarian system, the sector has carved its space in public life. Today the civil society eco-system includes well-funded Kyiv advocacy groups, think tanks, youth associations, local CSOs promoting democratic governance, several community regional foundations, human rights groups, and a new cohort of vol-unteer groups, many of which are informal and not registered. It also encompasses foundations established by oligarchs for various charitable purposes and aimed at improving their image, repu-tation, and fostering their political agenda.

Freedom House rates Ukraine as a "party free" country and its civil society is recognised by the USAID NGO Sustainability Rating as one of the strongest in the region (USAID 2014). There are no severe restrictions on civic activities. Citizens are free to associate and create organisations around their interests. The distribution of CSOs is patchy. Many of the groups are concentrated in Kyiv, but regional centres can also boast a myriad of organisations that observe elections, and work on local development, environment, and human rights.

Official Ukrainian statistics list over 130,000 civil society organisations, including citizen associ-ations, charities, trade unions, local apartment-owners' associations, and self-organised community groups, of which around 30% are considered active (Ukrainian State Statistics Committee 2014). The most popular sectors of CSOs' activities in Ukraine are youth and children, human rights, civic education, social issues, and support to the third sector. Around 40% of CSOs are engaged in advo-cacy, while only 20% provide social services (CCC Creative Center 2014). In terms of numbers, the sector has lost some organisations due to the occupation of Crimea and the Donbass. Many had to flee and close down their operations due to threat of imprisonment or harassment by the pro-Russian separatists or Russian authorities in Crimea.

The economy of the Ukrainian civil society is rather small. Overall, in 2014 the sector accumulated around UAH 4 billion (GBP £160 million) (Ukrainian State Statistics Committee 2014). In comparison, the annual income of UK charities is around GBP £69 billion, and over 164,000 charities report to the Charity Commission (Charity Commission 2014). Ukraine has only around 15,000 charitable foundations.

In the post-Euromaidan period, and especially triggered by the war with Russia, volunteering and charitable donations to the army increased substantially. Society saw it as the only way to defend state sovereignty when public institutions, including the Ministry of Defence, have such low trust of its citizens. Within two weeks, the Support the Ukrainian Army campaign attracted US$13 million in donations from legal entities and private individuals. In addition, many small chari-table campaigns were held every day in various regions of Ukraine (USAID 2014, 239). This added a new dimension to civil society, a security dimension. Civil society intervened to fill the gap created by the state's failure to fulfil key functions, such as the provision of security and defence (Puglisi 2015).

Existing mechanisms of influence

What avenues currently exist for active citizens to exert influence on policy-making to advance reforms in Ukraine?

The state formally recognises the importance of the civil society sector and has declared its willing-ness to cooperate. In February 2016 President Poroshenko approved a new Strategy for Support of Civil Society in Ukraine, which was developed in close cooperation with many CSOs. It paves the way for new funding programmes from the state, opens access to public procurement, and calls for new mechanisms of public policy consultations (President of Ukraine 2016).

At present Ukrainian civil society has several tracks of influence. Some of these are more devel-oped and some should be explored further. They include public hearings, public councils, public expertise of legislature, participation in working groups, and more indirectly influence via media. Advocacy for legislative changes at the national level is one of the strongest tracks. The new President and Government are open to the expertise and opinion of civil society experts about sectoral reforms. They have included civil society representatives in a newly created platform for reforms, the National Reform Council.[3]

The Council is a reform coordinating body with its Secretariat located in the office of the President of Ukraine. It holds regular meetings with the top leadership: President, Prime Minister, Speaker of the Parliament, and the leadership of party groups in the ruling coalition. It also officially includes four representatives of civil society: the European Business Association, Civic Initiative New Country, Reanimation Reform Package (REP),[4] and Professional Government Initiative.

Reanimation Reform Package is one of the most active civic coalitions that push reforms. It unites around 300 experts from various NGOs and think tanks. The network emerged right after the victory of Euromaidan. It has prepared its own agenda in the form of an "emergency reforms road map", which includes a list of laws to be adopted by the parliament. For example, the group was active in pushing for new laws on renewal of judges, administrative reform, and on the prosecutors' office. Overall, over 60 laws advocated by the coalition were adopted by the parliament.

At the same time the International Renaissance Foundation (a member of Soros's network of Open Society Foundations in Ukraine) supported the work of individual ministries by creating strategic advisory groups. Such groups included CSOs and provided support, for example to the Ministry of Health and Ministry of Education. They assisted in developing reform concepts and provided independent research. Healthcare reforms were driven by the Patients of Ukraine organisation and included public discussions of the proposed reforms in major Ukrainian cities (Ministry of Health of Ukraine 2014). The group has produced a concept for healthcare reform, but the reform process stalled due to lack of political will. It could barely be pushed from the bottom despite the fact that 72% of citizens negatively rate the work of local governments in providing healthcare services (Association of Ukrainian 2015).

The presence of new members of parliament from civil society also facilitated exchange about reforms between the lawmakers and CSOs. Twenty-five new lawmakers have created a new all-party group called EuroOptimists. They are open to ideas from think tanks, often utilise CSOs platforms, attend public events to communicate with citizens, and seek expert advice on key reforms.

There are also examples of successful advocacy and cooperation at the level of individual ministries. Either via public councils or through various working groups, CSOs could promote their ideas and advocate for change. The Reform Office created at the Ministry of Defence includes activists supporting the army. Another example includes the work of DIXI group, an energy think tank that since 2010 has been advocating for transparency in extractive industries. Thanks to their work with the Ministry of Energy, the creation of the coalition of 18 energy experts and active public awareness campaign, DIXI managed to achieve the publication of the first public report in December 2015. It was prepared by Ernst & Young with the funding from the World Bank. The report discloses the income of the oil and gas industry and its role in Ukraine's economy.[5]

The Ministry of Economy, in cooperation with anti-corruption NGOs such as Transparency International, successfully pioneered a digital procurement system called Prozoro (Transparent).[6] All central agencies are now using the system for tenders and it will be introduced at the regional level in 2016. Since its introduction it has allowed savings of over UAH 479 million (GBP £13 million). It has also opened up new data for watchdog groups, which monitor corruption in public procurement.

In addition to advocacy, the national government engages CSO representatives in selection commissions for leadership positions of key anti-corruption agencies. This opens up the process to public scrutiny and provides more legitimacy to newly created institutions. For example, out of 11 members of the commission to select the anti-corruption prosecutor, six were from civil society, including a vocal critic from the Anti-Corruption Action Centre. CSO leaders are also board members of a newly created public television channel.

Finally, CSOs try to influence the reform agenda by being present in national and regional media. Surveyed public officials believe that think tanks in particular have policy influence via shaping public opinion using media (Democratic Initiatives Foundation 2015). Because most citizens get their news from TV, it is important that CSO experts are invited as guests of national talk shows. Leading news outlets often seek comments from CSOs experts on particular reforms and provide space for blogs and comments from think tanks.

In spite of the fact that in Ukraine the press is viewed as free, the media landscape is distorted. In the post-Soviet period, major TV stations were privatised by oligarchs and used as levers of political influence. At the current stage of reforms, where government is trying to create a level playing field in business and clean up the system from vested interests, Ukrainian tycoons use their media resources to undermine reforms that threaten them. This impacts the quality of debate and politicises information. It also means that there is only a narrow public space for non-biased debate.

New members of parliament and CSOs were successful in 2015 in passing a new law that obliges media outlets to disclose their ownership and finances. This could be the first important step to increase scrutiny over leading media channels. It will also require monitoring to ensure that the companies follow the law.

The space for media and information is also distorted by the presence of many civil society experts who are paid to serve political interests. Presented as independent experts, they are in reality hired by political parties to promote certain agendas. The mapping of such experts shows the corruption of civil society that runs deep into the system. It lists 76 polling groups and 77 experts, many of whom are presumed to be independent CSOs, that spread fake polling data and biased analysis.[7]

The list of CSOs sustainability challenges could be further expanded. Other experts also highlight external threats to the territorial integrity of Ukraine, polarisation and radicalisation of society, complex regulatory environment, cumbersome taxation, and inefficient financial resources. The sector could also weaken if current progressive CSO policies are reversed and issues of taxation and regulatory imperfections remain unchanged (Ghosh 2014).

Actors without society: the risk of leaving citizens behind

Despite the high-intensity activism of formal CSOs and growing volunteering, there is a hidden potential for sustainability and social change that the sector could tap into: citizens themselves. Widening the base of supporters and increasing local legitimacy will better position CSOs to be effective organisations.

The experience of post-colour revolution societies shows that regression in freedoms and reforms is possible. The strategy of relying solely on expertise and national advocacy could backfire if the new government is less open to cooperation. The current cooperative environment enables a cohort of strong advocacy CSOs to advocate policy changes at the national level. Their leaders are recognised experts by the national media. But in order to "finish the revolution" and advance structural reforms CSOs have to reinforce their advocacy approach by closing the gap between their organisations and citizens. This was not done after the 2004 Orange Revolution and led to the marginalisation of the sector from the policy process (Lutsevych 2013).

The post-Euromaidan approach of CSOs differs from 2004, but only marginally addresses the constituency problem. CSOs continue to keep on the frontlines and pushing for change, as the lessons of post-Orange revolution demonstrated that the new leadership could continue playing by the old rules, and mobilisation of society has to continue beyond the protests in the squares. However, reforms are moving slowly and the policy influence of the sector is weak. The current "theory of change" of many CSOs is to exert influence via its Western donors, the EU, or the US embassy. While this could work for some time, Western attention spans are short, Russian propaganda, including in the West, is sapping belief that Ukraine can make a reform breakthrough, and "Ukraine fatigue" is increasing. This is why such an approach is risky and unsustainable.

There is an overwhelming belief among CSO leaders that neither a membership base nor strong constituency define CSO influence. CSO leaders believe that the factors which matter for success are linked to the reputation of the leader of the CSOs, the will for change, a focus on addressing the needs of target groups, dialogue skills, ability to manage conflicts, collaboration with the authorities, and persistence. Think tanks in particular focus on quality of analysis and reputation of their experts.[8]

Such positioning means that national CSOs can push for reforms only within the so-called comfort zone of the current political leadership. When there are higher issues at stake that threaten the system or vested interests it is hard to achieve such pressure. A good example is a failure to start administrative reform, despite good expertise existing within the CSO sector. The same is true about healthcare reform. CSOs direct their efforts at influencing government officials and members of parliament, and forget to build pressure from below and increase understanding among key interest groups about the need for these reforms and the cost of not reforming.

Civil society sustainability and impact is impeded by shallow citizen engagement. In most cases, citizens have no stake in these organisations. This is particularly true with regard to democracy and human rights groups. The levels of formal members in CSOs are dismal. Seventy-two per cent of Ukrainian CSOs have fewer than 100 members (CCC Creative Center 2014), while only a handful of CSOs have active members across the country that represent their stakeholders. The social sector is an exception. Socially oriented groups and those working with various disabilities tend to have a stronger and more active constituency. These social groups rely on their members for advocacy and collect membership fees. One such example is the Patients of Ukraine association that unites 30 members representing 120 organisations, including people with serious illnesses themselves.

Citizen participation in public life, which is rather high, bypasses CSOs. Citizens either do not believe that participation in CSOs can change anything, or do not know how to join CSOs (Association of Ukrainian Cities 2014). Awareness and knowledge about formal CSOs among citizens remains low. At the local level 67% do not know a single CSO (Association of Ukrainian Cities 2014). The most recognisable logos are Hromadske TV, Femen, and the Rinat Akhmetov Foundation.[9]

Only a few organisations offer a membership perspective to citizens in Ukraine.[10] Even with such a pressing issue as corruption, only 10% are ready to seek help from CSOs if their rights are violated (PACT UNITER 2015). Therefore, they are much less active in pushing for reforms via CSOs. Even one of the strongest networks, the REP, has weak regional links and most of its work is concentrated in the capital.

The volunteering surge is also channelled via other routes. A UNDP survey shows that 67% of those who volunteered in Ukraine did so on their own or via educational or religious organisations, or the Red Cross (UNDP 2014). The share of those volunteering for formal CSOs in Ukraine is only 10%, compared to 45% in Germany. Most advocacy campaigns are run by the paid staff of CSOs, rather than by volunteers. On average each Ukrainian CSO engages 16 volunteers per year (CCC Creative Center 2014).

At this point of time, when demand for change is high and activism on the rise, CSOs could reinforce their local legitimacy in order to strengthen impact and long-term sustainability. Poor stakeholder connection weakens the pressure that CSOs can exert on decision-makers. CSOs lack legitimacy vis-à-vis policymakers because many CSOs leaders represent a small group rather than a wider constituency.

In addition to strengthening CSOs, increased civic engagement is indispensable for inclusive participatory democracy and sustainability of the sector. Ukrainian CSOs have a crucial role to play in forming critical minds of citizens and shaping consensus across various reform sectors. Different types of CSOs could find different linkages to citizens. Not all groups are fitted for a broad membership base. But all could reinforce linkages to their stakeholders, broaden participation, outreach, aim for individual donations, and try widening the public consultation process to reinforce the legitimacy of their policy recommendations.

Walk the talk: what about governance and accountability?

Many Ukrainian CSOs emerged not around concrete issues and communities, but rather around big policy ideas like a free media, political freedoms, human rights, environment, and transparency, with only vague sets of beneficiaries. This is particularly relevant for the human rights and democracy sectors, where CSOs could conduct various kinds of consultancy-type projects and share knowledge with government, media, or citizens. Such services are particularly interesting to Western state and private donors, who are trying to push transformation in Ukraine.

Therefore, Western donors fund most of the advocacy work in Ukraine. The situation is more diverse with other CSOs, were Western donors contribute on average 35% of organisational budgets (USAID 2014). Overreliance on Western donors for advocacy fuels suspicions and undermines the legitimacy of the sector. This could be the right time to capitalise on growing public trust in civic organisations, where for the first time in 10 years the balance of trust for CSOs is positive and rather high compared to other institutions (Kyiv International Institute of Sociology 2015). At the same time, growing trust is not reflected in increased practical support to the sector. For the last 10 years the proportion of individual donations in the budget of an average CSO has remained unchanged at around 12% (Kyiv International Institute of Sociology 2015). Membership fees provide, on average, only 11% of organisational budgets (Ukrainian State Statistics Committee 2014).

CSOs' low downward accountability to their target groups remains a significant problem for broadening support and funding bases. Fewer than 50% of CSOs prepare annual reports in Ukraine, down from 58% in 2009 (CCC Creative Center 2014). When surveyed about whom CSOs report to in Ukraine, 19% of CSOs report to international donors and 38% do not report to anyone. Only 9% report to their boards.[11]

CSOs that comply with the principles of internal democratic governance based on accountability to their members, as well as having check-and-balance mechanisms built into their operations, are more effective in promoting change. This is especially important for groups that fight corruption. If they demand integrity from the state, they themselves should be implementing what they preach. For example, the Centre for Political Studies and Analysis, which advocated for a transparent budget and is a member of National Agency for the Prevention of Corruption, has no annual financial report publicly available online.[12] There are only six Ukrainian think tanks listed on global transparency initiative "Transparify", with only one meriting a five-star transparency rating.[13] Transparency remains rudimentary.

There is a certain shift in an increased focus on governance among some donors that provide institutional funding, such as the Swedish International Development Cooperation Agency (SIDA). SIDA encourages its partners to conduct institutional change by setting up truly independent boards, separating executive management and oversight powers, and reinforcing connections with CSOs' stakeholders. Several large national CSOs have undergone such reforms, including a few think tanks and the civic TV station Hromadske.

A similar approach, focusing on the organisational development of regional human rights hubs, was applied by the UNDP democratisation project in Ukraine that was funded by the Denmark Development Corporation, Danida. Many local CSOs updated their statutes to upgrade oversight and accountability. Some groups, who modified their governance structures or developed volunteer engagement policies, report satisfaction with such change. In terms of benefits they report the ability to tap into new human resources, increased capacity for wider country outreach, improved image, increased effectiveness of project management, and better sustainability thanks to less dependency on a single charismatic leader. These inspiring examples could become potential role models for others.

From protest to creative collaboration

Even after the "Revolution of Dignity", Ukrainian civil society's approach to change is focused on institution building and structural change at the national level. Little resources and efforts are invested in helping change the mentality of the post-Soviet society. Transformative change requires careful reflection on Einstein's warning that "we cannot solve problems using the same kind of thinking we used when we created them".

Watchers of civil society note that even in developed democracies, the transformative impact of civil society is declining due to a lack of participation of people in politics and civic life (Edwards 2014). At the same time, many high impact CSOs achieve systemic change by combining services with advocacy, having a strong ethos of democratic participation and accountability, practising shared leadership, and active networking (Crutchfield and McLeod Grant 2012).

If Ukraine wants to see sustainable social change, the successful strategy should entail more openness from the sector to society, more transparency, and a more egalitarian and less elitist approach to citizens themselves. Existing and new CSOs should open their organisations to citizens, both as members and as points of targeted attention. The change from post-authoritarian system to deliberative participatory democracy requires a different kind of citizen, one with a deeper engagement in civil society beyond just protests.

Qualified citizens should be joining CSOs as board members and trustees. Annual general assemblies should perform the function of a democratic, collective, decision-making body. Effective membership and participation could create face-to-face, ongoing, and potentially transformative activities. Such interaction could be challenging as people come together with different views, and finding some common ground is crucial. That common ground could then be translated formally into laws and policies by voting in reforming governments. CSO leaders should learn moderation and facilitation skills to run public consultation and events that help identify the positions and problems of their key target groups. Such fieldwork is rare, but much needed.

This experience could have a transformative impact by shaping an active citizen with a critical mind, a quality that is very important for open democratic society. CSOs can perform an important role of helping citizens ask the right questions and provide critically needed, politically neutral, public space to share opinions.

To achieve this, a new set of capacity skills is needed. Western donors could help create the right incentives to help CSOs engage with citizens and provide technical assistance to reinforce citizen participation. At present larger donors are mostly funding projects that finance advocacy activities vis-à-vis the state, and have few indicators that measure citizen engagement. One possible model could be the Popular Account Model promoted by the Danish Development Assistance programme to involve more Danish citizens in state-funded development cooperation. Here, major groups, such as IBIS, were employed where recipients of development grants were monitored for fee-paying members, supporting members, volunteer hours, and funds raised in Denmark.[14] As the result of such an engagement strategy IBIS increased the number of paying members, active volunteers, and funds raised locally for international projects.

Local and national media could also conduct more scrutiny of local organisations and demand transparency. Local communities, especially if CSOs receive more state funding, have the right to know more about these groups. Such public oversight could lead to a higher quality of services and subsequently better sustainability.

CSOs are currently playing an essential role in helping the political leadership to reform Ukraine, and most experts believe the country is now moving in the right direction.[15] However, the current political crisis, and growing dissatisfaction with the slow speed of reforms, raises concerns about the sustainability of the process. If CSOs want to have a substantial and lasting impact, regardless of the political forces ruling the country, they should also reform themselves and reinforce their legitimacy. In that case, more sustainable CSOs could also lead to more sustainable change.

The modernisation of Ukraine requires not just an overhaul of the country's corrupt political elite: the entire polity, including CSOs, needs to improve its democratic standards and increase transparency, accountability, and participatory decision-making. If successful, Ukraine could be an inspiring example and have a transformative impact on the wider post-Soviet space.

Notes

1. For the full strategy, see www.reforms.in.ua/Content/download/Strategy2020updUA.pdf

2. Maidan is the name of central square in Kyiv called Independence Square.
3. See http://reforms.in.ua/en
4. See www.rpr.org.ua/en
5. See full report at www.slideshare.net/uaenergy/2013-56237321?ref=http://blog.liga.net/user/obelkova/article/20324.aspx
6. See http://prozorro.org
7. See pseudo-sociology infographics at http://texty.org.ua/d/socio/
8. Author's research for DANIDA and IRF Foundation in Ukraine.
9. Unpublished GFK study for PACT, September 2014.
10. Author's interviews with Ukrainian CSOs.
11. Ukrainian Catholic University, Social Marketing Research, 2013.
12. See www.cpsa.org.ua
13. See www.transparify.org
14. See IBIS Education for Development, http://ibis-global.org
15. See expert videos about reforms at Ukraine Forum of Chatham House: www.chathamhouse.org/about/structure/russia-eurasia-programme/ukraine-fo rum-project

Disclosure statement

No potential conflict of interest was reported by the author.

References

Association of Ukrainian Cities. 2014. "Association of Ukrainian Cities." Accessed March 12, 2016. http://auc.org.ua/sites/default/files/mon18_1.pdf.

Association of Ukrainian Cities. 2015. "Results of Opinion Polls on Issues of Local Government and Relations to Decentralization of Power." Accessed March 12, 2016. http://gurt.org.ua/blogs/Тарас%20Тимчук/1493/.

CCC Creative Center. 2014. *Civil Society Organisations in Ukraine: The State and Dynamics 2002–2013*. Kyiv: CCC Creative Center.

Charity Commission. 2014. "Recent Charity Register Statistics: Charity Commission." Accessed March 12, 2016. https://www.gov.uk/government/publications/charity-register-statistics/recent-charity-register-statistics-charity-commission.

Crutchfield, L. R., and H. McLeod Grant. 2012. *Forces for Good: Six Practices of High-Impact NGOs*. San Francisco: Jossey-Bass.

Democratic Initiatives Foundation. 2015. "Independent Analytical Centers of Ukraine Developing Policies: Obstacles, Perspectives and Mutual Expectations in Cooperation with Public Authorities." Accessed March 12, 2016. http://dif.org.ua/modules/pages/files/1423840398_3402.pdf.

Democratic Initiatives Foundation. 2013. "Maidan 2013: Who is Protesting? Why and Demanding What?" Accessed March 12, 2016. http://dif.org.ua/ua/polls/2013-year/mogjorjghoeoj

Edwards, M. 2014. "When is Civil Society a Force for Social Transformation?" *Open Democracy*. Accessed March 12, 2016. www.opendemocracy.net/transformation/michael-edwards/when-is-civil-society-force-for-social-transformation.

Ghosh, M. 2014. *In Search of Sustainability. Civil Society in Ukraine*. Berlin: Friedrich Ebert Stiftung. Accessed March 12, 2016. http://library.fes.de/pdf-files/id-moe/10862.pdf.

Hall, J. A. 1995. *Civil Society: Theory, History, Comparison*. London: Polity Press.

Krastev, I. 2014. *Democracy Disrupted: The Politics of Global Protest*. Philadelphia: University of Pennsylvania Press.

Kyiv International Institute of Sociology. 2015. "Trust in Institutions and Social Groups." Accessed March 12, 2016. http://kiis.com.ua/?lang=ukr&cat=reports&id=579&page=2.

Lutsevych, O. 2013. *How to Finish a Revolution: Civil Society and Democracy in Georgia, Moldova, Ukraine*. Chatham House research paper. London: Chatham House.

Ministry of Health of Ukraine. 2014. "National Health Reform Strategy for Ukraine 2015–2020." Accessed March 12, 2016. http://healthsag.org.ua/wp-content/uploads/2015/03/Strategiya_Engl_for_inet.pdf.

PACT UNITER. 2015. "Corruption in Ukraine: Comparative analysis of nationwide surveys of 2007, 2009, 2011 and 2015." Accessed March 12, 2016. http://uniter.org.ua/upload/files/PDF_files/Anticorr-survey-2015/CorruptionFULL_2015_Eng_for%20public.pdf.

President of Ukraine. 2016. "Strategy for Support of Development of Civil Society, 26 February 2016." Accessed March 12, 2016. www.president.gov.ua/documents/682016-19805.

Puglisi, R. 2015. *A People's Army: Civil Society as Security Factor in Post-Euromaidan Ukraine*. Rome: Institute of International Affairs. Accessed March 12, 2016. www.iai.it/sites/default/files/iaiwp1523.pdf.

Soros, G. 2015. "Ukraine and Europe: What Should be done?" *New York Review of Books*. October 8. Accessed March 12, 2016. www.nybooks.com/articles/2015/10/08/ukraine-europe-what-should-be-done.

Transparency International. 2015. "Transparency International Index: Ukraine." Accessed March 12, 2016. https://www.transparency.org/country/#UKR.

Ukrainian State Statistics Committee. 2014. "Statistical Bulletin: The activities of citizen's associations in Ukraine 2014." Accessed March 12, 2016. https://ukrstat.org/uk/druk/publicat/kat_u/publpolit_u.htm.

UNDP. 2014. "UNV Annual Report 2014." Accessed March 12, 2016. www.unv.org/annual-report-2014/.

USAID. 2014. "The 2014 CSO Sustainability Index for Central and Eastern Europe and Eurasia." Accessed March 12, 2016. www.usaid.gov/sites/default/files/documents/1863/EuropeEurasia_FY2014_CSOSI_Report.pdf.

World Justice Project. 2015. "Rule of Law Index." Accessed March 12, 2016. http://data.worldjusticeproject.org/.

Russian civil society and development challenges in Eurasia

Charles Buxton

ABSTRACT

What are the prospects for development and for civil society as an actor in development processes in Russia's poorer, more remote regions and among neighbouring states that were once Soviet Republics? This viewpoint assesses the situation today from the author's vantage point working for a civil society support organisation in Kyrgyzstan, and taking into account the tense international situation and the crisis in Russia's economy.

Quelles sont les perspectives pour le développement et la société civile en tant qu'acteur des processus de développement dans les régions les plus pauvres et les plus isolées de la Russie, et parmi les États voisins jadis républiques soviétiques ? Ce « Point de vue » évalue la situation actuelle du point de vue de l'auteur, qui travaille pour une organisation de soutien à la société civile au Kirghizistan, et en tenant compte de la situation internationale très défavorable et de la crise de l'économie russe.

En los procesos de desarrollo que transcurren en las regiones más pobres y remotas de Rusia, así como en los países vecinos que años atrás eran repúblicas soviéticas, ¿qué perspectivas existen para el desarrollo y para la sociedad civil como actor? El presente punto de vista valora la situación existente hoy día desde el observatorio del autor como empleado de una organización que apoya a la sociedad civil de Kirguistán, tomando en cuenta la muy desfavorable situación internacional y la crisis atravesada por la economía rusa.

Introduction

In my article for *Development in Practice* three years ago (Buxton 2013), I gave a short account of the history of civil society development in Russia, and in particular its difficult path from Tsarist autocracy and the Soviet state-dominated period into a new "time of troubles", the crisis-ridden transition period after 1991. The analysis pointed to a dilemma facing Russian NGOs today – whether to collaborate with the government authorities through a variety of new mechanisms like social contracting or participation in consultative structures like the Public Council system: or alternatively, to protest energetically against the problems of corruption, democracy deficit, attacks on workers' rights, and so on.

The problems I wrote about then have not gone away. In early 2012, Vladimir Putin was elected as President and immediately opened an offensive against Western-funded NGOs working in the area of democracy and human rights. A law was pushed through labelling organisations "foreign agents" and within a year a number of leading Russian NGOs had been identified as such. Some of them closed down, but others have continued to work while lobbying against the new law and its tough reporting procedures. However, this has been very difficult while Putin's popularity increases as a result of the crisis that erupted in Ukraine in autumn 2013 and the consequent events in Crimea and Donbass.

Putin's actions to support the Russian-speaking population and Russian-majority regions in Ukraine have been very popular at home. The deepening rift with the USA and Europe makes it harder for Russian NGOs to accept money or political support from abroad. The events in Ukraine led to the imposition of sanctions on Russia by the USA and European Union, and after Russia retaliated with its own sanctions in autumn 2014, the economy took a battering and government budgets at all levels were reviewed and in many cases reduced.

The key issue in Ukraine in autumn 2013 was whether to sign an association agreement with the EU. Broadly speaking, the western half of the country was in favour, while the eastern half was not so sure. Since Putin's election as President one of his key priorities has been to build cooperation and alliances in the Eurasian region under Russia's leadership. Ukraine's support would have been highly desirable, not just as a "brotherly" Slavic country but the second most powerful ex-Soviet economy. In the event the Eurasian Economic Union (often referred to as the Customs Union) now has two other, much smaller members – Armenia and Kyrgyzstan.

In my recent book (Buxton 2014) I took the analysis of Russian civil society eastwards and southwards. My aim was to try to consider the Russian development model historically and in the present – and the place of civil society in it. The geographical focus was the Urals and Siberia regions (which have stayed in the Russian Federation), and Central Asia (whose five countries are now independent). There are many interesting comparisons between the Tsarist Empire (a land empire colonised over a long period and with Russians now in the majority in most regions) and other European empires; and between the effects of the Soviet period on different regions within the former USSR. Indeed, revolution and collectivisation affected "backward" regions like Central Asia and the Far East no less than urban/western regions, but in different ways – and arguments continue as to whether this was an "empire" in the usual sense. In brief, I concluded that the Russian model (at least up till recently) was notable for its state-led element and for the history of socialist revolution. In contrast, the Putin regime now explicitly characterises itself as "conservative" – that is in alliance with the Orthodox Church, nationalist-patriotic, and national bourgeois elements of the Russian elite.

What are the prospects for development and for civil society as an actor in development processes in Russia's poorer, more remote regions and among neighbouring states that were once Soviet republics? This article tries to assess the situation today from my own vantage point working for INTRAC in Bishkek, Kyrgyzstan, and taking into account both the very unfavourable international situation and the crisis in Russia's economy. There are a number of different strands that need consideration.

The effect of war and security policies

In Russia no less than USA and Europe, the "war on terror" and security issues are never long out of the news. The violent events in the Middle East, where Russia takes a different view from the West on many issues, have strengthened the hand of the military in demanding a continuation of the arms build-up that President Putin has presided over since the early 2000s. Russia is now heavily involved in the war in Syria, along with the troubles in Donbass and Islamic radicals in North Caucasus. Security is an issue in Central Asia too, with a large amount of international aid diverted away from social and civil society development into strengthening police forces and national borders. Security concerns (around drugs trafficking as well as terrorism) foul the atmosphere in Russia, leading many Russians to see their southern neighbours as a "security risk".

NGO strategies for coping with crisis

The 2000s saw an effort by the Russian government to develop social programmes (national, regional, and local) in which NGOs could play a role as delivery agents. In many parts of the country state-funded grants programmes have been operating successfully for more than 10 years. The rapid growth of the Russian economy in those years, bolstered by high prices for Russian's oil exports, seemed to indicate a good time ahead – until the sanctions, the collapse of oil prices, crisis of the rouble, and new costs of supporting Crimea and Donbass and fighting in Syria. National philanthropy was beginning to develop in Russia, but has been hit badly. A short analysis of the strategies adopted by NGOs suggests that many are experiencing difficulties in sticking to their mission and diversifying sources of support (Gnevasheva 2015; Higher School of Economics 2015).

Civil society, social, and local development

The aim of the Russian authorities is to reduce Western influence within civil society, and in particular with regard to issues that concern "conservatives" – such as excessive democracy, challenges to ruling classes, sexual freedom, and secular competition with the Church. The dividing line is expressed in the phrase "political activities" and in late 2015 the Ministry of Justice, the Human Rights Commission, and various others were engaged in an analysis of what "political activities" means and which ones should be stopped or restricted by the law on foreign agents. At the same time well-known NGOs like Memorial (working on human rights) and SOVA (working on the rights of national and racial minorities) have successfully defended their right to exist and have even been able to gain some government funding. For example, Memorial is now working on a project on migrants and the law (Bearr Trust 2015).

The Putin government's attack on democracy and human rights organisations was balanced by an offer of increased collaboration with what are called "socially oriented" NGOs. During autumn 2015, the government announced new money and procedures for "SONGOs". Thus the Public Council system may take over the funding of social programmes from the ministries and agencies that run them now; and President Putin has suggested that up to 10% of social programmes might be delegated to NGOs. He said, for example, that NGOs can run them more cost-effectively and with better heed of the population's needs, especially where specialised services are concerned. Against this, it should be noted that the government system continues to be very centralised and local municipal budgets are very limited, especially in "dotational" (subsidised) areas of the country. Regional NGOs are increasingly active in lobbying for a larger share in government social development funding vis-a-vis the Moscow-St Petersburg "elite" NGOs (Muravieva et al. 2011; Ivanushkin 2015a, 2015b). Here we see a range of different interests existing within civil society.

New countries entering the Eurasian Economic Union at a difficult moment

The history of post-1991 regional collaboration in the former Soviet Union is not so positive. The Commonwealth of Independent States (CIS) created in the early 1990s could perhaps be viewed as more a way of legitimating centrifugal processes than integration – that is, as a way in which the divorcing partners could "stay in touch" with each other. The coloured revolutions in Georgia and Ukraine weakened the CIS seriously, but at the same time it became clear that the economies of the region needed a coordination process with which to compete with external players like the EU and China. This is very true of Central Asia where natural markets for the sale of agricultural produce are to the North, and where links with the Russian educational, scientific, and government apparatuses are still strong. This can be illustrated by the choice made by Kyrgyzstan where, despite being the most liberal democratic of the five states, an elite consensus strengthened in the late 2000s that Russia was a "strategic partner" and the country should join the Customs Union. In summer 2015 Kyrgyzstan formally signed the relevant treaties, with big hopes of gaining an immediate economic advantage. For example, during 2014–15 there was much talk of Kyrgyzstan's agricultural producers being able to fill the gap left by European suppliers no longer able to sell fruit and vegetables in Russia. The Russian government set up a Russia-Kyrgyz development fund, Gazprom bought up the gas industry in Kyrgyzstan, and Russian companies launched new projects to develop hydroelectric power stations on Kyrgyzstan's mountain rivers. However, the hopes that people had have by no means been realised. Economic growth was very sluggish in 2015. Kyrgyz exporters of milk and meat products found that quality standards for their exports were hard to meet and their counterparts in Russia and Kazakhstan were not willing to make exceptions for their poorer southern neighbour. Some energy sector projects have also been postponed as the Russian economy struggles. A section of Kyrgyzstan's civil society campaigned against the EEU but now the country has joined this does not look like a very easy campaign to sustain.

Migration within the CIS

Around a third to a half of the working age population in Kyrgyzstan and Tajikistan are estimated to have worked in Russia or are working there now. The numbers of Uzbek work migrants are similarly very high. This is one group of people who will likely gain from the EEU – that is, it will be easier to get documents, residence registration, and social benefits. Migration is a very controversial issue in Russia – but perhaps slightly less difficult than in Europe. For example, citizens of the ex-Soviet Republics have the right to take up Russian citizenship and many hundreds of thousands have done so. However, migrants typically live in very poor conditions in Russia's cities, they are exploited by employers as cheap labour, and they face hostility from nationalist/fascist youth. Migration is an issue of supreme importance for the development of poorer countries. Migrants' remittances to Tajikistan are said to exceed the total for development aid to the country, and they were hit badly by the recession (Central Asia on the Move 2016). Migration is vital for the Russian Federation too (with its low birth rates and deficit of labour) and attitudes to it are a key indicator in the development of a tolerant, progressive civil society. Russian government support for programmes easing the access of migrants and their families is increasing, but public opinion remains divided, with reactionary politicians and media agencies playing an unhelpful role.

A new "foreign agents" law in Kyrgyzstan

One of the big worries among NGO activists in Kyrgyzstan in 2015 was whether Parliament would pass a new law on foreign agents. This law was drafted by a previous ombudsman with a conservative agenda and public discussion focused on the so-called danger emanating from democracy, human rights, and minority groups. The President adopted a rather ambivalent position but many hoped that if the law went through Parliament, he would veto it. This seemed like a test case for Russian political influence in Kyrgyzstan after recent setbacks for US influence in the country (in summer 2014, the US air base at Manas was closed and in summer 2015 the Kyrgyz government cancelled a number of USAID projects). The law on foreign agents did not get through Parliament before the national elections in October 2015, which resulted in a victory for the governing Social Democratic Party. In early 2016 it passed a second reading in Parliament and most observers concluded that it would be adopted with stringent reporting requirements for foreign funded NGOs, but without forcing them to adopt the label of "foreign agents". In the event the law was defeated on its third reading with a roughly 60-40 majority, to the great relief of NGOs and development agencies alike.

Three peripheries within the Russian space

In considering the development challenges in the Russian Federation and neighbouring countries in Eurasia, I developed the idea of "three peripheries". This is based around the well-established notion that development in its colonial and capitalist mode demands a division between the centre and the periphery: that is, the centre requires and creates a periphery of poorer, dependant, less well-informed or empowered regions. In *Russia and Development* I defined these as follows: (1) the outer periphery – Central Asia and other ex-Soviet independent countries, significantly less developed on economic and social indicators than the Russian Federation; (2) less well-developed regions in Russia itself (e.g. remote areas in Siberia and the Far North); and (3) dispossessed and alienated elements in Russian cities (Buxton 2014). This provides a simple way of looking at the problems of poverty and inequality in the wider Eurasia region. Is it possible to compare conditions in these three peripheries? This is a complex question, but certainly one can say that the newly independent countries have some advantages as well as challenges. Also, in some ways urban populations have suffered worse, but in other respects we can see major developments in the cities while rural areas are in decay.

Russian development policy as a BRIC

This short survey ends with a consideration of Russia's new development policies as a member of the BRIC grouping. As I noted in *Russia and Development*, positioning Russia as a BRIC has some ideological and political advantages for the government. First, it moves the discussion away from the complex of issues around Russia and the West (so often an unprofitable or circular discussion). Second, it focused on modernisation issues for a number of states that have a big combined economic weight and are trying to catch up the richest countries. Third, it begins to create an alliance for changes in the system of international development (at the UN, IMF, World Bank, etc.) or even for the creation of a number of alternative BRIC agencies (Brezhneva and Ukhova 2013). There are a number of main ideas in the BRIC's emerging development policy. First, the primacy of the state in development. Second, national sovereignty and a critique of the conditions that Western governments impose on developing nations. Third, a focus on horizontal cooperation rather than aid from donor to recipient. While we can easily see that this may be an attractive offer for some poor countries, what is the practice in Russia? At the risk of over-generalisation, we can see that indeed, most Russian development cooperation is from state to state. The involvement of the private sector and Russian NGOs in development programmes is very limited. However, in 2014–15 Russia hosted international civil society gatherings in connection with meetings of the G20 and BRICs and the government has come up against the challenge of how to ensure some kind of citizens' engagement and accountability. Here the experience of the other senior BRICs – Brazil, India, and China – is quite varied, as are their interests, geographical, political, and economic focus. The challenges for prioritisation, coordination, and effective development in the BRICs are very significant.

The sustainability of CSOs

The analysis provided above indicates that Russian civil society will have to rely mainly on national resources for the foreseeable future, and CSOs in poorer urban and rural settings in Russia face a struggle to survive and maintain the pressure for development. At the same time, history shows that the Russian intelligentsia has almost always maintained a Westernising stance. International links are vital to face global environmental, social, and economic challenges – as well as to oppose the badly thought out, destructive, and unnecessary wars that we see going on at the present time.

Note

1. Below is further useful, background reading on this subject.

Abashin, S. et al. 2008. *Historia Rossica – Central Asia in the Russian Empire* (in Russian). Moscow: Novoye Literaturnoe Obozrenie.

Boiko, V. (ed.) 1998. *Siberia in the geopolitical space of the 21st Century* (in Russian). Novosibirsk: Siberian Branch of the Russian Academy of Sciences.

Bykov, A. 2009. *Post-soviet space: strategies of integration and new challenges of globalisation* (in Russian). St Petersburg: Aleteia.

Chatterjee, S. et al. (ed.) 2009. *Asiatic Russia: partnerships and communities in Eurasia*. Delhi: Shipra.

Clement, C., O. Mirasova, and A. Demidov. 2010. *From bystanders to activists* (in Russian). Moscow: Tri Kvadrata.

Dobronravin, N. 2010. "Globally superfluous: non-government peoples and the resource state." In *Paths to modernisation* (in Russian), edited by V. Gelman and O. Marganiya. St Petersburg: European University.

Eurasia Heritage Foundation and UNDP Russia. 2010. *Engagement of Russian Business in International*

Development Assistance in CIS Countries (Kyrgyzstan and Tajikistan). Moscow: Eurasia Heritage Foundation and UNDP Russia.

Evans, A. 2006. "Vladimir Putin's Design for Civil Society." In Russian Civil Society: A Critical Assessment, edited by A. Evans et al., 147–157. London: ME Sharpe.

Hohmann, S. et al. 2014. Development in Central Asia and Caucasus: Migration, Democratisation and Inequality in the Post-Soviet Era. London: I.B. Tauris.

Humphrey, C. 2010. Post-Soviet transformations in the Asiatic part of Russia (in Russian). Moscow: Natalis.

Jakobson, L., I. Mersianova, O. Kononykhina et al. 2011. Civil Society in Modernizing Russia. Moscow: CIVICUS World Alliance for Citizen Participation and HSE.

Kubayeva, G. 2015. "Economic Impact of the Eurasia Economic Union on Central Asia." Central Asia Security Policy Brief No.20. Bishkek: OSCE Academy.

Romanov, P. and E. Yarkskaya-Smirnova. 2009. Social movements in Russia (in Russian). Moscow: Library of the Journal of Social Policy.

Tiulegenov, M. 2015. "A Certain Path to an Uncertain Future: Kyrgyzstan's Accession to the Custom's Union / Eurasian Economic Union." Bishkek: Friedrich Ebert Foundation.

Zubarevich, N. 2010. "Socio-economic variations between ethnic regions and the politics of redistribution" (in Russian). In Federalism and Ethnic Diversity, Russian Political Encyclopaedia.

Disclosure statement

No potential conflict of interest was reported by the author.

References

Bearr Trust. 2015. "Socially-orientated NGOs can spend State resources more effectively than Government agencies, says Vladimir Putin." November 5, 2015. Accessed March 1, 2016. www.asi.org.ru/news/vladimir-putin-nko-sotsialnoj-napravlennosti-mogut-luchshe-tratit-gosudarstvennye-resursy-chem-gosstruktury/.

Brezhneva, A. and D. Ukhova. 2013. Russian as a Humanitarian Aid Donor. Moscow: Oxfam Russia.

Buxton, C. 2013. "Russian civil society – background, current, and future prospects." Development in Practice 23 (5&6): 771–783.

Buxton, C. 2014. Russia and Development: Capitalism, Civil Society and the State. London: Zed Press.

Central Asia on the Move. 2016. "Update on Migration by the Partner Platform Involving NGOs in Kyrgyzstan, Tajikistan and Russia" (in Russian). Accessed March 1, 2016. http://camplatform.org/en/newsroom/item/521-obzor-migratsionnoj-situatsii-na-nachalo-2016-goda.

Gnevasheva, A. 2015. Antirecessionary Management for NGOs. Perm, Russia: Grany Centre for Civic Analysis and Independent Research.

Higher School of Economics. 2015. "Materials from Summer School for Civil Society Researchers on NGO Sustainability." Moscow: Center for Study of Civil Society and the Non-Commercial Sector, Higher School of Economics. www.grans.hse.org.

Ivanushkin, G. 2015a. "Results of the 2nd Presidential Grant Contest for NGOs." October 23, 2015. Accessed March 1, 2016. www.asi.org.ru/news/podvedeny-itogi-vtorogo-konkursa-po-raspredeleniyu-prezidentskih-grantov-dlya-nko.

Ivanushkin, G. 2015b. "The Ministry of Economic Development's Grants Fund can be Transferred to the Public Chamber." November 5, 2015. Accessed March 1, 2016. www.asi.org.ru/news/grantovyj-fond-minekonomrazvitiya-mozhet-byt-peredan-obshhestvennoj-palate.

Muravieva, V. et al. 2011. Socially Oriented Non-Commercial Organisations (in Russian). Moscow: Agency for Social Information (ASI).

Crises in civil society organisations: opportunities for transformation

James Taylor

ABSTRACT

This viewpoint explores the possibility of successful civil society formations using a crisis of opportunity for transformation. Such crises reflect the need and creative energy for transformation emerging out of internal development processes. These are important moments for innovative change, not top-down or bottom-up, but from the inside out. The paper uses the experience of a South African organisation (Community Development Resource Association) that has been serving the organisational development needs of civil society organisations for 28 years. It draws specifically from work with one of South Africa's most successful CSOs (Treatment Action Campaign) over the past two years.

Ce « Point de vue » examine la possibilité que des entités efficaces de la société civile utilisent une crise d'opportunité pour se transformer. Ces crises traduisent le besoin et l'énergie créative pour la transformation qui émanent des processus de développement internes. Il s'agit de moments importants de changements innovants, non pas descendants ou ascendants, mais à partir de l'intérieur. Ce document se sert de l'expérience d'une organisation sud-africaine (*Community Development Resource Association*) qui répond aux besoins en développement organisationnel d'organisations de la société civile depuis 28 ans. Il se base spécifiquement sur les travaux effectués par l'une des OSC sud-africaines les plus efficaces (*Treatment Action Campaign*) au cours des deux dernières années.

El presente punto de vista examina la posibilidad de que algunas agrupaciones de la sociedad civil exitosas utilicen una crisis de oportunidad para lograr un cambio. Tales crisis reflejan la necesidad y la energía creativa transformadoras que emergen de los procesos de desarrollo interno. Se trata de momentos importantes que pueden hacer posible el cambio innovador, no de arriba a abajo, o viceversa, sino desde adentro hacia afuera. En este sentido, el artículo destaca la experiencia de una asociación sudafricana (Community Development Resource Association-CDRA) que, durante 28 años, ha atendido las necesidades de varias organizaciones de la sociedad civil en el ámbito de desarrollo organizacional. El artículo se centra específicamente en el acompañamiento que esta asociación ha brindado durante los últimos dos años a una de las OSC sudafricanas más exitosas (Treatment Action Campaign).

Introduction

This viewpoint utilises the experience and approach of a South African organisation (the Community Development Resource Association – CDRA) that has been serving the organisational development needs of civil society organisations (CSOs) for the past 28 years. CDRA has worked in around 50 countries, but remains embedded in South Africa's continuing struggle to deliver on the needs and aspirations of the majority of its people.

The paper explores the need for organisational transformation in pursuit of sustainability from an organisational development perspective. It makes a case for civic-driven, social justice-type CSOs having a particular contribution to make in seeking new organisational forms more appropriate to addressing the challenges of our time. It also suggests that there are organisational crises that arise in effective growing organisations that could act as catalysts for transformation. After using a case from practice as an example, the paper shares three areas that have emerged from practice as key to maximising the potential for transformation towards increased sustainability.

The concept of transformation

The word "transformation" lives large in the history of the political struggle against the policy of apartheid in South Africa and in the aspirations of the majority of its people. Systemic and systematic discrimination, exclusion, and marginalisation are well understood as being mechanisms through which wealth and power are extracted and concentrated amongst an elite minority. From a South African experience, the concept of transformation is being presented as describing the need to find alternatives to systems of organised society that rely on impoverishment as a means of achieving purpose. Transformation is a response to the need to find alternatives to forms of organisation that are not sustainable because they undermine the ability of communities and the people within them to flourish and reach the fullness of their potential to contribute to the larger wholes of which they are a part.

As my work has taken me beyond my own country, I have learnt that the South African experience is not unique. Globally, many CSOs that have gone beyond the alleviation of symptoms in search of the underlying causes of social exclusion and impoverishment arrive at the realisation that the problems are systemic and require fundamental systems change. The urgency in the need for transformation has been further deepened by the growing focus on environmental impoverishment, and understanding of the need for the transformation of the systems and organisational forms that shape all of human enterprise.

As has been learnt in South Africa in the 22 years since the overthrow of the apartheid regime, there is more to transformation than a shift in power from a minority to a majority. Along with the first democratically elected government in the country, CSOs have played a significant role in successfully shifting power and control over access to resources to those who were previously excluded. The improvement in their lives suggests that such victories are an important first step. However, the fundamental societal systems continue to create and benefit elites, as the gap between the rich and poor and its attendant frustration grows. The South African experience is presented as an example of a system organised in ways that render it unsustainable and in need of transformation.

Transformation has now become an overused word, virtually synonymous with all significant change. From an organisation development perspective, it has a very particular meaning. It denotes a developmental process that takes place when an organisation can no longer effectively coordinate the functions required to achieve its organisational purpose through its present structure/form, and reaches a crisis. While growth entails quantitative increase – and may precipitate the need for transformation – transformation implies a qualitative change in structure. Transformation reflects the need to let go of old forms of organisation that have worked well in the past to find new forms that reflect the societal advances, new needs, and challenges of the time.

Civil society's role in contributing to the transformation of unsustainable societal systems

I have worked where civil society has mobilised and organised in response to impoverishment, exclusion, and discrimination of all types. I have seen CSOs innovate and bring to the world new services in response to unmet human need, as well as address the needs of other forms of life and ecological systems. I have experienced CSOs acting as a foundational generative source of human society. For the reasons, I am promoting the idea that civil society has a vital role to play in contributing to the transformation of unsustainable societal systems. I do not generalise this role to all CSOs or claim it as the preserve of civil society alone. I have experienced CSOs that undermine and act as a destructive counterforce to human and ecological development. And I know of businesses that are experimenting with more socially innovative forms of organisation than most CSOs.

Specific CSOs have a crucial role to play in exploring and experimenting with new and innovative organisational forms as a part of their creative societal function. There is the possibility of those organisations that promote empowerment, transformation, and civic-driven bottom-up change, playing a leading role through transforming their own organisations. Here, the focus is on social justice organisations active in challenging the inability of dominant systems to deliver to those who need services and resources most: in particular, organisations that include members of the targeted beneficiary communities as integral to shaping the organisation and delivering its services. In other words, this viewpoint explores how organisations that are already inclusive, are conscious of and constantly challenging dominant dysfunctional power relations, can contribute to systemic transformation through example.

As an organisational development practitioner I have learnt that organisational crises are times of opportunity for change and innovation. Organisations can face crises at any point in their development. Here, I wish to focus on successful civic-driven social justice organisations that have had rich human and financial resources invested in them, grown significantly in size, services, and complexity, and then faced a crisis. This type of crisis is common in the development of organisations. We refer to it as the crisis of the "over-ripe pioneer" organisation. In the business sector this crisis is well understood. When successful businesses outgrow the initial systems, strengths, and interest of their pioneer entrepreneurs they too face the prospect of starting to fail or making the choice to change. One option facing business comes through an established market served by brokers who sell these businesses into their next phase of differentiated professional management. The pioneering entrepreneurs leave for their next venture with capital and the experience of success. Their erstwhile businesses become assimilated into the more corporate world of business management. Although there is no market for social justice organisations, when arriving at this moment of crisis they too face the prospect of decline or the possibility of being assimilated into the dominant, more corporate and globalised, development industry. There is an alternative though: to see and use this crisis as a catalyst for transformation.

The view so far is that the dominant ways of human society organising itself include within them a threat to sustainability. New forms of organisation are being called for – organisations that include, and nourish, the parts towards contributing the fullness of their potential in the process of shaping and achieving the purpose and contribution of the organisation as a whole. One group of CSOs is focused on as having a contribution to innovation by transforming themselves – those organisations that have successfully brought together people previously excluded to effectively challenge systems that undermine their ability to flourish. There are points of crisis common to successful organisations that provide moments of opportunity for transformation.

The Treatment Action Campaign

My recent practice provides an example of an organisation arriving at a crisis laden with potential for transformation. The case of the Treatment Action Campaign (TAC) shows some of the successes, pressures, and tensions that bring it to this point of crisis.

As the newly formed first democratic government in South Africa took office in 1994 the full impact of the HIV/AIDS pandemic was being unleashed, with Southern Africa as its epicentre. As it was the impoverished part of the South African population, with scant access to health services, that was most devastatingly affected, civil society responded. Those marginalised in under-resourced communities (particularly women) had to organise in their families and communities as best they could to care for the sick and dying. Activists (many themselves infected) with a history in the political struggle and relationships with leaders in poorer communities established the Treatment Action Campaign (TAC) in 1998, one of the myriad CSOs formed to support the struggles of those infected and affected by HIV and AIDS.

To achieve its objective of accessing treatment, TAC was soon drawn into challenging (and winning against) the government in the constitutional court. From 1999 the government was led by a President (Thabo Mbeki) influenced by a minority of international scientists (known as HIV/AIDS denialists) who claimed there was no causal link between the HI virus and AIDS. TAC mounted numerous very high-profile, expertly conceived and led campaigns. It not only took on the government of the day, but also the global pharmaceutical companies and patent laws to get affordable antiretroviral drugs to those who desperately needed, but could not afford, them.

An account of the first 12 years of their history describes the crucial membership aspect of the organisation:

> "TAC set up its first offices in Johannesburg, Cape Town and Durban in 1999. TAC was able to mobilise and operate at a community level by establishing branches across the country. This model of social mobilisation and organisation was adopted from the struggle against apartheid. Branch members operated in their own communities, educating others on HIV science and establishing adherence clubs and support groups. 'TAC grew in members because people needed space to disclose their HIV status and get support. Members sustained branches. TAC is mostly the work of volunteers, Grassroots activists many with no income and no employment, who have given up their time,' explains Vuyiseka Dubula." (Treatment Action Campaign 2010)

The following captures the advocacy achievements:

> "TAC has mobilized a nation, made brilliant use of the courts, applied constant and consistent pressure on decision-makers, and saved millions of lives. Through its peaceful activism, TAC supporters forced their government to stop denying AIDS. They forced drug companies to stop denying HIV treatment to all but the wealthiest. They forced their urgent message – our members are dying; you must act – upon an indifferent world." (Treatment Action Campaign 2010)

The foundation on which all achievements are based emanates from this membership. TAC has been highly effective in maximising its impact through its ability to empower with knowledge, mobilise, and organise the voluntary activist energies of citizens against the system denying them access to what is most needed.

The purpose of this article is not to evaluate the impact of TAC. This has been thoroughly done in evaluations, articles, and books. Its success has been acknowledged by many, including the nomination of the organisation as a whole, along with one of its founders (Zackie Achmat), for a Nobel Peace Prize. TAC is used here as an example of many effective social justice campaigning organisations that come into being in response to the failure of dominant systems. Central to their purpose is the pursuit of systems that serve the priorities and interests of those most in need who are excluded.

Through the skilled pioneering leadership of individuals those infected and affected by the HIV and AIDS were mobilised into a highly effective force in countering the pandemic. As global institutions responded, amounts of funding way beyond what was originally imagined possible started flowing. TAC grew exponentially into a substantial national organisation with strong global connection and influence. The funding made it both necessary and possible to employ skilled, formally educated staff to complement the experienced and skilled community based activists who learnt from experience and on-the-job training.

During the pioneer phase TAC quite rapidly grew to reflect all the essential elements, systems, and functions of large budget organisation running complex programmes funded by international donors. It has offices and structures to coordinate and manage its work around the country. The organisational form that emerged is a complex one. In this hybrid membership/professional delivery/campaigning organisation, staff are accountable to line managers, and they to the membership through the General Secretary. Leadership resides in the National Council of the membership structure that elects national office bearers, including the General Secretary who is also the paid executive director of the organisation. In recent years, to ensure proper governance and financial accountability, all this is now overseen by an independent Board of Directors.

The growth in size and complexity of the organisation has made increasing demands on its systems of leadership and management. As funding and formalisation have grown, administration and management systems have been put in place and evolved. Over time the pioneer leaders have moved on to start other organisations. The pandemic itself has developed and needs have changed along with the priorities of the funders. TAC has evolved with, and played a significant role in influencing, the changes.

In recent years growing tensions in relationships internally and with its funders have started to hinder the ongoing development of TAC. It has become increasingly difficult to coordinate and mediate the complex array of relationships between externally recruited staff, members who had come up through the ranks to work and earn as a part of the team, and branch members who do crucial work in communities on a voluntary basis. Leadership and management systems have not managed to keep up with the increasingly complex development needs of the organisation as a whole, and of the individual members. At the organisational level the management systems were no longer bringing sufficient coherence to the complex array of tasks to be differentiated, delegated, coordinated, and adequately reported on and accounted for in the array of people, programmes, and departments. As previous personalised relationship-based ways of doing this have not been adequately replaced by effective management systems, passionate, committed individuals have started feeling undervalued and frustrated.

Tension in the organisation has increased as a result of pressure on management to account for results to funders. In the shift from the less formal, more personalised processes of the pioneer organisation to the more formally managed systems, reporting to managers started being experienced as a means of control through top-down authority structures rather than a source of support, empowerment, and learning. This has undermined the vital function of accounting for results to funders. The crisis can no longer be avoided when funders are forced to withdraw their support. But the decline in funding is a symptom. The underlying cause is the growing tension around organisational systems that are no longer able to effectively manage the growth in size and complexity of the organisation.

It is clear that from the outset TAC has been shaped by a particular set of civil society values. There is already a foundation of experience in operating an organisation experimenting with forms, structures, and systems in which power and authority functions differently from conventional organisations. The tensions that have brought TAC to the point of crisis arise out of a combination of unmet needs of staff and members on the one hand and funders on the other, at a time when important strategic leadership and re-positioning is required.

I pause here to insert a note on my use of the world "crisis" in describing TAC. I use it conscious of its negative connotations. I use it from the organisational development perspective earlier described, to highlight a moment of opportunity for development and transformation. It is not intended in any way to cast TAC in a poor light or suggest weakness. I see it as a great strength that TAC has fully embraced the challenges it is facing and using the opportunity to rethink its next phase of development. This was an important consideration in choosing the case of TAC to exemplify the point of this paper.

Institutionalising new organisational forms and practices

What makes this common organisational crisis different in an organisation like TAC is that it has an organisational form where authority resides in a previously excluded, under-resourced membership.

In TAC there is a foundational intention (and resultant tension) around shifting power to access and exercise control over the distribution of resources. The ability to resolve this tension through institutionalising new organisational forms and practices lies at the crux of the transformation challenge. What makes TAC an important example is that its commitment and ability to remain well-managed, civic driven, and membership-led and owned continues as a formative force. The question raised by this paper is how this pressure and the tensions surrounding it can be used as a creative catalyst in society's search for new organisational forms. TAC is an example of civil society's ability to pioneer new hybrid-type organisations in response to urgent needs that other institutions are unable to respond to. The question is whether it can use its present crisis to find a new form for itself in the post-pioneer phase that will be an inspiring example of what is possible.

In the closing of his book, in response to the title "Reinventing Organizations: A Guide to Creating Organizations Inspired by the Next Stage of Human Consciousness", Frederic Laloux suggested that:

> "All of this is very much emerging ... As more people and more organizations follow in the pioneers' footsteps, they will enrich and refine our understanding of this emerging model by pushing the boundaries a bit further, by inventing new practices, and experimenting in new directions." (Laloux 2014, 304)

This paper is not suggesting what the organisations of the future will look like, but making a case for social justice CSOs in transition playing a leading role in further pushing the boundaries suggested by Laloux. From the work I have done with TAC and other similar organisations, negotiating the crisis of letting go of ways of organising that no longer serve the needs of their organisations, I suggest three areas that require particular attention to contribute to transformed organisations. The first is to fundamentally rethink the function and practice of management and its role in future organisation. The second is to re-imagine future options for the financial resourcing of the civil society impulse in society. The final challenge is for civil society activists and their practice of mobilising and organising to develop beyond the vital role of challenging systems and institutions that are not sustainable – to become laboratories for new forms of organisation.

The seeds of the new in all of these areas are already germinating and starting to take root at the creative margins of society. CSOs are well placed to model new organisational forms, making practical the growing understanding that complex living systems are not based on hierarchies of control but on principles of self-management. As in the case of TAC, many of them have already been practicing alternatives that seek to shift control in their pioneer phase. The challenge of the next phase is to turn the underlying principles and values into new management systems, approaches, and disciplined practices. The focus needs to shift from control to connecting and coordinating the passions and commitments of empowered individuals into well-integrated, effective, and accountable organisations that do not extract and impoverish, but nourish.

Funding is the second area that requires focused attention to open up spaces for established CSOs to transform into, rather than be assimilated into, the present dominant system. Three funding related explorations have arisen as organisations I have worked with face the prospect of letting go of the old ways of doing things. First, the whole new arena of social enterprise is growing. The boundaries between business and civil society are being re-imagined and broken down. New models of pursuing social objectives are being experimented with that are strongly influenced by business thinking and approaches. Second, organisations that have been a part of the funded international development sector continue to look to existing funding agencies as well as the new concentrations of wealth generated from web-based industries. At the point of negotiating the post-pioneer crises, funders are being looked for that have specialist expertise in and a commitment to funding in ways that open up spaces and support for meaningful innovation and experimentation. This includes funders who understand the crucial need to adequately resource core organisational functions of leadership and management and their further development. Finally, there is increasing exploration into, and experimentation with, linking the dispersed web-based funding models, along the lines of crowdfunding, with membership-based, civic-driven, more social movement-type organisational forms.

Conclusion

I end with what I consider to be the foundation requirement for CSOs' ability to contribute to societal innovation and transformation more intentionally. Ultimately the ability to act with creative and innovative agency grows out of a particular quality of relationship to self and to the world. A confidence to take responsibility for testing new ways of being and doing is required. Social justice CSOs are at risk of getting stuck in and limited by the courage and skill they have developed to challenge and dismantle systems that abuse and impoverish. The risk is that, in the process, they become expert at countering the power of the system by exercising power over it in ways that replicate rather than transform the system. The challenge is to develop the creative generative experimental aspect of activism that uses courage to let go of and move on from the ways of organising in the past that are not sustainable. This lies at the crux of the broader societal challenge that is made clear in the ongoing struggle in South Africa.

Organisations like TAC have shown how civil society activism in its early phase can be highly effective in both countering sources of power like the state and the pharmaceutical industry, and in using innovative organisational forms and practices. The membership, the staff, and some of its funders are in the process of implementing a plan to pare down, rationalise, and re-focus the organisation. It is not yet clear if the crisis it has weathered will result in the ability to let go of enough of the old to find a new form that will be an inspiring example of its striving for social transformation.

What is clear to me is that "*emancipatory experimentalism that promotes permanent social transformation and perennial self-development toward ever increasing democracy and individual freedom*" (West 1988) is in the DNA of some CSOs. Those committed to transformation must learn to see it, support it, and grow its potential to contribute.

Disclosure statement

No potential conflict of interest was reported by the author.

References

Laloux, F. 2014. *Reinventing Organizations: A Guide to Creating Organizations Inspired by the Next Stage of Human Consciousness*. Brussels: Nelson Parker.

Treatment Action Campaign. 2010. "1998–2010; Fighting For Our Lives: The History of the Treatment Action Campaign." Accessed March 5, 2016. www.tac.org.za/files/10yearbook/files/tac%2010%20year%20draft5.pdf.

West, C. 1988. "Between Dewey and Gramsci: Unger's Emancipatory Experimentalism." *Northwestern University Law Review* 81 (4): 941–952.

Unpacking civil society sustainability: looking back, broader, deeper, forward

Rachel Hayman

ABSTRACT

More evidence is emerging about challenges many different types of civil society organisations around the world are facing relative to the sustainability of their organisations and functions. Valuable experiences and lessons are also emerging of how organisations are responding. This concluding article brings together themes from across the articles in this special issue, offering a broad understanding of civil society sustainability, exploring why this matters in the present geopolitical context, reviewing what has changed from previous analyses, and proposing ideas for what needs to change as we move forward.

Des données factuelles supplémentaires émergent sur les défis que de nombreux types différents d'organisations de la société civile de par le monde doivent relever en ce qui concerne la durabilité de leurs organisations et de leurs fonctions. Des expériences et enseignements précieux se dégagent par ailleurs de la manière dont les organisations réagissent. Cet article rassemble des thèmes de tous les articles figurant dans ce numéro spécial, et propose une manière large de comprendre la durabilité de la société civile, en examinant pourquoi elle revêt une importance dans le contexte géopolitique actuel, en se penchant sur ce qui a changé depuis les analyses précédentes, et en proposant des idées sur ce qui doit changer tandis que nous allons de l'avant.

Cada vez aparece más información acerca de los retos que una gran variedad de organizaciones de la sociedad civil enfrenta a nivel mundial en torno a la sostenibilidad de sus agrupaciones y sus funciones. Asimismo, están surgiendo valiosos aprendizajes y experiencias sobre las respuestas que han dado estos grupos. El presente artículo recoge los ejes temáticos examinados por los artículos de este número especial, los cuales se propusieron ofrecer una amplia comprensión en torno a aspectos como la sostenibilidad de la sociedad civil, las razones por las cuales este tema es de interés en el actual contexto geopolítico, así como considerar los cambios que se han producido desde los análisis anteriores y plantear ideas respecto a lo que debe cambiar en el futuro.

Introduction

"Would anyone notice if we closed tomorrow?" This comment from a workshop on civil society sustainability in Ghana in November 2015 (WACSI 2015) captures a mood that is prevalent among many established NGOs in different parts of the world. Pousedela and Cruz (2016, 606) in this special issue question: *"What would the world look like if poorly equipped civil society actors were unable to do their job?"* The former sentiment is symptomatic of reflection taking place within civil society organisations

(CSOs), who are looking inwards and asking themselves crucial questions about their future; the latter contemplates why this matters.

Sustainability of civil society and its organisations is gaining prominence within policy and practice, as awareness grows about challenges in relation to funding and political and operating space (CIVICUS 2015; Walker 2015). More academic research that explores civil society sustainability from different perspectives is emerging. This comes through in studies on: organisational development and management; North–South partnerships; exit strategies and aid withdrawal; civil society in middle-income countries; political and operating space; NGO legitimacy, accountability, and transparency; and various branches of area studies.

This special issue of *Development in Practice* has offered a space for academic and practice-based analysis as a way of pushing sustainability up the policy, practice, and research agendas. This concluding article brings together themes emerging from the articles with findings from INTRAC's research, advisory, and evaluation work. The article aims to unpack civil society sustainability, what it means, why it matters, what has changed from previous analyses, what needs to change as we move forward, and which questions remain unanswered.

Looking broader: a multi-dimensional understanding of sustainability

This collection provides evidence from different types of organisations in different contexts about a range of issues that are affecting their ability to function effectively and deliver on their missions. These include dynamics in the global political economy as well as international development. A first key trend is that of changing aid patterns for development generally, and for civil society specifically (Mawdsley 2012; Baobab 2015; Huyse and De Bruyn 2015). A second trend relates to political and regulatory space for civil society (Act Alliance 2011; CIVICUS 2013, 2015; Carothers and Brechenmacher 2014).

INTRAC began working on this topic out of a concern that the impact on civil society organisations of the changing environment was not being examined holistically (Lewis et al. 2015). For example, the index approaches used by USAID and CIVICUS to monitor the comparative health and strength of civil society across geographic spaces are highly valuable, including focusing attention at the global level on political and operating space.[1] These offer a big-picture understanding of civil society sustainability globally as well as within individual countries and regions. However, they do not provide detailed analysis rooted in empirical evidence about the specific challenges faced by organisations within particular contexts and how they are responding to them. Other studies had focused on specific aspects of the aid environment relative to civil society or to internal organisational and financial sustainability. We observed an absence of meaningful discussion across civil society, NGOs, donors, private funders, governments, social enterprises, and the private sector to cross-reference experiences, examine relative values attached to civil society, find innovative ways to support civil society differently, and share all these openly and publicly.

It was also clear to us that we need to look at sustainability in a broad way (Amagoh 2015; Hayman et al. 2015; WACSI 2015). The articles here contribute to a multi-dimensional framework for analysing sustainability that looks at the internal environment, the external context, and the relationships amongst different actors. Our explorations lead us to the following understanding of sustainability. CSOs require clear purpose, mission, vision and values to perform well and have legitimacy in their communities. They need progressive leadership and well-balanced accountability relationships with different stakeholders. They need to be able to demonstrate relevance and be credible. Critically, in order to operate freely, effectively, and sustainably, these organisations need resources, but again resources are multi-faceted. They include stable funding from a balanced set of sources, that also cover operational costs, in order to limit reliance on external funds or a single source; they also need relevant skills and capacities. Finally, they need sufficient political space, and a conducive governance environment that provides a regulatory framework that supports and protects the operating space for civil society. This covers both formal regulations and structures as well as the everyday practices of government and regulatory authorities. As the articles show, there are common themes, but across different contexts and times the configuration of how these aspects manifest themselves and affect civil society vary.

Within this understanding of sustainability, four elements are worth highlighting: credibility; legitimacy; regulatory and political space; and resource mobilisation.

Credibility

This emerges frequently as a foundation block for sustainability. The credibility of civil society organisations that are perceived as aid-dependent, donor created, professional, and formal – often, but not exclusively, classified or registered as NGOs – is most under scrutiny. NGOs globally are coming under immense pressure, both in the Global North, in the home countries of NGOs working internationally, and in the Global South among partners of those international NGOs (Arhin, Adam, and Akanbasiam 2015; Doane 2016; Farouky 2016). They are lambasted for being out of touch, unaccountable, irrelevant, and inefficient.

Legitimacy

This links closely with credibility, and relates to whether or not a given civil society organisation can claim to represent a group or cause. Without legitimacy or credibility, the value of the organisation comes into question and with it, therefore, the question of whether it is worth saving or is able to save itself. Legitimacy becomes closely intertwined with the ability of organisations to mobilise resources, particularly their ability to generate local support from the general population, local philanthropists, or businesses (see Wiggers 2016). Having identifiable "roots" and ideally a membership base is receiving scholarly attention as conferring legitimacy. Banks, Hulme, and Edwards (2015, 709), for example, define membership-based organisations (MBOs) as *"more traditional forms of civil society organizations such as social movements, political, or religious institutions, trade unions, cooperatives, small self-help groups, and campaigning organizations"*; this definition appears to explicitly exclude NGOs. Banks et al. pose the question of whether NGOs are too removed from the real sites of necessary social change, unlike these MBOs. However, legitimacy can originate from different sources, and we need to continually unpack and reflect on this. Is a "legitimate" CSO one that the government accepts as an interlocutor? In a context of restrictive legislation and closed political space this may be crucial to the ability of an organisation to function, but might lead to organisations being accused of being apolitical and mere service gap-fillers. Or is a legitimate CSO one that is grounded in a local community and that is responsive to local issues? Is it one that has global legitimacy in tackling global issues, and has recognised expertise and knowledge (Thrandardottir 2016), but does not necessarily have an obvious constituency? Or one that is faith-based, drawing legitimacy from its association with an accepted religion? Or one that funders consider to be efficient and effective?

Regulatory environment and political space

This is central to civil society sustainability, as explored by Claessen and de Lange (2016), Wood (2016), and Lutsevych (2016), but was arguably less prevalent in earlier analyses. Numerous regimes have used arguments about an absence of legitimacy and dependency on foreign funding to discredit NGOs (see CIVICUS 2015; Buxton 2016; Wood 2016). At the same time, there are very real questions about the blurred lines that many CSOs occupy between political action and civic action (Hayman et al. 2013, 2014; Lutsevych 2016) which renders this treacherous terrain for organisations to negotiate. An area that needs to be monitored is emerging evidence that private philanthropy may be at risk from tightening legislation in some contexts (Alliance Magazine 2016), which is mentioned by both Farouky (2016) and Buxton (2016). Given that private giving, local and international, represents a growing source of alternative funding for civil society, this is a worrying sign.

Resource mobilisation

Organisations will always be in need of support. Even the smallest organisations that rely primarily on voluntary input require resources to carry out or scale up their activities. This is therefore a critical component of the sustainability debate, as explored by Hailey and Salway (2016), Fowler (2016), and Wiggers (2016). Many organisations have always drawn on diverse income streams, but over-dependency on external, public aid is perceived as a key component of current sustainability problems. Diversification is important, and there are many new (and old) forms of resourcing that offer opportunities for CSOs, including from government, the private sector, philanthropic foundations, diaspora groups, venture philanthropy, social enterprise, crowdfunding, and direct giving. Diversification requires strong relationships (see Dawson 2016) and different capacities to access. However, some of these new avenues carry risks that CSOs have to navigate, including alternative dependencies, different forms of government control, and mission drift (see Batti 2014; Arhin 2016; Hailey and Salway 2016). Moreover, some of the actors are themselves directly involved in implementing development initiatives or tackling social justice issues, representing "competition" for NGOs and CSOs in a more crowded development landscape. As Wiggers (2016) shows, diversification is not straightforward, and requires a holistic approach to capacity building that focuses not just on funding but on internal systems and structures as well as external dynamics.

Looking back: what (if anything) has changed?

In his article, Fowler (2016) revisits sustainability issues from his work in the late 1990s and early 2000s; building also on Holloway's (1997) study examining southern NGOs. Holloway argued that their decision-making around funding at the time "*limit*[ed] *their ability to realize their full potential (which is to become effective, rooted and sustainable organizations of civil society in the South)*" (1997, 1). He sought to shift attention to the sustainability of organisations, not projects, promoting the idea of supporting partners and their organisations to gain traction, not just treating them as instruments to deliver projects. Many of these arguments are applicable to an exploration of sustainability today, as are some of the solutions proposed by Holloway: develop robust exit strategies to enable indigenisation; support the development of a Southern grant-making infrastructure; and look towards social enterprise. This raises the question of why organisations have not addressed these issues before. Northern donors and NGOs were advised to rethink how they support Southern partners; and Southern organisations had ample warning about the risks of dependency on external support and of losing touch with their local roots (Fowler 2000a, 2000b; Brehm 2001). Many good examples were available of organisations that sought to develop innovative income-generating activities which others could have learnt from (see, for example, DGIS/ICCO 1993; DGIS/HIVOS 1997). As Fowler states, NGOs have "*a large share of co-responsibility for finding themselves and local partners in a sustainability predicament*" (2016, 570).

The 1990s and 2000s were years where the CSO sector, particularly NGOs, continued a growth spurt that had begun in the 1980s, but so did dependency (see Buxton 2016; Mendonça, Aquino Alves, and Nogueira 2016; Pousedela and Cruz 2016). External resources received in this period were generally not aimed at developing sustainable organisations, but were often project-oriented and short-term. Where core and programme funding was more readily available as part of organisational capacity development approaches, this did not necessarily lessen dependency, as Arhin (2016) observes in Ghana and Mendonça, Aquino Alves, and Nogueira (2016) in Brazil. The adoption of the Millennium Development Goals (MDGs) and the major campaigns of the early 2000s to increase aid flows in support of the MDGs perpetuated this absence of serious attention to sustainability planning. While the late 1990s saw a short-lived moment where the end of aid was predicted (Aldaba et al. 2000; Van Rooy 2000), this changed with the adoption of the MDGs. Concerns shifted towards effectiveness, governance, and accountability as NGOs benefitted from increased aid flows. As aid effectiveness took centre stage, NGOs gradually gained a seat at global development policy tables (Hayman 2012). However, this appears to have damaged the credibility of NGOs in the eyes of many stakeholders. They were criticised for following the money (Fowler 2016), becoming too close to donor agendas (Banks, Hulme, and Edwards 2015), focusing on service delivery (Buxton 2016; Pousedela and Cruz 2016), and taking an instrumental approach to partnership (Elbers 2012). As Pousedela and Cruz observe in Latin America, the current sustainability crisis for many organisations is taking place during a period when ironically *"CSOs are for the first time ever officially recognised as relevant development actors"* (2016, 614).

A structured literature review on civil society sustainability that we undertook in early 2016 threw up references that fell broadly into two time periods: late 1990s/early 2000s; and 2011 onwards. Although sustainability was inherent in much of the NGO management and organisational development literature during the 2000s, the terminology and concept received less attention than impact and effectiveness (Lipson and Hunt 2008; Fowler and Malunga 2010). With the global financial upheavals of the late 2000s, sustainability re-emerged, but with little significant sign of organisations paying any more attention (at first) than in the late 1990s. A head-in-the-sand mentality seemed to persist even as the warnings of significant change began (INTRAC 2011; Tandon and Brown 2013). Research on exit strategies demonstrates that even when donors and international NGOs began withdrawing support from partners and countries, local partners often failed to grasp the significance and the need to consider their futures (Hayman 2015; Lewis 2016).

Looking deeper: sustainability of who and for what?

Sustainability therefore touches on many different aspects of organisations and their environments; some are long-standing or even perpetual issues, while others are newer and reflect contemporary geopolitics. This exploration leads to another set of fundamental questions, namely sustainability for what, and of what? A first assumption that we need to tackle is whether we are primarily talking about the future of a self-perpetuating professional sector of formal international NGOs in developed countries and national NGOs in countries experiencing economic growth where funding patterns are changing rapidly. While evidence is emerging about sustainability challenges for NGOs in these contexts, the cases presented in the articles of this special issue and elsewhere demonstrate that – when we look at sustainability from multiple angles – a wide range of types of organisations across many contexts need to take stock of what is affecting their sustainability and seek ways to tackle this. This is as pertinent to community-based CSOs (see Taylor 2016) as to large national NGOs (see Wiggers 2016) and major international NGOs; it is happening across Central and Eastern Europe, Latin America, South-East Asia, and Africa; it is also relevant in conflict-affected and fragile contexts where CSOs are constantly under pressure (INTRAC 2015).

For many funders, it would seem that the sustainability of impact and outcomes remains as important, if not more important, than the sustainability of organisations. While this obviously matters, an over-emphasis on impact and outcomes of the project, programme, or intervention has often happened to the detriment of organisations. We therefore need to find a balance between the sustainability of individual organisations – provided that they are relevant, useful, and effective, etc. – and the sustainability of the sector as a whole, and its functions and purpose. Such a view allows for the fluidity and fluctuation that characterises civil society over time, a recognition that there are some organisations that should cease to exist, but that many others will expand and contract or continually re-invent themselves to respond to changing needs in society. Some of the oldest associations have been doing this for decades, and look considerably different today than when they were first established (WACSI 2015); others are going through a process of transformation now (Taylor's (2016) article provides a very strong example of this in South Africa). This takes us beyond the rather tired debate about whether NGOs should "do themselves out of a job", and focuses on the value of organisations that genuinely act in solidarity and struggle for social, political, and economic transformation in multiple arenas and spaces.

With this in mind, the emerging evidence that organisations focused on rights and advocacy, as well as networks, are most affected by sustainability challenges is worrying (CIVICUS 2015; Mendonça, Aquino Alves, and Nogueira 2016; Pousedela and Cruz 2016; Wood 2016). It also highlights a contradiction. As noted above, civil society has been recognised as critical to development within global agendas. CSOs are considered to play an important intermediary role in promoting empowerment, participation, inclusion, and citizen-state engagement (Carothers and Brechenmacher 2014; Fox 2014; Lutsevych 2016). External aid has been crucial to supporting and promoting work on human rights and democracy, governance and accountability, and citizen voice and participation. Legitimacy and protection has also been conferred on organisations carrying out such work by their external connections. This function of civil society organisations may be in jeopardy as alternative sources of funding are limited for such work. This is not area that governments provide significant funding for; nor or do many private funders, neither corporate nor philanthropic.

Looking forward: what are the prospects?

Taylor (2016) proposes that what might be considered as a moment of crisis for CSOs, actually presents an opportunity for organisational transformation (see also Buckley and Ward 2015). For Sriskandarajah (2016) this is also a necessity. From an organisational development perspective many of the challenges that organisations are facing are not new. The question is whether the situation is sufficiently critical for CSOs and their supporters to address it.

A recurrent theme in the articles of this special issue is the need for diversification and flexibility, for organisations to build new relationships that will offer a sustainable future and forge roles for themselves that are valued and relevant. Organisations need to learn new skills, adopt new thinking, and embrace new strategies (Hailey and Salway 2016). These articles offer examples of how some organisations are embracing new approaches, adding to a small but growing pool of empirical research and case studies (see also Constantinovici 2012; Abouassi 2013; Arhin, Adam, and Akanbasiam 2015; INTRAC 2015). But they also demonstrate that diversification is a long-term process (Wiggers 2016). Pousedela and Cruz (2016) observe that many organisations in Latin America have gone from dependency on external resources to dependency on government, which reduces some of their capacity for advocacy and governance work; access to private sources of funding are limited, with many private funders having low confidence in CSOs and preferring to implement their own programmes. A similar situation is evident in many countries of the Middle East and North Africa (Farouky 2016). At the same time, organisations need to get the balance right between flexibility and adaptation, and professionalism and responsibility. This depends on what the expectations are in a given context. It is interesting to note that in the Middle East, there is a call for greater professionalisation among both NGOs and philanthropic foundations for better practice, but on local terms (Farouky 2016); and both Pousedela and Cruz (2016) and Mendonça, Aquino Alves, and Nogueira (2016) argue that the labour rights of third sector workers are being undermined as their job security becomes ever more precarious.

While personal giving, philanthropy, corporate giving, social investment, and social enterprise are important areas for CSOs to explore, they are also no magic bullet. There are often barriers to the expansion of these types of activities with lack of clarity on regulations and incentives. The evidence from different contexts shows that many private foundations prefer to steer clear of advocacy, rights, and governance activities. Emerging middle classes are not necessarily driven to donate. In fragile contexts, engaging in politically sensitive activities is sometimes only feasible with external support and often with very limited overt internal legitimacy. There are many contexts where private funding prospects are slim, especially remote, rural, poor, and volatile parts of countries where private capital is scarce. Furthermore, we need deeper exploration of whether private giving can tackle the *"messy stuff"* (Lewis et al. 2015). In particular, more evidence is required on civil society sustainability in contexts of conflict and fragility, where the options of social enterprise, philanthropy, or government support are less viable, and where activists, communities, and organisations are splintered. Once conflict comes to an end, and the aid begins to flow, how can organisations avoid falling into the same dependency traps (Hayman et al. 2013, 2014)?

Diversification needs to come from deep internal reflection about the organisation, its purpose and future, and should also include reflection on the balance between growth and sustainability. Arhin (2016, 555) raises a concern about CSOs adopting a business-minded approach as they latch onto a *"social enterprise craze"*, doing this in a way that is potentially *"mission-twisting"*. Pratt (2016) likewise reflects on the earlier microcredit craze. Organisations need to strike a fine balance between diversification and following the money, which can undermine their credibility. If diversification happens through a deep review process, that also seeks to build new coalitions between CSOs, NGOs, philanthropy, social investment, and government, then organisations can potentially make a shift without losing sight of their mission and character.

Another recurrent theme is the need for organisations to revisit their roots to enhance their legitimacy and their potential for sustainability. In Ukraine, Lutsevych (2016) sees this as crucial to enabling CSOs to continue pushing for political reform. Claessen and de Lange (2016, 544) note that overcoming and resisting a restrictive environment is feasible where organisations have a *"strong support base that is sympathetic to the cause"*, where there are strong national coalitions of CSOs, as well as external support. Dawson (2016) and Buxton (2016) likewise show that there are organisations in Ethiopia and Russia that are managing to find ways to resource such work locally despite a generally hostile government environment. Developing a membership base is one option, although what is meant by membership will differ across types of organisations. More important, perhaps, is being able to make the case for the benefit that a given organisation brings in its context. In West Africa this appears to be as much about ensuring that stakeholders understand better what NGOs do. There is a perception that many national NGOs are removed from communities and the people they claim to support; yet many have strong connections with grassroots groups, acting constantly in intermediary roles (Arhin, Adam, and Akanbasiam 2015; WACSI 2015).

The issue of connectedness and rootedness throws up different areas of tension in debates around the future of civil society. To overcome legitimacy and resourcing challenges, some international NGOs have begun to organise themselves differently, including decentralisation and devolution (International Civil Society Centre 2014). Yet this can be controversial, with new national branches of international NGOs undermining existing national organisations (Buckley and Ward 2015). Some are trying to redefine themselves to connect closer with broader civil society and shake off the label of "NGO". Many are trying to explore ways to work with newer, more fluid forms of civil society, something that funders are also increasingly keen to do. This thrusts larger, national and international NGOs further into the intermediary role (see Banks, Hulme, and Edwards 2015), particularly as funders struggle to balance accountability demands with a desire to fund civil society more directly. Yet this could perpetuate many of the sustainability problems for organisations across the board.

Going forward, there are new trends to watch. First, a number of new civil society initiatives offer prospects for different forms of engagement and support for civil society organisations. These include the Civil Society Innovation Initiative, and the Civic Space Initiative. Several donor agencies are also exploring new ways to work with civil society.[2] Second, the adoption of the Sustainable Development Goals (SDGs) offers prospects of new resourcing and roles, but also risks for CSOs. Fowler (2016) contemplates whether the SDGs will have the same impact as the MDGs in terms of corralling NGOs with new funding and donor-driven agendas; he concludes that it is unlikely. Arhin (2016) considers that there are assumptions that NGOs will play roles in service delivery, advocacy, and facilitation to help achieve the SDGs, but that the challenges they face in funding, capacity, and identity will undermine this. The emphasis in the SDGs on inclusion, security, and fragile contexts will present those organisations that specialise in these areas with many opportunities for new partnerships and funding (see Dawson 2016). We already see organisations repositioning themselves around inclusion, fragility, and climate change mitigation. However, the long-term sustainability of these organisations may be at risk if they are swamped with new resources without taking into consideration all the issues under discussion here.

Conclusion: what do we still need to know and what should we do?

Civil society organisations need to be focused on their mission not their own survival if they are to enable citizens to claim their rights and hold those with political and economic power to account. Sustainability is not an end; it is a process. It needs to be built into the fabric of organisational management. But it also needs to be built into the policy and funding fabric of those who support and enable civil society, as well as the governance fabric of the given context.

In many parts of the world organisations that do crucial work in support of the poor, marginalised, and disenfranchised have faced harsh shocks; they have been ill-prepared for the new political and economic conditions. These changes should not have come as a surprise; there was ample warning. But many did not act. As Pratt questions in the overview to this issue, was this because of poor communication, an unwillingness to face up to the inevitable, or poor planning for the future? Some organisations have adapted, as case studies presented in this special issue show, while others are struggling. We are beginning to build up a picture of what is happening, with more research emerging, some policymakers and private funders beginning to engage, and capacity builders developing new tools and training options. There are critical lessons to share across these contexts for organisations facing major change; such sharing can help to fill gaps in knowledge and thinking about what makes for a healthy and sustainable civil society. Funders and supporters of civil society – whether they are governments, international NGOs, corporate givers, or private foundations – need to ensure that they are taking sustainability seriously in their policies and programmes, including recognising the unintended consequences of their actions, as Wood (2016) highlights. This needs to be demonstrated through rethinking capacity building support, through robust – not tokenistic – exit strategies focused on those at the sharp end, and through a commitment to reviewing the sustainability of partners and interventions long after the funding has ended (INTRAC 2016).

A 12-country programme on capacity building for sustainability that INTRAC facilitated between 2013 and 2015 highlighted that organisational development has to be planned in ways that enable CSOs to be independent entities capable of mobilising support in their own societies from the early stages of intervention. But how do we get this message across when funds are available and the urgency lies in achieving the objectives of the intervention? What is the tipping point that brings this message home? And when change is required, what do organisations need to know and need to access in order to make the necessary shifts, including mentally? For those of us who exist to support civil society, our challenge is to understand and prepare for these moments, and support organisations through them with appropriate forms of capacity building for sustainability that take into account all the many aspects outlined here.

Many organisations are going through a real moment of introspection about their future. According to Interaction, the umbrella organisation for NGOs in the United States, the NGO sector there has been through this, emerging different but stronger, recognising alternative roles that they have to play in a much more crowded development landscape.[3] The same is happening across many European countries and in other parts of the world also, and is not just confined to aided, formal NGOs. This process of regeneration needs to be viewed positively, as a real opportunity for profound shifts in how we understand and tackle sustainability. What we do not want is to be having the same conversation in another 15 years' time when we will be reaching the end of the "SDG era". Nor do we want organisations to squander the chance to really change themselves, as the secretary general of CIVICUS is calling on them to do (Sriskandarajah 2016). It could be that there is enough of a "disruption" happening that civil society organisations have a chance for genuine transformation into organisations with a renewed sense of purpose. There is a note of optimism in some of the articles presented here, one that draws hope for the future of many different types of organisation from the commitment of an activist core that will continue to fight for civil society.

Notes

1. See USAID CSO sustainability index and the CIVICUS Civil Society Index, the CIVUCUS Enabling Environment Index, and Enabling Environment National Assessments.
2. The Civil Society Innovation Initiative is supported by USAID, Sida, OSI, and AKDN; the Civic Space Initiative run by CIVICUS, ICNL, Article 19, and the World Movement for Democracy. New donor explorations include the EU Country Roadmaps for Engagement with Civil Society, and Danida's work on multi-donor funds (Danish Ministry of Foreign Affairs and INTRAC 2014).
3. Presentation by CEO of Interaction at Bond Annual Conference, London, March 2016.

Acknowledgements

The following people have helped shape the work and ideas covered in this article: Rowan Popplewell, Albert Arhin, Marcelo Marchesini, Kanykey Jailobaeva, Erla Thrandardottir, Brian Pratt, and many of my colleagues at INTRAC.

Disclosure statement

No potential conflict of interest was reported by the author.

Funding

I am grateful to the following organisations that have provided support to INTRAC to conduct work on this topic: Broederlijk Delen, CBM, DanChurchAid, ICCO, Save the Children International, Norwegian Church Aid, Cordaid, Plan Sweden, and Wild Geese Foundation.

References

Abouassi, K. 2013. "Hands in the Pockets of Mercurial Donors: NGO Response to Shifting Funding Priorities." *Nonprofit and Voluntary Sector Quarterly* 42: 584–602.

Act Alliance. 2011. "Shrinking Political Space of Civil Society Action." Geneva: ACT Alliance.

Aldaba, F., P. Antezana, N. Valderrama, and A. Fowler. 2000. "NGO Strategies Beyond Aid: Perspectives from Central and South America and the Philippines." *Third World Quarterly* 21 (4): 669–683.

Alliance Magazine. 2016. "Closing Space for Philanthropy: Survey Findings." *Alliance Magazine* 10 May. Accessed 28 May, 2016. www.alliancemagazine.org/article/closing-space-survey-findings/.

Amagoh, F. 2015. "Improving the Credibility and Effectiveness of Non-governmental Organizations." *Progress in Development Studies* 15 (3): 221–239.

Arhin, A. 2016. "Making a Difference in a Changing Development Landscape: Challenges of NGOs in Advancing the Sustainable Development Goals in Ghana." *Development in Practice* 26 (5): 555–568.

Arhin, A., M.-A. S. Adam, and A. C. Akanbasiam. 2015. "The State of Civil Society Sustainability in Ghana: Striving, Surviving or Thriving?" Accra: WACSI. Accessed May 4, 2016. www.wacsi.org/en/site/publications/2756/The-State-of-Civil-Society-Organisations%E2%80%99-Sustainability-in-Ghana-sustainability-civil-society-Ghana-STAR-Ghana.htm.

Banks, N., D. Hulme, and M. Edwards. 2015. "NGOs, States, and Donors Revisited: Still Too Close for Comfort?" *World Development* 66: 707–718.

Baobab. 2015. "*Civil Society Aid Trends* 2015." Baobab Briefing Number 3. Accessed May 4, 2016. www.baobab.org.uk/wp-content/uploads/2015/01/BBAidTrends2015.pdf.

Batti, R. C. 2014. "Challenges Facing Local NGOs in Resource Mobilization." *Humanities and Social Sciences* 2 (3): 57–64.

Brehm, V. 2001. "Promoting Effective North-South NGO Partnerships: A Comparative Study of 10 European NGOs." Occasional Paper Series Number 35. Oxford: INTRAC.

Buckley, L., and H. Ward. 2015. "Getting Good at Disruption in an Uncertain World. Insights from Southern NGO leaders." London: IIED. Accessed March 29, 2016. http://pubs.iied.org/pdfs/11505IIED.pdf.

Buxton, C. 2016. "Russian Civil Society and Development Challenges in Eurasia." *Development in Practice* 26 (5): 657–662.

Carothers, T., and S. Brechenmacher. 2014. *Closing Space: Democracy and Human Rights Support Under Fire*. Washington, DC: Carnegie Endowment.

CIVICUS. 2013. "State of Civil Society 2013: Creating an Enabling Environment." Johannesburg: CIVICUS: World Alliance for Citizen Participation. Accessed May 1, 2016. http://socs.civicus.org/wp-content/uploads/2013/04/2013StateofCivilSocietyReport_full.pdf.

CIVICUS. 2015. "State of Civil Society Report 2015." Johannesburg: CIVICUS: World Alliance for Citizen Particpation. Accessed May 1, 2016. http://civicus.org/images/StateOfCivilSocietyFullReport2015.pdf.

Claessen, A., and P. de Lange. 2016. "Lessons for Supporting Policy Influencing in Restrictive Environments." *Development in Practice* 26 (5): 544–554.

Constantinovici, A. M. 2012. "A Study on Sustainability of Non-Governmental Organizations in Tamilnadu." *Golden Research Thoughts* II (Vi): 0–5. http://aygrt.isrj.org/ArchiveArticleList.aspx?id=23.

Danish Ministry of Foreign Affairs, and INTRAC. 2014. "Study on support to civil society through multi-donor funds." Accessed May 1, 2019 www.globaltfokus.dk/images/Pulje/Arkiv/Fagligt_Fokus/Study_on_Support_to_Civil_Society_through_Multi-Donor_Funds.pdf.

Dawson, E. 2016. "Gender, Diversity and Sustainable Civil Society Strengthening: Lessons from Ethiopia." *Development in Practice* 26 (5): 629–636.

DGIS/HIVOS. 1997. " …el grupo meta somos nosotros. Programme evaluation on income generating activities of counterparts of HIVOS in Central America (Costa Rica and Guatemala) and Grenada." The Hague: DGIS/HIOVS.

DGIS/ICCO. 1993. "Se dice … exigimos créditos ágiles y oportunos. Programme Evaluation on income generating activities of counterparts of ICCO in El Salvador." The Hague: DGIS/ICCO.

Doane, D. 2016. "The Future of Aid: Will International NGOs Survive?" Accessed May 2, 2016. www.theguardian.com/global-development-professionals-network/2016/feb/23/the-future-of-aid-will-international-ngos-survive?CMP=ema-1702&CMP=.

Elbers, W. 2012. "The Partnership Paradox: Principles and Practice in North-South NGO Relationships." PhD thesis, Radboud Universiteit, Nijmegen.

Farouky, N. 2016. "The State of Arab Philanthropy and the Case for Change." *Development in Practice* 26 (5): 637–645.

Fowler, A. 2000a. "Introduction Beyond Partnership: Getting Real about NGO Relationships in the Aid System." *IDS Bulletin* 31 (3): 1–13.

Fowler, A. 2000b. *The Virtuous Spiral. A Guide to Sustainability for NGOs in International Development*. London: Earthscan.

Fowler, A. 2016. "Non-governmental Development Organisations' Sustainability, Partnership, and Resourcing: Futuristic Reflections on a Problematic Trialogue." *Development in Practice* 26 (5): 569–579.

Fowler, A., and C. Malunga, eds. 2010. *NGO Management: The Earthscan Companion*. London: Earthscan.

Fox, J. 2014. "Social Accountability: What does the Evidence Really Say?" GPSA Working Paper. Washington, DC: World Bank.

Hailey, J., and M. Salway. 2016. "New Routes to CSO Sustainability: The Strategic Shift to Social Enterprise and Social Investment." *Development in Practice* 26 (5): 580–591.

Hayman, R. 2012. "The Busan Partnership: Implications for Civil Society." INTRAC Briefing Paper 29. Oxford: INTRAC.

Hayman, R. 2015. "NGOs, Aid Withdrawal, and Exit Strategies." *Journal für Entwicklungspolitik/ Austrian Journal of Development Studies* 31 (1): 48–61.

Hayman, R., et al. 2013. "Legal Frameworks and Political Space for Non-Governmental Organisations: An Overview of Six Countries. Phase I." Oxford: INTRAC. Accessed May 2, 2016. www.intrac.org/resources.php?action=resource&id=771.

Hayman, R., et al. 2014. "Legal Frameworks and Political Space for Non-Governmental Organisations: An Overview of Six Countries. Phase II." Oxford: INTRAC. Accessed May 2, 2016. www.intrac.org/resources.php?action=resource&id=801.

Hayman, R., et al. 2015. "Building Sustainability of Civil Society: Beyond Resourcing. Reflections from INTRAC staff and associates." Oxford: INTRAC. Accessed May 2, 2016. www.intrac.org/data/files/resources/830/Sustainability-blog-series-copyright-updated.pdf.

Holloway, R. 1997. "The Unit of Development is the Organization, Not the Project. Strategies and Structures for Sustaining the Work of Southern NGOs." Baltimore: John Hopkins University.

Huyse, H., and T. De Bruyn. 2015. *New Trends in Governmental Funding of Civil Society Organization: A Comparative Study of 9 OECD-DAC Donors*. Leuven: HIVA-KU Leuven.

International Civil Society Centre. 2014. "Diversify, Adapt and Innovate – Changing ICSO Business Models." Berlin: International Civil Society Centre. Accessed May 1, 2016. https://icscentre.org/downloads/14_09_12_Diversify_Adapt_and_Innovate_web.pdf.

INTRAC. 2011. "Civil Society at a New Frontier: Challenges and Opportunities Presented by Economic Growth." Oxford: INTRAC. Accessed May 1, 2016. www.intrac.org/data/files/resources/735/Civil-society-at-a-new-frontier-conference-report-Dec-2011.pdf.

INTRAC. 2015. "Finding Space to Manoeuvre: Local and National CSOs in Complex and Politically Charged Contexts." ONTRAC No. 60. Oxford: INTRAC. Accessed May 1, 2016. www.intrac.org/data/files/resources/874/ONTRAC-60-FindingAspace-to-manoeuvre-local-and-national-CSOs-in-complex-and-politically-charged-contexts-September-2015.pdf.

INTRAC. 2016. "Post-closure Evaluations: An Indulgence or a Valuable Exercise?" Oxford: INTRAC.

Lewis, S. 2016. "Development a Timeline for Exit Strategies: Experiences from an Action Learning Set with the British Red Cross, EveryChild, Oxfam GB, Sightsavers and WWf-UK." INTRAC Praxis Paper 31. Accessed April 24, 2016. www.intrac.org/data/files/resources/890/INTRAC-Praxis-Paper-31_Developing-a-timeline-for-exit-strategies_FINAL.pdf.

Lewis, S., et al. 2015. "Building Sustainability of Civil Society: Debates, Challenges and Moving Forward." Accessed April 24, 2016. www.intrac.org/resources.php?action=resource&id=831.

Lipson, B., and M. Hunt. 2008. *Capacity Building Framework: A Values-based Programming Guide*. Oxford: INTRAC.

Lutsevych, O. 2016. ""Civil Society vs." *captured state: can citizens push for change in Ukraine?" Development in Practice* 26 (5): 646–656.

Mawdsley, E. 2012. *From Recipients to Donors: The Emerging Powers and the Changing Development Landscape*. London: Zed Books.

Mendonça, P., M. Aquino Alves, and F. Nogueira. 2016. "Civil Society Organisations and the Fight for Rights in Brazil: Analysis of an Evolving Context and Future Challenges." *Development in Practice* 26 (5): 592–605.

Pousedela, I., and A. Cruz. 2016. "The Sustainability of Latin American CSOs: Historical Patterns and New Funding Sources." *Development in Practice* 26 (5): 606–618.

Pratt, B. 2016. "Special Issue Overview: Civil Society Sustainability." *Development in Practice* 26 (5): 527–531.

Sriskandarajah, D. 2016. "Civil Society must Change Itself before it can Change the World." 26 April 2016. Accessed April 27, 2016. http://oxfamblogs.org/fp2p/civil-society-must-change-itself-before-it-can-change-the-world.

Tandon, R., and D. L. Brown. 2013. "Special Issue: Civil Society at Crossroads: Eruptions, Initiatives, and Evolution in Citizen Activism." *Development in Practice* 23 (5-6): 784–796.

Taylor, J. 2016. "Crises in Civil Society Organisations: Opportunities for Transformation." *Development in Practice* 26 (5): 663–669.

Thrandardottir, E. 2016. "Legitimacy and Knowledge Production in INGOs." In *Negotiating Knowledge: Evidence and Experience in Development NGOs*, edited by R. Hayman, S. King, T. Kontinen, and L. Narayanaswamy, 47–58. Rugby: Practical Action Publishing.

Van Rooy, A. 2000. "Good News! You may be out of a Job Reflections on the Past and Future 50: Years for Northern NGOs." *Development in Practice* 10 (3/4): 300–318.

WACSI. 2015. "Report on Regional Workshop on Civil Society Sustainability in West Africa, 17 November 2015." Accra: WACSI.

Walker, D. 2015. "What's Next for the Ford Foundation?" 11 June 2015. Accessed April 14, 2016. www.fordfoundation.org/ideas/equals-change-blog/posts/whats-next-for-the-ford-foundation.

Wiggers, R. 2016. "Action for Children: A Model for Stimulating Local Fundraising in Low and Middle-income Countries." *Development in Practice* 26 (5): 619–628.

Wood, J. 2016. "Unintended Consequences: DAC Governments and Shrinking Civil Society Organisation Space in Kenya." *Development in Practice* 26 (5): 532–543.

Index

For Product Safety Concerns and Information please contact our EU
representative GPSR@taylorandfrancis.com
Taylor & Francis Verlag GmbH, Kaufingerstraße 24, 80331 München, Germany

www.ingramcontent.com/pod-product-compliance
Ingram Content Group UK Ltd.
Pitfield, Milton Keynes, MK11 3LW, UK
UKHW051831180425
457613UK00022B/1200